Java
Professional
Interview Guide

*Learn About Java Interview Questions and
Practise Answering About Concurrency, JDBC,
Exception Handling, Spring and Hibernate*

Mandar Maheshwar Jog

www.bpbonline.com

FIRST EDITION 2022

Copyright © BPB Publications, India

ISBN: 978-93-91030-056

LIMITS OF LIABILITY AND DISCLAIMER OF WARRANTY

To View Complete
BPB Publications Catalogue
Scan the QR Code:

Dedicated to

My wife Tejaswini and my lovely son Ojas
&
My beloved Parents

About the Author

Mandar Jog is a passionate Java trainer and conducting training for the last 15+ years. His expertise areas are Java & J2EE-related technologies like Spring, Spring Boot, and Hibernate. Along with training Mandar is also a freelance author and has written a book entitled "Java 9.0 to 13.0" under BPB publications. He also works as the technical reviewer for some books based on Java. He is also one of the key panelists in many of the organizations that conduct the technical interviews of Java for fresher and experienced candidates.

Along with this Mandar is also connected with different organizations and institutions for designing the curriculum of computer engineering. He also conducts Train-the-Trainer sessions for many colleges to connect them with cutting-edge technologies.

About the Reviewer

Abhijeet Rathod is working in the software industry since 2006, and now working as a hands-on Software Development Manager-Architect involved in the architecture, design, and implementation of microservice architecture, distributed systems, and deployment over different clouds. In his career, he has successfully delivered several projects for various product-based organizations using Agile methodology, code reviews, DevOps, and CI-CD.

Also, he is actively involved in hiring team members with different skillsets and grooming them as part of proudly leading successful teams.

To the challenges of budget, incomplete requirements, he kept focusing on having clarity on the basics of every language/technology that is required in the project.

For delivering big value in small packages, he believes to have good knowledge of OOPS, SOLID principles, and design patterns.

In addition, Abhijeet thinks one should develop an X-Ray vision to understand – "How data is flowing through various layers of application from UI to the database?"

Acknowledgement

Writing a book is creative work. This can't be accomplished without support, guidance, and inspiration from people around you. During this journey right from thinking of a book and publishing a book, there were many such people who helped to achieve this.

To begin with I am thankful to the entire team of BPB for their continuous support and guidance. I would also like to thank my wife Tejaswini for her inputs during this process. She has been always an inspiration to me right from my first book. I would also like to thank my students, my friends who constantly kept me motivated by suggesting that this book is needed for everyone.

I would also like to thank my parents for their blessings and of course last but not least to my lovely son, Ojas for his patience during this wonderful journey.

Preface

This book is the complete digest about how you can crack Java interviews. Getting successful in an interview is the result of a lot of systematic preparation. Of course, you should have the knowledge, but along with that, you should know how to represent your knowledge in the interview. You should know what type of questions would be asked and how to answer them precisely. This book covers all the aspects of Java interviews which you can come across in top IT companies.

This book provides you information about the entire interview process right from how your profile is shortlisted and how should you prepare for a non-technical interview round. Though this book does not give you much scope for hands-on, you will get enough interview questions on Java, J2EE, and so on. As in the case of an actual interview, the interviewer is most interested in conceptual knowledge rather than implementation this book talks about all the concepts of Java. Instead of teaching you concepts in Java and then sharing the questions, the book teaches you all the concepts through the questions.

The attempt has been done so as to cover all the concepts of Java which are important for the interview. To achieve this, the book is divided into 14 chapters. These chapters cover Java architecture, OOPs, Exception handling, Concurrency, and lot many other features. Along with Java industry is also using different frameworks like Spring, Spring boot, Hibernate, and so on. The book also covers different interview questions on these frameworks.

Chapter 1: The Preparation Beyond Technology

This topic covers mostly nontechnical stuff for fresher candidates. What are the opportunities, how should they present themselves, and what roles they are fit in, are discussed in this topic. The focus of this topic is to bridge the gap between the industry and the candidates.

Chapter 2: Architecture of Java

This topic is a general topic that will discuss the architectural information about Java. It will start the journey right from the version information of Java and different new concepts introduced in those versions. This topic will also cover how java internally works from converting the source code to executable files and also some of the other file systems which are available in JDK or JRE.

Chapter 3: Object Orientation in Java

This topic will describe the different concepts of an object-oriented language. And this will discuss in detail every implementation of the same in terms of Java. This topic will cover all the concepts of OOPs including abstract classes, interfaces, and so on, which forms one of the most important parts of the interview for freshers.

Chapter 4: Handling Exceptions

This topic first will cover the entire concept of how to handle exceptions in Java. It will cover all the concepts like try, catch, finally, throws and throw keywords. Along with this, it will also take care of the new features of exception handling like automatic resource management, and so on.

Chapter 5: File Handling

This chapter talks about how to connect with files to execute different operations on File. The topic also covers IO concepts in Java in detail. Apart from traditional IO, it also covers the new java.nio package i.e. NIO and deals in detail study of buffer and channel, and so on.

Chapter 6: Concurrency

This chapter walks through from basics of multithread to advance concepts of the concurrent application development approach. Along with basic thread creation, it also talks about Executor Framework, fork & Joins, Locks and Barriers, automic integers, and so on.

Chapter 7: JDBC

This topic discusses the JDBC API in Java. We will be connecting to the MySQL database and discuss different concepts in JDBC. The topic talks about database connections, retrieving data, inserting data, and updating the records. In the later part of the chapter, it talks about the transaction, RowSet, CachedRowSet, and so on.

Chapter 8: Collections

Collections are one of the most important topics for interviews. This topic starts the discussion with the basics of collection and its necessity. Further, the chapter also discusses the different types of collections and scenarios in which it can be used and different techniques such as sorting and searching data using collection API.

Chapter 9: Miscellaneous

There are many concepts/classes in Java, which are hard to put into any hierarchy. This topic is focused on all such concepts in Java which might not be covered in any other topics but they might be important as far as interview is concerned.

Chapter 10: Functional Programming

Functional programming is a new approach to programming nowadays. This chapter starts with the need for functional programming and how it is important in the modern era of programming. Further, it talks about the functional interfaces, lambdas, and stream implementation.

Chapter 11: Design Patterns

Software development is not about only writing the code and generating the solutions. Along with this, we need to be also sure of creating a flexible ad robust architectural design of the application. Design patterns provide such an approach to application designing. This topic covers a few of the design patterns which are important for the interview.

Chapter 12: Basics of Web

This topic is focused on the basics of web application development. Before going into the advanced topics like spring and spring boot, the reader must be aware of this basic concept. The topic covers some introduction to HTTP and related concepts on the web. The chapter also gives a brief solution about how to create the web application using Servlet and JSP.

Chapter 13: Spring and Spring Boot

Spring framework is one of the most popular and lightweight frameworks nowadays for dependency injection. The chapter uses the spring framework 5.0 to explain the concepts from the basics of spring, different projects from the spring framework. Along with this topic, the chapter also talks about Spring boot which is used for created REST endpoints nowadays.

Chapter 14: Hibernate

Hibernate is one of the most important frameworks which simplifies database connectivity with its concepts of ORM. The topic covers the basics of hibernate to advanced features like HQL and caching.

Downloading the coloured images:

Please follow the link to download the
Coloured Images of the book:

https://rebrand.ly/7eb340

Errata

We take immense pride in our work at BPB Publications and follow best practices to ensure the accuracy of our content to provide with an indulging reading experience to our subscribers. Our readers are our mirrors, and we use their inputs to reflect and improve upon human errors, if any, that may have occurred during the publishing processes involved. To let us maintain the quality and help us reach out to any readers who might be having difficulties due to any unforeseen errors, please write to us at :

errata@bpbonline.com

Your support, suggestions and feedbacks are highly appreciated by the BPB Publications' Family.

BPB is searching for authors like you

If you're interested in becoming an author for BPB, please visit **www.bpbonline.com** and apply today. We have worked with thousands of developers and tech professionals, just like you, to help them share their insight with the global tech community. You can make a general application, apply for a specific hot topic that we are recruiting an author for, or submit your own idea.

The code bundle for the book is also hosted on GitHub at **https://github.com/bpbpublications/Java-Professional-Interview-Guide**. In case there's an update to the code, it will be updated on the existing GitHub repository.

We also have other code bundles from our rich catalog of books and videos available at **https://github.com/bpbpublications**. Check them out!

PIRACY

If you come across any illegal copies of our works in any form on the internet, we would be grateful if you would provide us with the location address or website name. Please contact us at **business@bpbonline.com** with a link to the material.

If you are interested in becoming an author

If there is a topic that you have expertise in, and you are interested in either writing or contributing to a book, please visit **www.bpbonline.com**.

REVIEWS

Please leave a review. Once you have read and used this book, why not leave a review on the site that you purchased it from? Potential readers can then see and use your unbiased opinion to make purchase decisions, we at BPB can understand what you think about our products, and our authors can see your feedback on their book. Thank you!

For more information about BPB, please visit **www.bpbonline.com**.

Table of Contents

CHAPTER 1
The Preparation Beyond Technology

Introduction

"We are pleased to inform you that you are selected for the position of Java Developer." This was the sentence I used to dream every alternate day before I got placed in a top multinational company. There is nothing more you could ask than get rewarded by getting hired for your education, or in real words, for your knowledge. I know most of you have some goals set up in your mind, for companies you are going to get selected. Of course, to get selected in any company and to be part of that company, you need to go through a rigorous process of interview. The interview is not only about how good you are technically, but also to test how good you are in pressure situations and how good you are as a person with whom other employees of the organization would love to work.

This book is specially focused on how to get through the technical interviews. We will discuss different questions on different concepts throughout the book. But, this chapter is something going beyond that. In this chapter, we will discuss about how you can represent yourself better at interviews. By representation, I do not mean I will teach you what to wear and what not to. But, I will be sharing my knowledge about different psychological aspects of how you can get successful in interviews. Let me reiterate, technical knowledge is the first priority. You will not work in a psychological clinic, but you will be working in the development company. But, if you know the mindset of interviewer and if you also know what mindset you should have during the interview, you will be increasing your chances to get selected.

Structure

Learning technology is always important, but prior to that, you must prepare yourself for behavioral skills as well. You should know how to present yourself, how to prepare yourself, and how to build up the mindset to appear for the interview confidently. The interview process starts long before you actually appear in front of interviewer. The better you prepare, better are the chances to get selected for your dream job. In this chapter, we will discuss such non-technical aspects of an interview.

Objectives

At the end of this chapter, you will know how to prepare for interviews non-technically. We will focus our discussion on the following:

- Types of recruitments
- Java career opportunities
- Selection process: pipeline
- How to choose your career or role
- How well are you prepared
- How to practice for interview
- Common interview mistakes that you should avoid
- What analysis interview normally do

Let us begin the fascinating journey.

Types of recruitment

It is also important know as a job seeker from where companies do the recruitment. Will you get a job in college or university itself? Or, you get it once you complete your graduation. There are two types of recruitment that normally occur.

On-campus recruitment

This is the most easy way to get selected in an organization. Normally, company representatives visit some good colleges and conduct the interview when you are in the final year of your graduation. Such interviews are typically based on your aptitude and the knowledge of C, C++ programming skills. To get selected in an on-campus recruitment, you need to maintain a good track record in your curriculum and perform well in the aptitude and technical test, which will be followed by a personal interview.

Off-campus recruitment

If you are not selected via the on-campus recruitment world, it is not the end of the world. You still have another option available through the off-campus recruitment process. Here, companies will publish advertisements in the newspapers or job portals like **naukri.com**, **indeed.com**, or sometimes on their websites. You can apply per the company norms, and you will be called for the interview. Sometimes, there will also be walk-ins where you can see thousands of job seekers waiting in a queue for their turn. Off-campus recruitment will be also have similar rounds like on-campus interviews, but often, it is observed that off-campus recruitment is technically more tough than an on-campus interview.

Java career opportunities

The IT world is a huge. What we see from outside is just a tip of an iceberg. If we need to discuss what are the different career opportunities in IT, then, probably, one needs to write a separate blog or book to cover it thoroughly. In this chapter, we will concentrate only on the job roles that are aligned with Java technology. Following are the different job roles you can expect if you are a Java developer.

Java full stack developer

Probably, this is one of the most challenging job roles you will come across in the IT industry nowadays. A **full stack developer** is a developer who not only develops applications, but will also design the UI and test it. So, you should have the knowledge of programming, UI designing like HTML, CSS, jQuery, Bootstrap, Angular or React JS, and testing to apply for this position.

Java Web developer

To become a Java Web developer, you should know the overall architecture of the Web application. Your job would be mostly consisting of generating the responses for the requests that are generated from the UI. You must have some knowledge of HTML, and along with that, you should know servlet and JSP. Though the technology of Web has evolved beyond servlet and JSP, unless you know these two technologies, you will find yourself in a bitter position to learn other technologies.

Java mobile app developer

This is one of the most rapidly growing fields nowadays. You talk about any business and then you immediately think about the app for that business. There are different frameworks for mobile application development. But, as far as Java is concerned, you should learn Android if you would like to make your career as an app developer.

Java EE developer

Enterprise developers take care about large-scale application developments. Unlike normal Web applications, these applications have a lot of features like logging, messaging, Web services. These applications may be Web applications or normal applications, but they need to be more scalable, maintainable, and flexible. The technologies that form such applications are EJB, Spring, Hibernate, REST, and so on.

Java API developer

Evolution of REST has really made a shift in the way applications are created. Instead of you creating everything as an application developer, now you can just utilize the services created by an API developer. As an API developer, you can create an API to update the database, respond to a request, consume data, and so on. The major technology you can use as a part of API development is Spring Boot.

Selection process: pipeline

The selection process in IT companies is always a tough process. You need to go through a number of rounds to get selected for the position. The stakeholders obviously want the right person for doing the right job. During the selection process, you will come across the following rounds.

Telephonic interview

"Good morning!! This is Stella from Google Incorporation, am I talking with George?" This is what you can expect on early morning weekdays if you have applied for a position at Google Incorporation. Telephonic interviews are one of the most elementary interview rounds that follow after you apply for a particular position. If your educational qualification, skillsets, experience (if you are applying for higher positions) match with organizational expectations, someone from the HR team will connect with you. Sometimes, the interview will be a surprise interview, which is very rare though. Many times, the HR team member will block your calendar for a call for a telephonic round.

Telephonic interviews are suited for interviewee because it gives you the flexibility to attend the call from anywhere. The only thing you have to make sure is that the place you choose must be free from any disturbance and should not have any network issues. Telephonic interview is almost similar to your face-to-face interview; the only difference is that you are not sitting in front of the panel physically. That does not mean there is no panel at the other end virtually. Sometimes, you might expect that a project manager is going to call you for an interview, and during the process, there are some other people also getting involved in the call. This is now an era of technology. So, be wise enough to use the different tools available like Skype, Zoom, or GoToMeeting, which are now preferred ways to conduct interviews rather than conference calls.

Technical tests

If you are through from phone screening, the next round of interview will be a technical test. Technical tests can be of two types:

- Multiple-Choice Questions (MCQ) test
- Algorithm-based test

It is not always a case that both these tests are always conducted. Mostly, MCQ tests are conducted when you are applying for an in-campus recruitment process, that is, when you are applying from your college or university. So, when companies are scrutinizing thousands of candidates, they want to be absolutely sure that only the eligible candidates will get a chance to attend the personal interviews. This also makes a point that the senior persons will be conducting the interviews do not waste their valuable time to interview the candidates who are not up to the mark. Ultimately, these seniors are key persons in the projects, and they need to invest their time in more productive work.

Normally, an MCQ test is divided into two segments, aptitude test and technical test. The aptitude test segment is based on mathematical skills. The technical segment will consist of questions based on C, C++, SQL, and sometimes, even on Java. Our focus in this book is not C, C++, and we will be concentrating more ourselves on the interview questions on Java. As this round is one of the selection parameters for getting selected for a personal or face-to-face interview, it is better that you practice these tests. But, remember that aptitude is not overnight success; you need to live with it. You need to make it a daily practice to be an expert in solving the questions. Often, students do ask me, what is the reason of aptitude if I am a programmer? Why not knowing Java is the only ability to be checked when I am applying for the Java programmer job role? Is it only the process of rejection as companies want to reduce the numbers for actual interviews? If you observe this from 15,000 feet above the ground, you may be correct, but the ground reality is your aptitude skill is mapped with your problem-solving abilities. It is an indication about how your brain quickly reacts to different scenarios of business in day-to-day life.

Solving technical MCQ will be little bit simpler as it is based on something that you are doing since years. After all, you have invested few years of your graduation to learn the programming languages. This should be your home ground where you can score freely. Still, sometimes, designing the problem solutions though code and solving MCQ could be a different perspective, so the more concepts your read and more programs you practice, you will be in better position to solve such MCQ.

Face-to-face interview

"Congratulations!! You have cleared your technical test and we are glad to invite you for face-to-face (F2F) interview on <date> at <time> IST." You should be proud of yourself if you get this email from the employer. Sometimes, it may happen that the technical test and the F2F interview happen on the same day. In the morning slot before lunch break, you might need to take up your technical test, and followed by that, post-lunch, you might get your chance to appear in front of a panel for an F2F round.

F2F is the most difficult aspect of your selection. You will not only be scrutinized for your technical knowledge, but there will be some questions that will be mapped with your behavioral skills. Most of the times, an interview will be conducted by a panel, which will comprise of technical evaluators as well as some HR representatives. The technical person could be your next manager with whom you will be working. He will be testing you on how good you technically are to be part of the upcoming or ongoing project under his leadership. And, the HR person will be monitoring your behavioral skills, which consists of your communication skills.

Though the views of HR are important, it is more important to make sure that you answer the questions of the technical manager satisfactorily. Ultimately, it will be his/her decision that will be more considered when it comes to a selection or rejection. He/she is a person who will be responsible for successful delivery of a project, and he/she has every authority to choose the right person to do the job effectively. Throughout this book, you will go through different questions that could be asked in the technical interview. It is very important to know what kind of questions will be asked during this round. Of course, there is no any thumb rule about it. But, based on my experience, I would like to add my two cents to this. One of the possibilities is that the interview will start on the basis of your performance of technical tests. If the technical test that you just cleared was about some algorithm implementation, then the interviewer will be interested to know the logic about the same. At times, the interviewer will ask you to change the algorithm on the fly to check how flexible you are and how quickly can you take up the challenge. Remember, it is not important at this point whether you complete the entire algorithm, but what is more important is your approach toward problem-solving. Interviewers are always masters in technology, even if you climb the first few steps of the ladder, they would know how fast and how effectively you will reach on the top floor using the same approach. So, do not worry about that end result, try to emphasize on the process of solving the problem statement, if asked. Such solutions are always expected to be produced on white paper or white board. Writing on a paper can be troublesome sometimes if you do not have practice of it. Nowadays, we are so fond of systems that we tend to forget the use of paper and pencil. This might be an irony, but this is fact. When I tried to recall when was the last time I wrote a program on paper, it took me 5 years back. So, make a practice of writing clean and tidy code snippets on paper.

The next few questions will be based on the different concepts on which the interviewer is interested in. You need to apply a thought process to guess which topics would be more important for which organizations or projects. For instance, if you are applying for a position in an organization that works in stock trading, then concurrency becomes the utmost important concept. If you are applying in an organization that works predominantly in online shopping, then database transactions could be more important. Of course, all these are wild guesses. You might expect few shocks from the interviewer in an actual interview. But then, you do not prepare for shocks, you can do nothing as a preparatory measurement for that. What you can do is expect a shock and be mentally prepared to handle it.

Another point to know here is it is not all a crime if you do not know something. Though, it is crime if you know nothing. Come on, I am kidding. If you know nothing, then why would you be sitting in front of the interviewer? But often, an interviewee panics about what will happen if I do not know something and is it fine to say that "I don't know about this?" It is absolutely fine if you are not an expert in everything. Ultimately, it is team work where the collective intelligence will matter significantly. So, if you are expert an in something, the other team member may be an expert in something else. Collectively, as a team, you will be able to solve a problem. So, if you do not know something, accept it with the grace and convey it politely to the interviewer.

This is supposed to be almost the last hurdle before you are selected for the role you have applied for. I am saying supposed or may be because sometimes the interview process could be so stiff that even if you cleared all the three rounds, that is, phone screen, technical tests, and F2F interview, there can be still the next round where you might need to deal with the HR manager. The round with the HR manager is normally to decide your salary scale and other terms and conditions. Normally, this happens immediately after your technical round if you are through your technical round.

How to choose a career or role?

Passion drives success. If you are passionate about something, you will find ways to get successful in that. Your career is not something that is a short-term game. You are going to live your life with your career. If I do calculate based on the number of productive hours you invest in your job, it comes out to be almost two-third. I know, someone might argue by claiming that sleep is the most productive work because that is where the dreams are generated from. But, let us talk about a time span when you are awake. And then, I am sure that most of you will agree about the fact that most of the time you will be investing in your job. So, before you apply for a job, make sure that it is matching with your passion. If that is not the case, you will be in resentment after a few years. It will be difficult for you to shift the job role after 4–5 years. So, before you apply, check if the job description suits you. For example, if you are fascinated about how the UI is developed for an application, probably you are someone who loves to do the UI designing job. But if you are keen know how the dashboard is getting filled by different posts on Twitter, you a developer who loves coding. Or sometimes, you might be more inclined toward the database designing approach. So, knowing yourself is the one of the most critical parts in the interview process.

How well are you prepared?

No matter if you are a fresh graduate from a university of repute or experienced candidate looking for a change, you must prepare well. Preparing well must be organized and should cover everything that is going to be a part of interview, right from applying for the job. The first thing you should do once you come across the advertisement in a local newspaper or website that suits your qualification is to send the resume or CV to the concerned HR representative. Hold on there. Is it resume or CV?

One of the important things to understand when you apply to any of the position is what should you put forward? Should it be a CV or resume? Well, most of the interviewees do not know the actual different between these two. Let us get this clear first! CV is curriculum vitae. It is a representation of your journey as a part of your graduation. Such kind of documentation contains information that is more focused on your achievements in universities, your final year projects and any publications, and so on. you have achieved during your graduation. On the other hand, a resume is a documentation about how you have resumed your career till date. A resume normally describes your experience, your roles, and achievements during your earlier job and if you have done any professional certification during this period. So, if you are applying as a fresher, you will be sharing your CV, and if you are experienced, you will be sharing your resume.

Once you share your resume or CV, you can expect an interview call or online test according to the policy of the HR department. You will get this intimation via a phone call or an email. But, do not wait till you get a call. Think positive and assume that you are going to be called for interview for all the jobs that you have applied for. The main reason for this is you might not get enough time for preparation after the intimation. Few companies will call you on a Tuesday evening and expect you be in front of the interview panel on a Wednesday morning. That is where continuous preparation will help you. Be always in a first gear so that you can drive your car quickly. Keep revising all the concepts regularly and check your knowledge, may be with your friends or on online portals, regularly even if you are not going to face any interview immediately.

How to practice for interviews

A tough thing to do really is practicing for interviews. How would you do that? If you feel that you are technically strong and are ready for an interview, how would you confirm it? Are there any agencies that prepare you for interviews? I am afraid there are not. Even if there are, they are in very small numbers. So, practicing for an interview is a really tough job. However, you can do so in three different ways:

By attending real interviews

If is often said in sports that "No matter how well you play in nets, your real ability will come in the pressure situation when you play actual match. "The same is true in case of the interview process as well. You may be good technically, or feel that you will perform confidently in interviews. But reality can be different. So, go and play a match to test yourself and practice in a real match. Attend more interviews. You will feel nervous in first couple of interviews. But, after that, you will gain confidence, you will able to understand the mindset of interviewers. You will, in fact, able to find out how the interview is going on and how much chance you have to get selected. As a seasoned interviewee, then you will improve your chances for getting selected.

By creating mock interviews

"A friend in need is a friend in deed." Who does not know this world-famous phrase? Preparing for interviews can be practiced by creating a mock interview session. You can form a group of friends and create a set of hundreds of questions that can be asked during an interview. Post that, you can literally attend the interview, which will be conducted by your friend (make sure that you forget that he/she is your friend and treat him/her as would be a manager of yours). Such practices will certainly create more comfort for you to face the actual interview.

By collecting feedback post-interview

Every interview panel maintains a performance sheet of the interviewee, which they submit to the HR department. When you get notified that you are not selected for the desired position, you may ask politely about the feedback of the interview. Many a times, this may sound as a rude behavior as the person at the opposite end might feel that you are asking a proof about why you are rejected. But, if you ask politely to the HR division that such document will help you to improve yourself in upcoming interviews, they will probably help you. Remember, how you interact with HR from day one of your connection matters here. If you have already created some positive relationships with HR through emails and support, HR will certainly help you by providing the right feedback about your interview.

Interview mistakes that you should avoid

Mistakes are inevitable. After all, you are graduates in technology and not in how to face interviews. Probably after reading this book, you get to master in how to face an interview, but at this moment, you are a beginner. Mistakes are ought to happen. You will stumble in difficult questions, but the managers know that you are a fresher. Even Mike Tyson had lot many punches on his face in his initial days; he fell but stood up and kept hitting back. But, as I already mentioned, try to avoid mistakes as early as possible. Let us now list out some of the common mistakes.

Complex and confused answers

Often, when you are facing the interviewer, you are stressed. Because of this stress, many times, you might get confused while forming the sentences. Though the interviewer at times will try to understand what you want to say, sometimes, they might not be in good mood to accept that. So, keep it simple. As far as possible, form simple and short sentences to elaborate your answers.

Loosing calmness

Getting stressed at the time of an interview is not uncommon. In fact, psychologists say that it is good to get some stress at interviews, but at the same time, you should learn how to control it. Such stress situations may push you to the brain blockage stage, where you will not remember what you have prepared. Make sure that you find out how to control your stress to perform better in an interview.

Giving mugged answers

Mugged answers can probably get you through the MCQ, but not from the face-to-face interview. Remember the interviewers are masters of technology, and they have years of experience in their field. They do now expect someone to talk about the bookish definition of concept, if they cannot explain what it is all about. Try to find out different scenarios in which you can use the concept. Though the theoretical information about the concept does not change, the real-time examples could be your own.

Trying to be heroic at an interview

Never try to be extra smart at an interview. Many times, you make an attempt in an interview by telling additional information when it is not required. Such additional information may put in trouble if you do not have a really good knowledge. Also, this might go against you when the panel is judging you as a person. Be yourself. You must prove that you can do that rather than only giving a feel of that.

What analysis interviewers normally do?

As an interviewee, you know that you will be tested for your technical skills, communication skills, or behavioral skills. But, knowing only this is not sufficient. You should also know what is it that will appear in your performance sheet, based on which you will be selected or rejected. What is it that the interviewer is trying to read from your answers? Though there are many aspects on which an interviewer is scaling you, but I am sharing with you some of the very basics and generic scale factors that will help you to prepare your answers.

How good are you to do the job?

This is a fundamental analysis to be done by the interviewer. To do this analysis, interviewers might asked you questions related with your skillsets and the depth of knowledge you have for those skillsets. Your behavioral skills are always secondary requirements, so the interviewer will invest most of the time in these types of questions. The questions in this will normally comprise of the projects you have done, the challenges you faced, and how you came out of those challenges as a winner, or may be what effort you did irrespective of the result.

Are they comfortable to work with you?

None of the organization would like to have a resource who tries to break its barriers. Every organization has its own set of rules, style of working. This involves how to follow hierarchy while escalating the issues, or may be how to get connected with immediate managers or bosses. The interviewers normally are aware of these parameters of companies, which may impact the working culture of organization if not followed by individual. So, you can expect a couple of questions that will lead to understand you better in this regard.

Are you motivated enough?

Motivation is a key to success. A motivated person always finds a reason get the things done rather than finding the reason why it cannot be done. An interviewer is always keen to know if you are motivated about the position you are applying. You might get a question like "Why you are applying for this position" or "What makes you feel that the job is made for you?" Get ready to answer such questions as they are mapped with your interest to the job that you are applying.

How good and quick are you to learn new tools/ technologies?

Sometimes, the job role that you are applying might require some extra knowledge in your basket. Be sure that you answers indicate that even though you are lacking some skills, you are still keen to learn new things so that you can justify the job profile for which you are going to get paid. It is not only important to have the interest to learn, but you should also emphasize that you are someone who is quick in learning. Organizations nowadays do not have a prolonged time to wait for your progress. In fact, most of the organizations have their Learning and Development (L&D) department that takes care of all the training needs of their employees. But, the duration allocated for such training is really crisp. For example, in your graduation, you might have invested 100 hours in a course to learn Java, but in an organization, the same or more advance content of Java will be taught to you in 20–30 hours at the max and still your manager would expect you to be an expert in that.

Do you fit into the team culture?

Creating software is a team task. You will not sit in a cubicle for months and create software alone. There are different modules to be created by different personas. There is lot more communication between the team, which is one of the key aspects for developing a better product. So, the interviewer will be keen to know about your interpersonal skills and how you cope up with the conflict situations with your team members.

Mantras to succeed in an interview

To be successful in interviews, you need to follow some rules or guidelines. Though you may be facing your first interview on a particular day, the interviewer might have been busy all day interviewing a number of interviewees. So, you should make every attempt to make sure that the interviewer is satisfied with your performance. Following are some of the key mantras to be successful in an interview.

Answer the questions correctly and in your own words

Preparing for an interview is an art. When you get a schedule for your interview, you often choose to practice for would be questions asked in an interview. Of course, this is not a wrong approach at all, but while doing so, there might be one threat. Many a times when you are over-prepared for an interview, you will come up with mugged answers for questions. Remember, the interviewer is an expert. He/she can always figure out from the answers if the answers are mugged from some books. So, as you practice for the questions, try to frame the answers in your own words. Also, listen to the question properly. Do not create the answers even before the question is completed by the interviewer.

Body language matters

Apart from how good you are technically, how you present yourself also matters. You may presume though that this is a secondary aspect of an interview, it is important. The way you sit, the way you speak will have an impact on the interviewer. The interviewer might get distracted by your body movements (nail biting, tapping, scratching, and so on.) and miss some of the parts of your answers, which you should not let happen. As far as possible, try to add the warm smile while speaking. Some candidates feel that adding a smile might give an impression of overconfidence, but it is not. Also, it is not totally wrong even if you show some nervousness on your face. Interviewers understand that giving an interview is not playing a game. It is sometimes interpreted that you are serious about the interview, job.

Research about company

This is obvious, isn't it? If you are applying in a company, then you must know what the working area of company is. What are main or related products of the company? It is even better to know about the stakeholders or the board of directors of the company from the public domain. You might not get a chance to meet them in your interview process, but knowing such details might help you to prepare better as, in few companies, directors have the important role to play in selecting the fresher, though from behind the scenes. Sometimes, you might get one of the panelists in the interview panel who would like to know "What you know about our company."

Check your skills

Skills are most important parameters for your selection. Make sure that you have the required skills for the job you are interviewing for. For example, if you are applying for the full stack developer role, you must have the skills for that role like UI designing, database, and programming. You will be shortlisted for the interview only when these skills are mentioned in your CV or resume. A few of the companies have the system where they will check the skills by assignments or online tests as a preliminary round. It is always advisable to revise the required skills before the interview. Sometimes, it is also better to add some domain knowledge in which the company is working. For example, if you are applying for the financial organizations like CITI or JPMorgan, the interviewer would like to test your technical skills mapping with some concepts related to finance or trading.

Understand the job description

You probably know the famous quote "Time is money." When you opt for an interview, you are investing not only your time but also the time of the interviewer. So, make sure that you know about the position, role, and responsibility of the job for which you are facing the interview. Though it is not always possible to know everything about the job, make an attempt to understand the details as you can. You may talk to the HR or the recruiting agency about it, to get more information about the same. Do not waste your or the interviewer's time if the job role does not suit you. You will get enough other opportunities to grab.

Relationship of your personality and job role

What does a personality have to do with a job of a developer? After all, you are going to work on a system in an isolated cubicle. That is what is the case most of the times. But, there are some job roles where you need to be a part of a team. Particularly, if a company works in agile approach, you have to be vocal. You should have the courage to speak in daily standup, which will help in improve the quality of the software that you or your organization is developing. So, if the interviewer finds that you are not someone who can merge in a team or not extrovert to share your views proactively, then you might lose your chances to get selected.

Your expectations matter

Your expectations are always mapped with your performance. If you have expectations aligned with the policies of the organization, you will always perform well. The top management is always aware about the horizontal or vertical growth in terms of the position or even in terms of hikes in the organization. So, during an interview, you might get a question, "where would you like to see yourself down the line 5 years from now?" Such questions will always make your expectations clear for employers, and he/she understands whether you will get satisfied within the organization in the set policies of the organization or not.

You have to be flexible

Being affirmative is sometimes good. But, in the real-time world, situations are always different. You may have your life principles to which you can stick. But, work cultures are not the same. An employer might expect you to be flexible in terms of timings, technologies, or even policies that you have been using for some time. During the interview, you will get some questions to check your flexibility and how open are you to shift from traditional strategies depending upon the situations.

You have to be proactive

Proactiveness should not be at the cost of the organizational policies. Managers always want someone who works within the boundaries defined by the organization. At the same time, you should be a decision maker at your level. You should act proactively in a situation that can be handled by you. You have to be a go-getter and get the work done.

Know your resume/CV

A resume or CV is the first impression about you. You get shortlisted based on how effective you resume is. But, that does not mean that you decorate your resume with the skills that are not known to you. Though the first objective is to reach in front of the interview panel, the expected outcome is to get selected. Will you be only satisfied by only appearing for interview or getting selected for the job role? Not only the skillset but your hobbies, academic projects are also counted in the interviews if you are a fresher. Make sure you know your resume. You should know what all things are mentioned in your resume. If you cannot talk about the points mentioned in the resume, then the interviewer might get a feel of cheating. No organization will be interested to hire someone who is trying to cheat on them knowingly or unknowingly.

You should be trustworthy and a good team player

Once you get cleared off the technical process for interview, this will be the last step where the interviewer will be interested to know how good you are for the organization in terms of a team player as well. Are you a person who will be able to get merged with the existing teams? The interviewer will be keen to know how good you are as a person while working in a team.

Conclusion

In this chapter, we discussed about how you should prepare for the interviews. Now, you know the key points that you should take into consideration while appearing for an interview. You also studied what is the mindset of an interviewer, and what the interviewer wants to see in you sitting across the other side of the table. We also talked about what are the common mistakes that you will do and how that will affect your selection. We had a walkthrough about different rounds that you will go through in entire selection process. This is relatively the non-technical or behavioral study of an interview. Further chapters are more focused on technology. In the next chapter, we will be discussing in detail what is the architecture of Java and interview preparation that you can do for the same.

CHAPTER 2
Architecture of Java

Introduction

A developer is a savant. He/she has a lot of knowledge about the domain, algorithms, and also how to combine both of them to create an efficient application. Writing a code and compiling it is an idiomatic task. Once compiled, this program is executed on the underlying systems. And that is where the developers will stuck up. Developers are normally unaware about the internal working of operating systems. This might not impact the way of writing a program much, but sometimes that may lead to very unpleasant surprises.

Structure

Compiling and executing a Java program is just a matter of couple of commands. But, how the process happens internally must be taken into consideration. This chapter takes a gradual approach from how one writes a Java program, compiles it, and executes it. During the discussion of all these concepts, we will also discuss different interview questions that you might face while attempting your interview.

Objectives

At the end of this chapter, you will understand the architecture of a Java program. You will able to understand:

- Java program execution flow
- Key files in Java program
- JVM
- JRE
- JDK
- Bytecode verifier
- Just-in-time compiler

Java program execution flow

Writing a Java program, compiling, and executing it is a day-to-day task for you. But still, you need to make sure that you understand every bit of it. Let us discuss this in more depth along with the interview questions.

Explain the execution flow of a Java program

The most basic thing you need to understand is how a Java program gets executed. *Figure 2.1* gives a pictorial representation about how that happens:

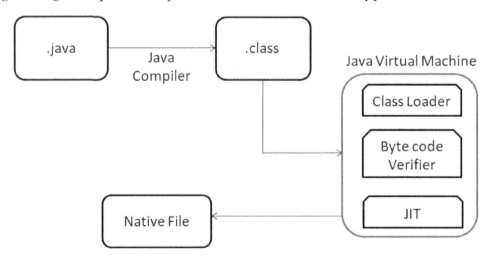

Figure 2.1: *Java program execution flow*

As we observe, the **.java** file, which is a source file, is provided to a compiler. The compiler compiles the file and converts it to a byte code file **.class**, which is a platform-independent file. This file is then passed to JVM, which takes the responsibility of executing it.

Key files in Java

While developing Java applications, we come across different file types. As a developer, you must aware of all these files.

What are different types of files and their significance in Java programming?

When developers write an application code, they normally write a code in a human-readable file, which gets converted into the machine-compatible file. As a developer, you must understand these key files.

Source code file

This file is written by a Java developer having extension `.java`. This is normally as program written in a high-level programming language. The following code snippet will give you how a basic structure of such files looks like

```java
class Sample{

  int x;

  //other data members

  public void method1(){

  }

  //other member functions

}
```

Byte code file

Before Java converts the high-level code to a native compatible executable, it generates the same into byte code, which is a platform-independent code. This file has the extension of `.class` and is termed as a class file that can be executed. Though the interviewer does not expect you to read the class file, you may have a look at the snippet of the class file that gets created after compilation.

Why Java is termed as a platform-neutral or independent language?

Traditional programming languages generate platform-dependent files after compilation to execute the program. For instance, the C programming language if compiled on Windows generates the .exe file, which is compatible only with the Windows platform. This means that the file is not portable. On the other hand, Java generates the class file after compilation, which is platform-neutral. You can load this file on any JVM, and the corresponding JVM will take care to generate the native file to execute.

Java Runtime Environment (JRE)

One of the most common terminologies you come across while discussing Java is JRE. Though it is common, many of us do not know the internal working of JRE. An interviewer might have some tricky questions on JRE, which you might be unaware of.

What is the role of JRE?

JRE is typically a program that can communicate with the class file provided to it. A runtime environment is typically a kind of physical operating system on which the software runs traditionally. JRE is a software that runs on top of an underlying operating system. The main reason why JRE plays a vital role in the entire Java lifecycle is the programmer does not need to bother about the actual OS and need not modify the code or the process of execution depending upon the operating system. When you instruct Java to execute the program, the JRE accepts your code, merges the different dependencies via a Java class loader, and passes it to JVM.

What are the components of JRE?

JRE comprises of three components as follows:

- Class loader

- Bytecode verifier

- Interpreter

Class loader

Class loaders play a vital role in the entire Java application flow. The following are some of interview questions that you can expect about class loaders.

What role a class loader plays?

Java applications are complex by design. They contain different classes, which are related to each other. Most of the classes use the services from other classes. In other words, they are dependent on some other classes. So, in order to make sure that a class compiles or executes, the class must find the classes on which it depends.

The class loader takes the responsibility of searching and loading such classes in memory. These classes are not loaded at once in memory by the class loader; it is done on a demand basis.

What are the different types of class loaders?

There are different class loaders available in JRE depending upon from where they load the classes dynamically.

Bootstrap class loader

The monolithic version of JRE has a jar file **rt.jar**, which is a repository of all the system or internal classes in Java. This jar file is present in the lib directory of JRE. **The bootstrap class loader** is responsible to load the internal classes that are present inside this jar file. Additionally, the bootstrap class loader also acts as a parent for other class loaders, and somebody needs to take responsibility to initialize them. So, it is also called as a **primordial class loader** of Java.

Extension class loader

The extension class loader is termed as a child of the bootstrap class loader. The external classes in JRE are present in the **jre/lib/ext** directory. The extension class loader loads the classes from this directory if the classes are not loaded by the bootstrap class loader.

System or application class loader

This class loader is child of the extension class loader. Generally, developer sets up the class path to search the classes for an application. **The system class loader** loads the classes from the class path.

If you are keen to know which class loader is utilized to load the required classes, you can use the method **getClassloader()** of that class as shown next:

```
1. import java.util.Date;
2. class CheckClassLoader{
3.    public static void main(String[] args){
4.    System.out.println(CheckClassLoader.class.getClassLoader());
5.    System.out.println(Date.class.getClassLoader());
6.    }
7. }
```

```
D:\>java CheckClassLoader
sun.misc.Launcher$AppClassLoader@73d16e93
null
```

Figure 2.2: *Working with the class loader*

As you can observe, the **CheckClassLoader** class is loaded from **AppClassLoader,** and for the *Date* class, you are getting the output as null. This null represents that the class is loaded by the bootstrap class loader. The output null from the bootstrap class loader is generated because the bootstrap class loader is implemented by C or C++ libraries, which Java cannot read.

Can you select the ClassLoader manually?

While loading the class in an application via **Class.forName()**, we can provide the classloader. The **Class.forName()** method takes into argument the fully qualified name of the class in a string format, which you want to load as a resource.

Bytecode verifier

As all of you know, the process for compiling and executing a Java program is very simple and straightforward. Developers are doing chores to generate the class file and passing it to JVM for execution. Though, normally, this should not create a problem for JVM about inconsistency or vulnerability issues, it may not be the case always. Sometimes, the class files, which are uploaded for JVM, might not be coming from trustworthy resources. For example, the downloaded files from hot browsers often contain the class files that need not to be compiled by JVM as they are pre-compiled within an application. Such third-party class files might have some code in it, which can exploit the Java virtual machine. To make sure that no intruder can enter inside, JVM has a gatekeeper, bytecode verifier. As the name implies, the bytecode verifier verifies that there is no any breaching of constraints, which can harm JVM.

Which verification is carried out by the bytecode verifier?

The following verifications are carried out by the verifier:

- The operand stack present in the frame should not get overflowed, and it should not be underflow or underutilized.
- The variables must be initialized before the usage.
- Private data from the class is not accessed from outside of the class.
- The proper references must be used for the method calls.

- The stack should not get overflowed.

- The final classes are not extended, and the final methods are not overridden.

If the verifier finds that something is missing from the preceding list, the code execution is blocked for that file.

I know the immediate question which is peeing in your mind is "Hey, are you kidding me? All these tasks are done by the compiler. What role the byte code verifier has in this stuff?" A similar question might be thrown at you by the interviewer.

Why do we need the bytecode verifier along with compiler?

Though the compiler can check all these aspects and then create a class file, the class files CAN BE MODIFIED. If any pernicious person knows about assembly programming, then he/she can easily edit the class file and do the modifications. And that is where the gatekeeper will object such class files. This makes JVM more robust and reliable.

JVM

JVM is the heart of the entire Java ecosystem. Either you are a novice or expert Java developer, you should have enough knowledge of JVM. An interviewer expects that you know the role of JVM in depth. Let us walk through some of the interview question related to JVM.

What role JVM plays in Java execution flow?

"Virtual Machine," that is what we call it. But, when one says virtual machine, the perspective is different. Often, we know that we can install virtual machines on your existing machine. To give just an example, we can install a Linux virtual machine on our Windows and work in Linux on the top of our Windows system. On the same lines JVM is, in fact, an abstract machine installed on your system on which you can execute your Java programs. This approach of having a separate virtual machine on your system is to cater the platform independency approach of Java. Where most other high programming languages generate the executable file that matches with the operating system, Java creates a bytecode file that can be executed on JVM. JVM has all the characteristics like the system you have with you. The hardware devices contain registers, instruction pointers, and sets. All these features are imparted in JVM because of which we can execute programs on it, which are written in Java.

Memory management in JVM

Java program contains different segments like methods, local variables, references, objects, and many more. When we execute the class, all these segments get stored temporarily as long as the program is executing. These segments do not get stored at the same location in JVM, but they get stored in to different logical compartments. *Figure 2.3* shows the different memory blocks of JVM.

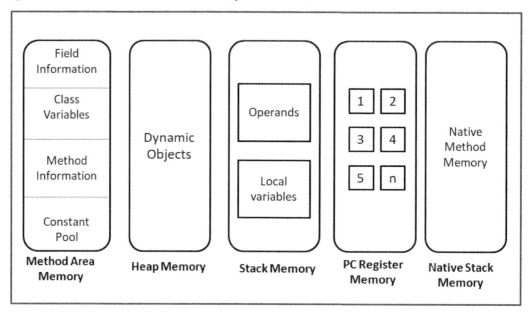

Figure 2.3: *JVM memory blocks*

Describe the different types of memory areas generated by JVM

The following are the different types of memory regions generated by JVM:

- **Method Area or Class Area**: This area stores the class information like variables, method data, or runtime constant pool.

- **Heap Memory**: This memory is utilized by the dynamic objects created during program execution.

- **Stack Memory**: The stack memory stores the frames created during execution for each thread. All the local variables, the method results are stored inside this. The frames gets deleted or removed whenever the method call is terminated or completed.

- **PC Register**: Every task that is being executed by JVM is executed within a thread. Program counter register is a memory that contains the instructions of a thread that is being executed currently by JVM.

- **Native Stack Memory**: Native stack memory is utilized by the native method if used in an application.

Can you increase the heap memory of JVM?

Or

What is "OutofMemoryException?" How can we handle it?

This **exception occurs** when JVM runs out of memory. To handle this, we need to increase the heap memory of JVM. We can increase the heap memory of JVM dynamically by providing additional attributes to the Java command. We can use the following attributes to modify the heap memory size:

-Xms: Setting the minimal heap size

-Xmx: Setting the maximum heap size

For instance, you can execute the following Java command to change the heap size:

> *java* `Sample -Xms512m -Xmx1024m`

Alternatively, you can also set up the environment variable in an operating system to change the heap size every time when a Java program executes as:

> `_JAVA_OPTIONS = -Xms512m -Xmx1024m`

How can you differentiate between stack memory and heap memory?

Stack memory is a memory that is utilized to store the local variable and references to object or arrays. This memory is expandable at runtime. The **heap memory,** on the other side, is a fixed size memory that is used to store the object or arrays. This memory can be changed at the time starting up of JVM or changing the setting of Java environmental variable.

How JVM executes class?

When we load a particular class to JVM by using the Java command, JVM executes it. But internally, many steps are being performed.

Let us assume that we are giving the following command:

java `Sample`

Immediately as a result of this command, JVM identifies that the class is not loaded in memory. So, with the help of the class loader, the binary representation of this class is found; if this is not found, the error will be displayed. If the class is found, JVM does not directly call the main method. Before that, the class must be linked by the linking process. Linking typically comprises of the verification, preparation, and resolution process. **Verification** is a process of verifying if the binary representation is a well-formed class. It also checks if the class obeys the semantic requirements of Java and JVM. After the verification, JVM initiates the preparation process. In this process, JVM allocates the static storage for the class and also generates the data structure, which is internally utilized by JVM. At the end, JVM initiates the resolution process. In this process, JVM checks the symbolic references that are generated from the current class to other resources by loading those resources.

Once the linking process is completed, JVM starts the initialization process. In this process, the class variables or static initialization blocks are executed. This process, in fact, happens recursively as classes might have super classes, and super classes still can have a cosmic super class. So, all these classes are initialized hierarchically before initializing the **Sample.class**. Once all these processes get completed, the main method of the Sample class is called.

JIT compiler

JIT, a famous acronym for **Just in Time** compiler, is a special compiler present within JVM, which converts the bytecode to native code. JIT plays major role to improve the performance of a Java application. It works in contrast to normal compilers. Normal compilers work before execution; on the other hand, JIT starts its work when the execution begins. It is dynamic in nature. Let us discuss the concept of JIT with the help of some interview questions.

What is importance of JIT?

We all know that a Java program contain classes that need to be executed. The class is nothing but the platform-neutral bytecode. When JVM starts executing this code, it has to interpret this bytecode so as to make sure that the underlying CPU understands that. This process is time-consuming, because of which the performance of application might be hampered as every method or code called has to be interpreted.

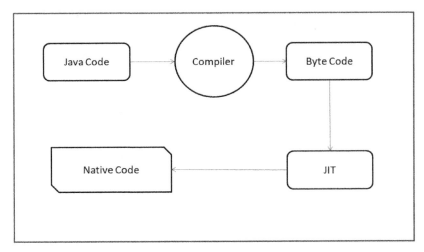

Figure 2.4: *Just-in-time compiler*

Figure 2.4 shows how JIT picks up the bytecodes and converts it to native code so that JVM can execute it.

Of course, like normal compilers, JIT is also bit expensive. It does require memory and other system resources. But, even if we consider this, JIT still improves the performance of an application as compared to the normal interpretation process by JVM.

How JIT works internally to choose methods to compile?

The way JIT works is interesting. The JIT compiler does not compile the method at the time the method is called. In fact, each method will be provided with a threshold compilation value. Each time the method is called, that threshold value is decremented by one, and the moment threshold value reaches zero, JIT compiles the method to native code.

Can we have different versions of JIT than the Java version?

JIT and JVM are integrated together. So, this option is not available where you can use different versions of JIT than JVM or Java. Normally, JIT comes bundled with JVM, so it is not possible to separate it and use as an independent component.

Can you disable JIT?

Yes, we can disable the JIT compiler by providing the options **-Xint** or **-DJava. compiler=NONE** to the Java command.

If you disable JIT, what consequences will you face?

Disabling JIT is not recommended as this will force to interpret the entire Java program. Because of this, the performance of the application will be hampered. So, normally, if someone wants to diagnose an application, then only the JIT is expected to be disabled.

What is the difference between JDK, JRE, and JVM?

JVM

Java virtual machine is a runtime environment provided by Java. The main task of JVM is to execute the bytecode, which is the platform-independent file format. JVM is platform-dependant, so we get different JVMs for different platforms. To initiate JVM, we need to execute the Java class.

JRE

This is typically implementation of JVM termed as **Java Runtime Environment**. The main job of JRE is to provide a runtime environment to Java. It comprises of the Java libraries that will help to execute the Java files.

JDK

JDK is an environment using which we can develop and compile Java applications or even applets. So, I would say this is a developer's bundle. JRE is essentially part of JDK nowadays.

What are the legal signatures of the main method?

JVM expects a main method in your program as a start-up method. The **main** method must be declared as **public**, **static,** and **void**. The **main** method must have arguments of type String. The arguments cannot be a single parameter, but you can have either an array of **String** or **var** argument of **String**.

The following are the legal signatures of the main method:

```
public static void main(String data[])
public static void main(String[] data)
public static void main(String… data)
static void main(String[] data)
static public void main(String… data)
```

Can we overload main( ) ?

Yes. Technically, we can overload the main method.

If you answer it as yes, the next question you can expect about it.

Will your program execute if you overload the main method?

The Java complier does not object the overloading of the method, which means that the compilation will be successful. But when we pass the generated class file to JVM, JVM will try to find out the signature that is known to it.

Consider the following code snippet:

```
1. public class TestIT{
2.    public static void main(int x){
3.        System.out.println("In overloaded main method");
4.    }
5. }
```

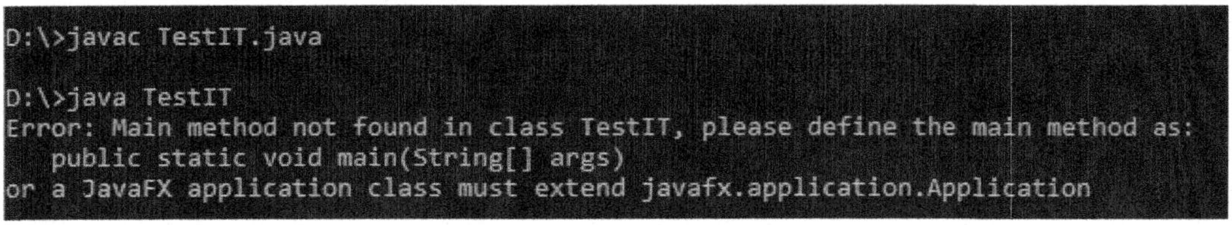

```
D:\>javac TestIT.java

D:\>java TestIT
Error: Main method not found in class TestIT, please define the main method as:
   public static void main(String[] args)
or a JavaFX application class must extend javafx.application.Application
```

Figure 2.5: *Overloading of main*

Here, the **TestIT** class contains the overloaded main method. This class will get compiled fine, but if executed, it will throw the error as shown in the preceding output screenshot.

Can we declare main() as private?

Again the answer is Yes!

The preceding question will be followed by the next question based on the access specifier rule of the private keyword.

But, if we declare any method, how will JVM find it?

We can declare the **main()** method as private. But, if you do so, it is not visible outside of the class. Because of this, JVM will not able to find it and will generate error that the main method is not found.

Can we declare main() as non-static?

Yes, we can do so.

Will your program execute successfully if you declare main as non-static?

If we declare the main method as non-static, then somebody needs to take the responsibility to initiate the class and then call the method by referring the object of that class. If we declare **main()** as static, then JVM loads the main method as **classname.main()**.

Conclusion

In this chapter, we discussed about the internal structure of Java. We talked about different components of Java that take an active part in the execution of a Java application. Along with this, we discussed different questions that could be asked on each of these components.

In the next chapter, we will cover the object orientation concepts of Java. We will cover the basic to advance features of object-oriented programming and the interview questions related to that.

CHAPTER 3
Object Orientation

Introduction

Object-Oriented Programming (OOP) language is a paradigm that has changed the approach of the traditional programming language. Earlier developers were frustrated by writing boilerplate code and maintaining it. In this modern era, developers can leverage the advantages of OOP and create applications that are easily extensible and maintainable. If you are not well versed with object orientation, then you will certainly fail miserably while developing your applications.

Structure

Learning OOP can be little bit boring. Object orientation principles are complex in nature theoretically as well as practically. There are many books available from which you can learn the OOP language. But, this chapter is focused on how you get successful in the questions asked about OOP. We will be covering the following concepts during this discussion:

- Class and objects
- Abstraction
- Encapsulation
- Inheritance

Objective

At the end of this chapter, you will be able to understand the core features of the OOP language, how to implement different concepts of the OOP language in Java. Also, we will discuss many interview questions as this is one of the most important segment of your interview.

Class and objects

The primary concept to understand about object orientation is a class and object. It is kind of "Evolution of Earth," which is then followed by the other living organism. So, one need to understand clearly about the class and object before proceeding to other concepts. Let us discuss what type of questions you will face and how to answer them.

What is a class?

A **class** is a factory of objects. The properties and behavior of objects are crafted by the class definition. We can also say that it contains the instruction about how your object will behave. It is a bridge between real-world entities and theoretical concepts. The variables declared in the class describe the physical properties of objects, and the methods of a class describe the behavior of an object. A good design of a class is always the most important part while designing the project architecture, as a wrong class design can lead to generate objects that might not work as per the expectations in the entire life cycle of the project as intended.

What are the conventions of designing a class?

Following conventions are followed while designing a class:

- Should have a capitalized name
- Should have camel Case methods
- Should be public, unless other access specifiers explicitly needed
- Should contain private data members
- Should contain public methods

Note: You might get a next question related with what are specifiers and their rules.

What is an object?

Where a class is imagination or expectation, an object is reality. An **object** is an entity created from a class. Every object has the values associated with the data members, which is termed as state, and the business logic to perform the tasks allocated to it, which is termed as behavior. Objects can be logical, or they may have physical existence in nature.

What are the characteristic of an object?

Every object has following properties associated with it:

- **State**

  The **state** is values against the properties that object possesses. The design of an object is normally achieved by this state. For example, when a car is blue, blue is a value of the color attribute that defines state of a car.

- **Behavior**

  Behavior is the functionality of an object. This is normally defined in a method inside a class. For example, starting an engine is a behavior of a car, which might have a process written behind it inside a method called `startEngine()`.

- **Identity**

  Every object of a type has a uniqueness associated with it, which is termed as the identity of that object. You may have any data members, which can be treated as an **identity,** or you may have the memory address of that object, considered as an identity, which is invisible to the programmer.

- **Responsibility**

  It is said that there is a reason for our birth. There is some task that is allocated to us by the almighty. Similarly, objects are created for a purpose; they are responsible for something. They must take part in the business logic for which they are created as a **responsibility**.

Detailed knowledge of an object is one of the most basic things that you must have. After all, an object is the core of OOP, and your entire development revolves around it. You should know how to create it, develop a relationship between different objects, and how to destroy it as well. If you fail to answer such basic questions, then you ought to fail miserably in your interviews. The answers of these questions are important, as the next journey of your interview will depend on this.

What is a constructor? Explain its role

A **constructor** is special method defined in the class, which has the same name as that of the class. Whenever the object is created, the constructor is invoked implicitly. The main reason of a constructor is to initialize the object, or in other words, to initiate the data members of object.

Can we have a private constructor?

Yes, we can write a private constructor. However, if we do so, there are some limitations we can observe as follows:

- You cannot create an object of this class.

- You cannot subclass this class.

- Normally, such practice is used in the singleton design pattern.

Why Java is not called as a 100% object-oriented programming language?

To consider any programming language as a OOP language, it should follow two principles. It must support all the pillars of the OOP language, which Java does. And second, everything of it must be an object. Unfortunately, this is where Java lacks. Java still has some features like primitives, which are not objects. Of course, Java has wrappers as counterpart objects of primitives, but the existence of primitives in an API makes is non-eligible for a complete OOP language according to many developers.

Why all the instance variables have default values in Java?

When we create an object by using the new keyword, the memory is reserved in heap. To initialize this memory, JVM provides the default constructor, which takes the responsibility to initiate the instance variables to default values. This constructor is always present when we create an object. So, if you provide your own constructor, it will be called after the constructor provided by JVM.

What are the accessor and mutator methods in Java, and what is their significance?

Every class has data members that take part in the business logic. Accessing and modifying such data members always require the help of methods. These methods can be used to initiate the data members or set the data members. But, if we write a single method to access and modify a data member, we are violating the abstraction rule of object orientation. So, the concept of **accessor** and **mutator** methods was introduced in Java. These methods are dedicated to single data members. So, every data member will have two methods that are **setter** and **getter**. The **setter** method is used to set the value of data member, which is called as **mutator** methods. And, **getter** is used to get the value of the data member for which it is declared, which is called as the **accessor** method. Apart from this, there is one more advantage of the **accessor** and **mutator** methods. Many of the frameworks like spring, hibernate communicate internally to the data members of your object. If the methods for accessing the data members are written by you, then it is not possible for the framework to search such a method. But, frameworks can find the getter and setter methods internally to communicate with the data members implicitly.

Object creation

Creation of an object is another basic but important area where an interviewer tests you. You should know what do you mean by creating an object, and what are the different ways of creating an object. The following section covers most of the questions related with object creation.

What are the different ways to create objects?

- Using the new keyword
- Using the new instance method
- Using the clone method
- Using de-serialization

The preceding answer will be followed by some more connected questions, for which you should be completely ready. Always be sure that you know answers to those questions as well.

How to create an object using the *newInstance* method?

This is termed as a reflective approach of creating an object dynamically. This method is present in the **java.lang.Class**. Normally, when we use the new keyword, we are creating the objects of the classes that are present locally. But, when we are creating objects of the class from a remote source, it is not possible to use the new keyword. Or, sometimes you want a user to provide information of the class for the object you want to create. In such a case, you will need to use the **newInstance()** method. This method is used in conjunction with the **Class.forName**. **Class.forName("")** takes in argument the fully qualified name of the class; a user can provide this as an input parameter as well.

How to create a copy of an existing object?

If you want to create a copy of an existing object, you have to override the clone() method in your class. The **clone()** method is declared in the object super class, and it creates and returns the physical copy of an existing object.

How the clone method is different from copying the reference of an object to another?

The **clone** method creates a physical copy of the existing object. The objects created by this method have their own memory space and separate existence. But, if you copy the reference of one object to another, you are indicating that you have two references pointing toward the same object. So, ideally, you are not creating a new object , but you are creating another reference that points to an existing object.

How to use the clone method to create a new object?

The method **clone()** from the object super class is used to create a new object from existing object. When we invoke **clone()**, JVM copies the entire content of an existing object into a new object. Before you use the **clone()** method, you must make your class eligible for cloning. To do that thing, your class must implement the **Cloneable** interface and override the clone method, which is shown as follows:

```
1.  public class Student implements Cloneable {
2.    int rollNo;
3.    String studName;
4.
5.    Student(int rollNo, String studName) {
6.      this.rollNo = rollNo;
7.      this.studName = studName;
8.    }
9.
10. public Object clone() throws CloneNotSupportedException {
11.   return super.clone();
```

```
12. }
13.
14. public String toString() {
15.   return this.rollNo + "," + this.studName;
16. }
17.
18. public static void main(String args[]) {
19.   try
20.   {
21.     Student s1 = new Student(101, "John Doe");
22.     Student s2 = (Student) s1.clone();
23.
24.     System.out.println(s1);
25.     System.out.println(s2);
26.   }
27.   catch (CloneNotSupportedException c) {
28.     System.out.println("CloneNotSupportedException occurred");
29.   }
30.
31. }
32. }
```

When your code will throw the CloneNotSupported Exception?

When we try to clone an object that does not implement the **Cloneable** interface, JVM throws this exception. You cannot invoke the clone method on an object if it is not implementing the **Cloneable** interface.

How to serialize an object?

When we want to serialize an object, the primary thing that we must do is to implement the marker interface **Serializable** to the class of that object. This makes the object of that class eligible for serialization.

Once you do this, you can open the file in the write mode and serialize your object by invoking the **serialize()** method.

Note: There are few more questions that can be asked on serialization, but we will cover those in *Chapter 5, File Handling*, in detail.

What is de-serialization, and how it generates a new object?

De-serialization is the process by which we can retrieve the serialized object. We do not need any constructor to create such objects, but JVM internally reads the entire bytecodes stored for that object when it was serialized. Then, the extracted data is wrapped in an object format and provided back to the user.

Note: Sometimes, the interviewer might walk a step ahead and ask you about whether you can de-serialize the object serialized from other frameworks, for example, if an object is serialized in C#, can Java de-serialize the same? The answer is NO! De-serialization is a language-dependent process, as in the serialization process, the language information is added in the serialized object.

What are the different access specifiers present in Java? Can you explain their significance?

Following are the access specifiers in Java:

- **private**

  When we declare any member as private, it is said to be having highest secure member. Such member is accessible within the class in which it is declared. Even if you import a class, such data members are not accessible. Only inner classes can access the private data members of outer class in which it is declared.

- **default**

  As the name indicates, it is a default access specifier. There is no specific way to declare it, but if you do not mention any specifier, the member is said to be having default access. The members with this specifier are accessible within the same package.

- **protected**

  When we declare a member as protected, the member is accessible within the package. It is also available outside the package as well, but only to the subclasses of that class.

- **public**

  When we want to declare any member that is exposed to the entire world, we can declare that member with a public access specifier. Of course, even though we use a public access specifier, it is compulsory that we import that class if we are using the member out of the package.

Can we apply a private modifier to class?

This is a tricky question. Because if you say that you can apply a private modifier to a class, the answer is incorrect. But, from a different perspective, you can apply the private keyword to a class if it is an inner class.

Encapsulation

Famous poet Fernando Pessoa once said "If after I die, people want to write my biography, there is nothing simpler. They only need two dates: the date of my birth and the date of my death. Between one and another, every day is mine." Everyone enjoys privacy in real world. Same is the case with objects, after all they represent the real world. Objects are recommended to be designed in a way that they hide the way they are built and the way they process the data to achieve something through encapsulation.

What is encapsulation, and how to achieve that?

Every object consists of data members and member functions. The value of data members denotes the state of an object, and the member functions define the behavior of an object. Behavior is normally controlled by the value of data members. So, if we want an object to behave as designed by the creator, then the data members should not be exposed directly to the end users. This hiding of internal structure or data members from external world is termed as encapsulation.

We can achieve encapsulation by declaring the data members as private and member functions as public. By this way, the users of the system will able to access only the member function and not the data members.

Can you explain why we should follow encapsulation, with real-time example?

Sure. Consider the class Rectangle in the code as follows:

```
1. public class Rectangle {
2.    int width,height;
3.    double area;
```

```
4.   public Rectangle(int width) {
5.    height=width*2;
6.   }
7.   public double calculateArea() {
8.    area=width*height;
9.    return area;
10. }
11. }
```

Here, we are expecting that the user will initialize the width of the rectangle, and the height will be calculated internally as per the logic written by the developer:

```
1.  public class RectangleApp {
2.  public static void main(String[] args) {
3.    Rectangle rectangle=new Rectangle(10);
4.    System.out.println(rectangle.calculateArea());
5.  }
6.  }
```

This preceding code will initialize width as 10, and internally, the height will be calculated as double the width, that is **20**. But, the problem with this approach is, as encapsulation is not followed, the object of the rectangle can initialize the data member height directly as:

```
1.  Rectangle rectangle=new Rectangle(10);
2.  rectangle.height=200;
```

We do not want this manual modification for the height data member. To achieve this, we need to declare the width and height as private data members so that they are not accessed out of the class as:

```
1.  public class Rectangle {
2.  private int width,height;
3.  //implementation code
4.  }
```

To achieve complete encapsulation, can we declare the class with a private access specifier?

One may find luxury to declare a class as private to achieve the encapsulation automatically. But, it is not permitted. The reason is obvious. If you declare a class with private, then it is not accessible to the outside world, not even to JVM, which accesses the class to load and execute the main method.

Inheritance

Java provides many concepts as a part of its inheritance mechanism. In fact, most of the interviewers will spend at least 60% of their interview duration on inheritance. You must be well prepared about inheritance if you want to get successful in your interview of Java. The next few pages are dedicated to inheritance-related questions.

What is association in Java?

When we develop an application, we deal with many objects. These objects can interact with other. In other words, the objects can utilize the services that are defined by other objects. Such type of relationship between the objects is called as an **association**.

What is composition in Java?

Designing a class is always a creative job. You define properties and behavior that control the overall working of an object. Some of the properties of an object itself can contain some behavior. Let us take an example where a car contains an engine. The engine is one of the properties of a car, but the engine itself can have its own attributes and behavior. So, we can have the engine defined as a separate class with its own properties and behavior, which can be declared as a property of the car. This concept is termed as composition or has-a-kind relation.

The following code snippet will demonstrate how the composition can be implemented:

```
1.  public class Car {
2.    String color;
3.    Engine engine;//composition
4.    public void drive() {
5.
6.    }
7.    public void start() {
8.
9.    }
10. }
11.
```

```
12. public class Engine {
13.    //data member
14.    //member functions
15. }
```

What is the difference between composition and aggregation?

Both these are types of association in Java. Both these concepts use the other object as a part of it. But, there is one difference. Once we use composition, if we destroy the main object, the object that is associated with it also gets destroyed or not meaningful. In case of aggregation, even if we delete the main object, the other object still exists in the system.

Can you give one example of composition and aggregation?

One of the simple examples of composition is about a car and engine. A car is composed of an engine, but if we destroy the car, the engine on its own cannot perform. On the other hand, if we take an example of a school and students, where the school will have students associated with it. In this case, even if we destroy the school object, students can still exist and perform their role in the system.

What is difference between is-a-kind relation and has-a-kind relation in Java?

Java supports two types of inheritance approaches, is-a-kind and has-a-kind relationship. The is-a-kind relationship demonstrates a classical approach of inheritance where you create a new type that behaves similarly to the existing type. In this approach, you create a new object that essentially inherits all the properties and behavior of an already existing object, which is called as its super class. The newly created object is termed as a subclass. For example, a car is of type vehicle. Here, vehicle defines the common attributes for different types of vehicles. A car is a subclass that can be designed as is-a type of car. This achieves reusability of the code, which is defined in vehicle. So, you do not have to redefine the common properties or methods that are already defined in the vehicle.

On the other hand, has-a-kind represents composition. In this approach, the one object has a reference to other object as a part of its attribute. Here, the newly created object does not inherit the properties and behavior of an existing object. But, it can use its services by the reference that is declared within it. For example, a car has a steering wheel, or a car has an engine inside it.

How do you explain the term coupling?

Software development is complex scenario, and we know it from our birth. As we are moving more toward advance features of programming, it is getting more and more complex. **Software** is essentially a collection of different components communicating with each other to achieve something. This communication often requires the relationship to be established between different components of a system with each other. This relationship or connection is termed as **coupling** in the OOP language.

What do you mean by loose coupling?

Often, when we create software, the components are dependent on each other, which is coupling. **Loose coupling** is the type of coupling in which, if one component is modified the other component of system does not get impacted. In a nutshell, the components are independent of each other, though there is some relationship between them.

What do you mean by tight coupling?

If two components in a system are dependent on each other in such a way that changes done in one component impact the other component, then such coupling is termed as **tight coupling**. In this case, if we change one component, the other component is also forced to be changed.

How do you achieve tight coupling, can you explain with a real-time example?

Tight coupling is a scenario in which a component is dependent on other component. If we change one component, the other component is required to be changed.

To explain this concept, I am considering two objects A and B where A is using services of B using the concept of composition, as shown in the following code:

```
1. class A {
2.    B b;
3.    public A() {
4.        b = new B();
5.    }
```

```
6.      public void display() {
7.          System.out.println("In A");
8.          b.display();
9.      }
10. }
11.
12. class B {
13.     public B(){}
14.     public void display() {
15.         System.out.println("In B");
16.     }
17. }
```

As mentioned, A is using services of B, which is tightly coupled with it. If you look at the **display()**method in class A, it is internally calling **display()** of B. So, any change in the **display()** method of B will produce a different output for A. Also, the code will completely fail if we rename the **display()** method from class B as the method is called from class A.

What if instead of using the services of class B, now class A wants to use the services from class C? Then, we need to modify Line number 2 of the preceding code as:

```
2.      C c;
```

This will obviously require recompilation of class B. This scenario explains tight coupling in a real sense.

Explain loose coupling in Java with a real-time example?

Flexibility is the main reason why loose coupling is introduced in OOP. When you design a component in such a way that you can plugin and plug out the components within another component, you are essentially talking about the loose coupling.

Consider the following code snippet:

```
1. interface Print {
2.   public void display();
3. }
4.
5. class A {
```

```
6.   Print s;
7.   public A(Print s) {
8.     this.s = s;
9.   }
10.  public void display() {
11.    System.out.println("In A");
12.    s.display();
13.  }
14. }
15.
16. class B implements Print {
17.  public B() {
18.  }
19.  public void display() {
20.    System.out.println("In B");
21.  }
22. }
23.
24. class C implements Print {
25.  public C() {
26.  }
27.  public void display() {
28.    System.out.println("In C");
29.  }
30. }
```

In the preceding code, we have introduced the interface Print. The Print interface is implemented by classes B and C. And, if you observe class A, instead of referring to B or C, which will create the glue code, it refers type of Print, which could be either B or C dynamically. This is a classic example of loose coupling. So, at runtime, we can decide which object A can refer, as shown in the following code:

```
1.  public class LooseCouplingDemo {
2.    public static void main(String args[]) {
3.      Print b = new B();
4.      Print c = new C();
```

```
5.
6.    A a = new A(b);
7.    a.display();
8.
9.    A a1 = new A(c);
10.   a1.display();
11. }
12. }
```

Can you explain when to use is-a-kind relationship and when to use has-a-kind relationship in Java?

Whenever you want to create a new entity that behaves like an existing entity, then we can create an is-a-kind relationship. This is termed as **inheritance**. On the other hand, when we want the services of other object within our object, then we need to create has-a-kind relationship. This is termed as **containment** in Java.

What is abstract class?

An **abstract class** is said to be an incomplete class. This class declares skeleton and not the stub. This means that the class declares methods but does not define the body of it. The class declares the incomplete methods by declaring them as abstract. Such abstract methods need to be overridden by the subclass that extends the abstract class.

What is a final class, and why one need to declare it?

A class when declared as **final** cannot be extended. When you want to make sure that your services cannot be modified by creating a subclass, you can declare the class as final. By declaring a class as **final**, all the methods implicitly become final. If you wish, you can apply the final keyword to selective methods.

What is a final method?

When a method is declared with the **final** keyword, we are restricting the overriding. That means the method is not permitted to override. Subclass cannot override such method.

Can the abstract class contain constructors?

Yes. An abstract class can have a constructor as a part of its definition.

Why abstract classes provide constructors even though they are not instantiated?

An abstract class does not represent only skeleton. Sometimes, it may have the concrete methods with some business logic. In order to execute the business logic of that method, the abstract class may require the local variables or the data members. So, to have the some default value for the data member, the abstract class gives your constructors where you or JVM can initialize the data members.

What are concrete methods and abstract methods?

Normally, when we define a class, we write the methods that describe the behavior of an object. These methods have a body associated with it in the boundaries of curly braces. Such methods are termed as concrete methods.

But, in some cases, instead of a class defining the behavior, it delegates the implementation to its subclasses. In such cases, the methods are declared, but the body is not defined. Such methods are termed as abstract methods, which are terminated by semicolon (;) instead of curly braces.

Even if the method is declared with empty curly braces, the method is still treated as a concrete method and not an abstract method.

Can we declare all the methods of abstract class as a concrete method?

Yes. We can have the class where all of its methods are concrete and still declare such class as an abstract class. But, as we know, we cannot instantiate an abstract class. Because of this, if you want to use the services provided by this class, you need to subclass this class and then instantiate it.

Can we declare an abstract class as final?

The whole objective of declaring any class as an abstract class is to subclass it. We always extend the abstract class and instantiate the subclass. A subclass also overrides the abstract methods that are declared by the abstract class. The final keyword makes the class non-eligible for the subclass; one cannot extend the class if the class is declared as final. Because of this, the declared abstract class as final is not permitted.

Can we have abstract methods as private?

When we declare any method as private, basically, we are snatching visibility from it. The method is not visible to the outside world. Abstract methods need to be overridden by the subclass for which they must be visible to the subclass. As private methods are not visible outside the class, you cannot override it. So, it is not permitted to declare abstract methods as private.

Can we declare abstract methods as static?

The **static keyword** is associated with a class and not with an object. On the other hand, the concept of overriding is establishing relations between the objects where you can override the methods of a super class. Because of this, anything that is not part of an object cannot be overridden, so the static keyword is not used while declaring an abstract method.

Who takes the responsibility to call the constructor of an abstract class if the abstract class cannot be instantiated?

An abstract class is extended by the subclass. Every subclass while getting instantiated calls its own constructor implicitly. And, the constructor provides the "super" keyword, which calls the constructor of the super class.

```
1.  public abstract class A{
2.    int x;
3.    public abstract void method1();
4.  }
5.
6.  public class B extends A{
7.    public void method1(){
8.      //body of method 1
9.    }
10.}
```

The preceding snippet is equivalent to:

```
1. public abstract class A{
2.    int x;
3.    public A(){
4.       //initialization of data members
5.    }
6.    public abstract void method1();
7. }
8.
9. public class B extends A{
10.   public B(){
11.      super(); //calls the default constructor of super class
          i.e. abstract class A
12.   }
13.   public void method1(){
14.      //body of method 1
15.   }
16. }
```

Can interfaces have a constructor? How it is different than the abstract classes?

Unlike abstract classes, an interface cannot have a constructor. As an interface does not have data members, there is no need for a constructor for it. One major difference between an abstract class and interface is, interfaces contain only abstract methods, whereas an abstract class can contain a combination of concrete and abstract classes.

What is the need for interfaces?

Java does not support multiple inheritances. Because of this, you cannot utilize the services declared or defined from multiple resources. Interfaces are a solution to this problem. You can extend a single class and multiple interfaces for your classes. **Interfaces** are real-time implementation of complete abstraction where you declare the methods, and implementation is left with the subclass. Interfaces also play a major role in implementing loose coupling.

What is polymorphic reference?

A polymorphic reference is used to control the behavior of a subclass dynamically. When the subclass object is referred by the super class reference, such reference is termed as a polymorphic reference. Any instance that takes part in is-a kind of relationship can take part in a polymorphic reference. So, any object can be referred by its immediate superclass, indirect superclass, interface it is implementing or even the cosmic superclass object.

What is significance of a polymorphic reference, and how would you achieve the same?

When we use an object reference to invoke a method, JVM searches that method in the object to which you are referring, and it executes that method. In case the method is not present in the subclass, then the method of super class gets executed if it is present in the super class. So, prima facie, a subclass is flexible enough to write and execute the method that is not present in the superclass. A subclass is a supreme boss traditionally, unless someone controls it.

Consider following code snippet, where **Dog** is a subclass of **Animal**:

```
1. public class Dog extends Animal{
2.   public void talk() {
3.    System.out.println("Dog is barking");
4.   }
5. }
```

Dog extends **Animal**, and it can override the methods from the **Animal** class. So, the reference to **Dog** when calls method **talk()** will invoke the implementation from **Dog,** and when the method **breath()** is called, then the method from the **Animal** class is called, as the method is not present in the **Dog** class. But, let us consider the implementation of **Dog** as follows:

```
1. public class Dog extends Animal{
2.   public void talk() {
3.    System.out.println("Dog is barking");
4.   }
5.   public void read() {
6.    System.out.println("Dog is reading Economic Times");
7.   }
8. }
```

Here, you can see the intelligent **Dog** can even read the Economic Times. You may like that, but economists might hate that. And, the most interesting thing is, as the subclass is being independent, nobody can object this.

Let us now change the reference of **Dog,** which is shown as follows:

```
1. Animal d=new Dog();
2. d.read()
```

The preceding code fails as the object of **Dog** is referred by **Animal,** and it is trying to call the method that is not known to **Animal**. This way, we can control the behavior of the subclass using the polymorphic reference.

If Object is a cosmic superclass, what is wrong if you refer every object by it?

Technically, there is nothing wrong in referring every object by the **Object** super class. But, this will create a very weird situation dynamically. Imagine the following statements:

```
1. Object one=new Employee();
2. Object two=new Car();
3. Object three=new Student();
```

Here, all the three objects are referred by the **Object** super class, which is perfectly fine for a compiler. But, when you try to invoke the methods of Employee, Car, or Students using the respective references, it will fail. The reason is quite obvious. Because all the objects are polymorphically referred, only those methods can be invoked that are known to the **Object** class.

Can we extend more than one class?

No, in Java, multiple inheritance is not supported. Though you can create hierarchical inheritance, you cannot create multiple inheritance.

How do you achieve multiple inheritance in Java?

The only way by which you can achieve multiple inheritance in Java is by using the concept of interfaces. You can create an interface and implement it in the class where you would like to have the multiple inheritance. Your class can extend one class, and it can implement any number of interfaces.

Can you implement more than one interfaces?

Yes, we can. One of the important reasons of using an interface is to achieve the cohesion effectively. You can implement more than one interface even if all the interfaces are not related with each other.

The other thing that you can do is you can create relationships between the interfaces and use them as a hierarchal inheritance.

Let us observe following code snippets for interfaces **First** and **Second**.

First.java

```
1. public interface First {
2.   public void methodFirst();
3. }
```

Second.java

```
1. public interface Second extends First{
2.   public void methodSecond();
3. }
```

In the preceding snippet, interface Second is extended from First. You can extend one interface from another.

InterfaceDemo.java

```
1. public class InterfaceDemo implements Second{
2.   //implementation of methods from interface First,Second
3. }
```

In the preceding snippet, the class **InterfaceDemo** implements the interface **Second**. But, as the **Second** interface extends First, the implementation class **InterfaceDemo** must implement the methods from interfaces First and Second.

If your class implements two interfaces and both the interfaces declare similar methods, which method will be invoked? Is it permitted?

Nothing is wrong in this. You can have two interfaces having a similar abstract method, which can be implemented by any class. Once the class implements both interfaces, it must override the method from both the interfaces. So, ideally, when a class implements or overrides such method, the method becomes the behavior of the class and not of interface. So, when you create an object of such class and invoke the method, it becomes irrelevant for the caller about the interface in which the method is declared. Even if you refer the object by any of the interfaces, it does not make any difference for execution.

Consider the following code snippet:

```
1.  interface First {
2.    public void method1();
3.  }
4.  interface Second{
5.    public void method1();
6.  }
7.
8.  class DemoInterface implements First,Second{
9.    @Override
10.   public void method1() {
11.    // TODO Auto-generated method stub
12.   }
13. }
```

In the preceding snippet, there are two interfaces, **First** and **Second**. Both these interfaces declare the same method as **method1()**. When **DemoInterface** implements the **First** and **Second** interfaces, it must override methods from both the interfaces. But, as both interfaces contain the same method, the class can have a single method that suffices the method declared in both the interfaces, so the program compiles fine.

> **Note: If the question is framed in different words like – can you have different interfaces with the same method signature implemented by a single class? The answer for this is still YES. But, if you come across some scenario like this, then there is something wrong in the design of your application. Make sure that you talk about this in front of the interviewer.**

What is use of the final keyword?

In Java, there is no **const** keyword, which is present in earlier programming languages like C, C++. The keyword **final** is used to mark something that cannot be modified. You can declare variables as final, which makes them constants. You can also declare classes as final, which makes them non eligible for extending. You can even declare a method as final. If you declare a method as final, the subclass is not permitted to override the same.

Can we make the reference as final? What does it mean?

We can make the reference as final. Making reference final does not mean that you are making the object that it refers final. When you declare any reference as final, you cannot reassign the object to the same reference.

Consider the code snippet as follows:

```
1. final String x="abc";

2. x="xyz"; //compilation error

3. x.concat("xyz");
```

In the snippet, String **x** is declared as final. This means we cannot reassign any object to the same. Because of this, Line number 2 will fail at compilation. But, as you can see, you can make the changes in actual object by invoking the **concat()** method on the object to which it is referring.

What is use of a static variable?

Static keywords are used to declare class variables. Normally, when we declare any data member, it is instantiated independently for different objects. It has different copies of variables allocated to different object. So, if one object makes any changes in that variable, the other object does not have any relation with that. The other object will have its own copy of that variable on which it can process.

On the other hand, if we declare variable as static, the copy of such variable is shared across all the objects of same type. So, if one object makes modification in such variables, the other object will get the updated copy of that variable.

What is use of a static method?

As we are aware, we can declare the static variables in a class. **Static variables** are class variables that have only one copy of variable shared across all the objects. When we want to process static variables, it is recommended to use the static method. So, essentially, static methods are used to process or return the static variables.

Can we use a non-static method to process static variables?

Yes. We can use a non-static method to process static variables. Though this might create confusion in a developer's mind, but technically, it is permitted.

Can we use a static method to process instance variables?

No. Whenever we declare static methods, the keyword this is never used within it. The instance variables are always prefixed with the **this** keyword by the compiler. But, static methods are not dedicated to any specific objects, they are termed as class methods, and they cannot process any business logic that is dedicated to a specific object. So, we cannot use non-static members within the static method.

Can we declare static and instance variables with same name?

No, you cannot have the same name for static and instance variable as it will create confusion for the compiler.

In what scenario can you use a static variable?

There are numerous scenarios in which you can use a static variable. Let us assume that you have an Employee class. If you are interested to count how many Employee objects are created, you would require a counter variable that can be increased by 1 every time the object is created. But, if you create declare counter variable as an instance variable, then if one object increases the value of the counter variable, then other object will still get the original value of the counter. In such case, you can declare the counter as static so that all the updates on the counter variable will be shared across all the objects of Employee as follows:

```
1.  public class Employee {
2.    int empId;
3.    String empName;
4.    static int counter;
5.    public Employee(int empId,String empName) {
6.      this.empId=empId;
7.      this.empName=empName;
8.      counter++;
9.    }
10. public static int getCounter() {
11.   return counter;
12. }
```

```
13. public static void main(String[] args) {
14.   Employee e1=new Employee(101,"John");
15.   Employee e2=new Employee(102,"Smith");
16.   Employee e3=new Employee(103,"Derek");
17.   System.out.println("Total Employees :"+Employee.getCounter());
18. }
19. }
```

Can I apply static anywhere apart from variables?

Certainly, apart from the variables, you can apply the static keyword at numerous locations. You can make any method as static. You can declare the static block, which executes before the **main()** method. Apart from this, there is a concept called as **static instantiation block,** which is executed just before the creation of an object. You can also use the static keyword with a class that is termed as a static class. But, you cannot make any class as static unless it is nested in some other class. Such class is called as a **static nested inner class**.

What is the use of this keyword?

The **this** keyword refers the current object. Normally, it is used to call another constructor of the same object. This is the only way to call the constructor of the same object. You can call a parameterized constructor from default or from default to a parameterized constructor using the this keyword.

Also,if there is any ambiguity with the local variables and instance variables, you can use the this keyword to denote the instance variables differently than the local variable.

Explain the significance of the super keyword

The **super** keyword refers to the super class. If you want to call the members of the super class explicitly from a subclass, then you can use this keyword. You can invoke data members or member functions of a super class. Not only that, you can also invoke the constructor of the super class explicitly from a subclass constructor.

Another use of the super keyword is done by JVM when it calls the default constructor of super class implicitly from the constructor of the subclass.

The super keyword must be the first line of the constructor.

Why the super keyword must be located as the first line of the constructor?

When we say that we are in a subclass, it obviously contains some data members. Many times, the data members of the subclass are dependent on the data members of the super class. So, unless the data members of super classes are initialized, the subclass data members cannot be initialized. So, to make sure that the super class data members are initialized prior to any member of the subclass, the super keyword is placed as the first line of the constructor.

In what sequence the constructors will be called if we create an object of a subclass?

When we create an object of any class, implicitly, the constructor of the same object gets called. But internally, that constructor calls the constructor of the super class by using the super keyword. So practically, though we can observe that the constructor of the super class is called first, theoretically, it is not like that. It is "not everything as it seems.". Always, the constructor of the subclass executes first, which internally invokes the superclass constructor.

Do we have the destructors in Java?

Unlike the traditional programming language like C++, we do not have a destructor in Java that matches with the class name. But, the method **finalize()** is termed as a destructor in Java. This method is called implicitly by JVM when the object memory gets deleted from the virtual memory. We can override this method to write the customized code to free up the resources connected with the current object.

Which methods are present in the Object class that can be overridden?

Following methods are part of the **Object** class that can be overridden by a subclass protected object **clone()**

- public Boolean equals(Object o)
- protected void finalize()
- public int hashCode()
- public String toString()

Once you list out different methods from the **Object** class, next, you can expect a series of questions based on these methods.

What is use of the toString() method?

As the name indicates, this method represents the object in the String format. It returns a string that consists of information about an object, which is easy to read for the user. If it is not overridden, then it returns the hexadecimal representation of the hash code of the object. We can override this method so as to return the string that we want to represent as an object information as per the business need.

What is the equals() method, and how is it used?

This method is used to check the equality of an object. Developers can override this method to implement the business logic to check the equality of the object. In this method, a developer can check member-wise equality and return true or false depending upon the result. If this method is not overridden, then the Object super class considers every object as unequal and returns false to the invoker.

Can we declare an interface with the abstract keyword?

We can declare an interface with the abstract keyword, but it is not required. Interfaces are internally, by default, abstract classes, so we can declare an interface as an abstract interface.

If an interface is internally a class, does it extend the cosmic super class, that is, the Object class by default?

There is no cosmic super class available for interfaces. As there is no scope of any business logic because of its abstraction approach, there is no need for the Object super class.

What is the default method in an interface?

The **default method** concept is introduced in JDK1.8. Normally, interfaces provide full abstraction, but default methods in an interface are implemented methods in an interface. It is as good as creating an abstract class with a combination of concrete as well as abstract methods.

Why default method is required in an interface?

Sometimes, we have an interface implemented by some classes. Let us assume that now the interface wants to declare one more method because of some business need. But, the moment we add some additional method in an interface, the class that is connected with that interface will fail, as it is not aware about the new method that is introduced in that interface.

So, in such cases, the newly created method or methods can be created as default implemented method. By doing so, the existing class, which is dependent on the interface, does not need to modify itself as the method in the interface has a body associated with it. The new class where your interface is going to be implemented can override the method if required.

Can an interface have more than one method as default implemented methods?

Yes, an interface can have as many methods as they want as default implemented methods.

What is a static method in an interface, and what is its significance?

Static methods in an interface are similar to default methods, which means that they have the body associated with them. But, the difference between both of them is, as the method is static, the subclass that implements that interface does not have permission to override it; on the other hand, the default method can be overridden.

What is a functional interface?

Function interfaces are interfaces with a sole reason. This means that the functional interface declares only one method as a part of its content. Any class that implements this interface will need to override this method so as to make sure that it provides the meaning to the service that declared by the functional interface.

Which is a cosmic super class in Java?

The emperor **Object** class is termed as a **cosmic super class** of every object in Java. Even if you do not explicitly mention any class extending Object, by default, JVM makes Object as a super class for each and every class.

What is the difference between an equal operator (= =) and equals method?

The equality operator = = is normally used with primitives to check the equality of the variables. On the other hand, the **equals()** method checks the equality of object comparing the data members. To check if the two objects are equal, we need to override the **equals()** method from the Object superclass. We can also use the= = operator with object references, but instead of checking the object, it will check the equality of references.

The = = operator will return true only if both the references are pointing toward the same object.

What is a var argument? Where can it be used?

When we overload a method, we modify the arguments of the method. Either we change the type of argument or number of arguments. If we want to overload a method that takes different number of parameters of same data type, instead of declaring different methods with different number of arguments, we can use var arguments.

```
1.  public class Calculator {
2.    public void add(int a,int b) {
3.      //body of method
4.    }
5.    public void add(int a,int b, int c) {
6.      //body of method
7.    }
8.    public void add(int a,int b, int c, int d) {
9.      //body of method
10. }
11.}
```

In the preceding code snippet, we have overloaded three different methods taking different number of integer arguments. This code snippet can be replaced with the var argument as follows :

```
1.  public class CalculatorWithVarArg {
2.    public void add(int... values) {
```

```
3.    //body of method
4.  }
5. }
```

What do you mean by method overloading?

Method overloading is also termed as compile time polymorphism where the method signatures are identified at compile time. Method overloading is essentially the same method name with different arguments. The arguments may differ in terms of number of arguments or type of arguments. The return type of the method, or the access specifier of method does not have any impact on the concept of method overloading.

What are the different rules for declaring the var argument method?

The following rules must be followed while using the **var** argument:

1. There must be one and only one **var** argument in the given method.

2. If you are using the **var** argument along with other primitive argument, then the **var** argument must be declared as a last argument of method.

What is the difference between using the var argument and array as a method argument?

Technically, there is no difference. The **var** argument internally arrays in Java. The only difference is the way the method is invoked. If you have the method with a **var** argument, you can invoke the method by passing the comma-separated values. But, if you have the method with array as an argument, then the invoker must first create an array and pass that array as an argument while invoking that method.

What is method overriding?

Method overriding is termed as dynamic polymorphism in Java. In this concept, the method declared or defined in the super class is redefined in the subclass. We need to make sure that the method signature must remain same, which includes the arguments and return type. Method overriding is observed only in case of inheritance.

What are rules of method overriding in Java?

The following are the rules for method overriding:

- The overridden method must have same name and same argument list.

- The overridden method must have same return type or the covariant return type (covariant return type is subtype of the original method's return type).

- The overridden method must not have more restrictive access specifier.

- The final method cannot be overridden.

- Private methods cannot be overridden as they are not visible outside the class where they are declared or defined.

- The overridden method must not throw new or broader checked exceptions.

- *Synchronized* modifier has no impact on the overriding process.

- The *Strictfp* modifier has no impact on the overriding process.

- Static methods cannot be overridden.

Can we overload a static method?

A static method can be overloaded, as the overloading concept is only limited to the types or number of argument. The other keywords applied to the method do not make any sense when you overload the method.

Can we override the static method?

This question is little tricky. If we declare the method in the super class as static and rewrite the same method declaration with different implementation, then there is no compilation error. But, this is not termed as overriding. The keyword static is not considered in any concepts of object orientation, especially that of inheritance. So, in a nutshell, we can say that we cannot override the static method.

What is a co-variant return type?

When we override the method in a subclass, we must keep the return type of the method same or subtype of the original return type. This subtype of return type is termed as a **co-variant return type**.

> **Note: In case the interviewer asks you about elaborating in detail, then you can produce the following code snippet to him/her.**

```
1. public class A {
```

```
2.   public Number returnSomething() {
3.     return 10;
4.   }
5. }
6. public class B extends A {
7.   public Integer returnSomething() { //
     overridden method with covariant return type
8.     return 10;
9.   }
10. }
```

In the preceding snippet, class B is a subclass of A, and it overrides the **returnSomething()** method, which is defined in its superclass A. If you observe the return type of the method in the super class, it returns Number. But, in the subclass, the method is returning Integer, which is a subtype of Number. Such type of return type is termed as a co-variant return type.

Can we change the return type of the overridden method?

By the rule, the return type of the overridden method must be same. However, there is one more alternative available to you. Instead of having the return type exactly the same, you can keep the method return type as subtype of the method that is defined in the super class.

Do we have any restrictions on the access modifier when we implement method overloading?

Precisely, the concept of method overloading is only connected with the method signature. In method overloading, we need to strictly maintain the same method name with a different argument list. Method overloading has nothing to do with an access modifier, so there is no any restriction whether you need to keep the access modifier same or different while overloading.

> **Note: Sometimes, the interviewer might share some code with you on a white paper where method overloading is implemented with different access modifiers, so make sure that you know what has to be observed while reading the overloaded method.**

What is the difference between an abstract class and interface?

The following are the differences between an abstract class and interface:

1. An abstract class can contain abstract as well as concrete methods; an interface can contain only abstract methods.

2. An abstract class may contain a constructor, but an interface cannot contain a constructor.

3. An abstract class may contain data members, but an interface can declare and initialize only constants.

4. An abstract class does not support multiple inheritance, but an interface can extend multiple interfaces.

5. An abstract class can have members that may private, protected or even public. Interfaces, on the other hand, have everything as public by default.

What is a marker interface?

A **marker interface** is a special type of interface that does not have any method declared within it. It even does not have the field associated with it. This interface is also called as a tagging interface.

What is use of a marker interface?

Marker interfaces are used to instruct the compiler about the special behavior that can be applied to a class at runtime. You do not have to override any method to implement interface; it is just some extra information provided to the compiler. Of course, there are certain other ways than a marker interface to provide extra information to the compiler like declaring some flag inside the class. But, if we use a marker interface, it adds more readability to the class.

Can you list out some marker interfaces that you have worked with?

There are different marker interfaces that I have worked with like **Serializable**, **Cloneable**, and so on.

Can you create your own marker interface? How to declare it?

There is no any special magic in creating a marker interface. We can just create an interface without any method, which will be treated as a marker interface. And then, you can implement this interface on some class so as to denote that the class is of type of a marker interface you have denoted. Furthermore, in your business logic, you can check if the class is of type declared by you and then permit the object to do some processing.

What is typecasting in Java, and which are the different types of typecasting available in Java?

Converting one data type to another is termed as typecasting. There are two types of typecasting available in Java:

1. Down-casting
2. Up-casting

Down-casting is changing the type from the current data type into the lower data type. This has to be done explicitly by a developer, as converting the data type to lower data type might generate data loss or precision.

On the other hand, **up-casting** is converting the current data type into a higher data type. This can happen implicitly as there is no precision loss in this process.

Can you elaborate any situation where you can apply up-casting to objects or references?

One of such scenario in which we can use up-casting is implementing the **equals()** method from the *Object* super class. The **equals()** method from the Object super class declares the argument of type Object as its signature, which is shown as follows:

```
1. public boolean equals(Object obj)
```

That means, any object can be referred by the *Object* reference as **Object** is the cosmic super class for all the objects.

Consider the **Employee** class, which is shown as follows:

```
1. package casting;
```

```
2. public class Employee {
3.   int empId;
4.   String empName;
5.   public Employee(int empId,String empName) {
6.     this.empId=empId;
7.     this.empName=empName;
8.   }
9. }
```

If we want to check the equality of the Employee object, we need to override the equals method.

```
1. public boolean equals(Object o) {
2.   if(this.empId==o.empId)//error
3.     return true;
4.   else
5.     return false;
6. }
```

If you observe, Line number 2 uses the reference of the **Object** class to access data member of Employee, which is not possible because of the polymorphic reference. So, to achieve this, you need to up-cast the reference of the **Object** class to **Employee**, which is shown as follows:

```
1. public boolean equals(Object o) {
2.   Employee e=(Employee)o;//Downcasting
3.   if(this.empId==e.empId)
4.     return true;
5.   else
6.     return false;
7. }
```

What are the types of variables in Java? Also explain their scope.

Java provides following types of variables:

1. **Instance variables**

    An **instance variable** is a variable that is declared within class and not in any method. When we create an instance of that class, a copy of such variable is created for each instance. Modifications done by one instance do not impact the value of the same instance variable in other object. One of the most important features that an instance variable provides is: it is accessible within all the member functions of the class. The instance variables always have a default value.

2. **Local variables**

    When the variables are declared within a method or block, they are termed as **local variables**. The main property of local variables is they are visible only within the block or method where they are declared. You can declare a local variable in a method, loop, or even if condition. Unlike instance variables, local variables do not have a default value.

3. **Static variables**

    Static variables look almost similar like instance variables, but with one difference; they need to be declared with the **static** keyword. The static variables are also called as class variables, as they do not have separate copy for separate object. A single copy of the variable is shared across all the object of the same class. Modification made by one object will be reflected in other object of the same class. Similar to the instance variable, all the static variables have a default value.

4. **Reference variables**

    Reference variables are the variables that point to an object. We can declare these variables locally in a method as well as we can use it as an instance variable in the concepts of composition. If they are used as instance variables, they are accessible to all the methods of that class. But, if declared within any method, they are accessible only within that method.

What is an instance initializer block in Java?

An **instance initializer** block is a block that gets executed before the creation of object. The moment JVM identifies a new keyword while execution, it immediately jumps to the **static initializer** block and executes it.

What is difference between a static initializer block and instance initializer block in Java?

A **static initializer** block is used to initialize the static members, and an **instance initializer** block is used initialize the instance variables. The major difference between the two is, a **static initializer** block is called only during life cycle, while an **instance initializer** block is called each time the object is created of that class.

Can you explain the concept of wrapper classes in Java?

Wrappers, as the name implies, wrap the data. They wrap data and convert it to an object. So, essentially, a wrapper class is an object form of the primitives. For instance, for int primitive, there is an Integer wrapper. Similarly, we have Byte, Short, Long, Double, Float, Character, Boolean.

What is the significance of wrapper classes?

Wrappers provide two important facilities:

1. There are some concepts in Java like collections where you can use objects and not the primitives. So, in such a location, if we want to make the use of primitives, we can use the wrapper form of the same.

2. Wrappers provide methods for parsing the data types from one type to other.

What is auto-boxing and auto un-boxing? In which scenario are they observed?

Auto-boxing is the process of converting the primitive into a wrapper automatically. And, **auto un-boxing** is the process of converting the wrapper into primitive.

If you push primitive to collection, then primitives are automatically converted into wrappers and then they are added to collections, as collections only permit an object to be part of them.

Auto un-boxing happens when you try to access or modify or process the wrappers. For example, consider two Integer wrappers and you want to add them, which is shown as follows:

```
1.  Integer i1=new Integer(10);

2.  Integer i2=new Integer(20)

3.  int add=i1+i2;
```

In this case, you cannot add **i1** an **i2** directly as they are objects. But, at runtime, JVM un-boxes the wrappers and pulls value out of it, and then, it does the process of addition.

What is an immutable object? Can you list out some immutable objects that you have worked with?

Immutable objects are the objects whose state cannot be modified once it is created. In Java all wrapper objects and String are immutable.

What is the use of an immutable object? Why we should create such an object?

Immutable objects are created if you do not want your object to get modified after creation. When we create a multi-threaded application, sometimes, an object created by one thread can be modified by other thread because of which the system might perform in an unexpected way. So, to make sure that your object is not modifiable by other thread, you can create an immutable object.

Can you create your own immutable object? How to create that?

Yes. We can create an immutable object. To create an immutable object, you need to follow the following norms while designing a class:

- All the data members of the class should be private. Because if they are not private, they might get modified outside the class.

- You must have a parameterized constructor for your class so as to initiate the data members.

- Convert your class to final so that no one will be able to subclass it and try to modify the data members. (Though this is not assumed to be very strict norm, it is better to have it.)

- The class must not have the setter methods. It may contain the getter methods.

- If the class contains other object reference, then the getter method should not return direct reference of an existing object; instead, the cloned copy of that reference should be returned.

What is an enum to you?

An **enum** in Java is a special class that contains a group of named constants. This enum class is a subclass of a predefined Enum class. In Java, enum can also contain variables, methods, and constructors.

Can enum extend any other class?

No, *enum* cannot extend another class as it is already extending the Enum class. This is against the policy of Java, which says "multiple inheritance is not supported in Java."

Can we write an enum that implements an interface?

Yes, enum can implement any other interface like class as it is internally a class. The only thing that you need to remember is that you must override the methods that are declared in that interface.

What is the connection of the toString() method with enum?

When you try to access the constants that are present in enum, Java provides you the **toString()** method internally, which returns you the string representation of that constants or object. You can even override the **toString()** method and return the customized string to represent the object.

Can we declare constructors within enum?

We can declare constructors in **enum**. But, the constructor must be private. For each constant, this constructor is executed while the **enum** class is loaded.

Why the constructor of enum is kept as private?

An **enum** is kept as private so that the values or constants that are present within it should not be modified outside **enum**.

Can we instantiate enum using the new keyword?

As **enum** does not have the public constructor, you cannot create an instance of **enum** by using the **new** keyword.

Explain some important methods of enum in Java

There are three important methods in enum of Java:

- **values()**

  This method returns all the values that are present in enum.

- **ordinal()**

  This method returns the index numbers of all the constants that are present in enum.

- **valueof()**

  This method returns the constants in enum, which are specified as an argument.

Packages

Packages are used in Java to group the related classes together. The services that are written inside classes can be utilized by importing the packages to other class. We will discuss a few interview questions based on packages.

Which package is available as a default package for every Java class?

Whenever we create any class in Java, the **java.lang** package is available by default to that class. So, all the interfaces, classes, and their methods are implicitly available to all the classes that we declare.

If you import the parent package, does the compiler automatically import sub-packages as well?

No. If you want to use the class from the sub-packages, you have explicitly import them.

Can we have same classes in two packages of an application?

Yes. We can have the same class with same name. You can utilize the services from this class, by importing the class separately. But, you cannot import both the classes within a single class.

Explain the use of static import

When we define a class, we use static members inside it. To import such static members, we can use static import statement. When you use static import, you do not need to write the complete class name while using that member inside the class where you have imported it. Here, instead of importing the entire class, we import only the members that we want to use in our class.

Conclusion

In this chapter, we discussed different concepts of object orientation that can be implemented in Java. We started the journey from very basic terms like class and object and then discussed every detail of the same. We discussed different concepts like abstraction, inheritance, and polymorphism and the different questions that can be asked on these concepts. We also discussed a few concepts that are important, like enum, wrapper, which will give an added advantage at the time of actual interview. In the next chapter, we will discuss how to handle exceptions in Java.

CHAPTER 4
Handling Exceptions

Introduction

To err is human. And, everyone accepts it as a fact. We as a human being are generous enough to ignore the errors done by others. Most of us live in the culture of *"forgive and forget,"* which is a key to happy and longer life. Unfortunately, things are different when we talk about software. Clients always prefer to have the reliable, robust software for their business. Error-prone software may cost the client millions from their businesses. It is a developer's prime responsibility to develop software that will not fail or generate unwanted results for which he/she paid. The question is, why would one create faulty software in any case? Developers will make their at most efforts to create flawless software. But, still, there might be some cases because of which the software might fail. Software is created by human beings, installed on machines, and used by human beings. So, there might be something wrong with hardware or some wrong doings from user of system, which will cause the system to fail. Such situations are termed as exceptions. As a developer, we need to be sure of controlling such situations. Or, even if it occurs, we need to make sure that the application should not get abruptly terminated. This process of controlling the abrupt termination of application is termed as exception handling.

Structure

Java is known for its robustness. This is achieved by implementing the concept of exception handling. **Exceptions** are runtime errors that can be handled. Every application must have an efficient way to handle such exception. We will learn the following concepts in this chapter:

- What are the different types of exception

- How to handle an exception

- What are the different keywords in exception handling

- How to create and handle custom or user-defined exceptions

- What are the different interview questions and their answers

Objective

Exception handling is one of the important features in a Java interview process. You must know the need for exception handling and the way to achieve it. In this chapter, you will learn the very basics of exception handling, like what is handling exception, how to handle it, to the updates in exception handling. Also, you will know how to answer real-time interview questions, which could be asked during interviews.

What do you mean by handling an exception?

Handling an exception is not rectifying an exception. By handling, we mean to provide sufficient information to the client about the type and reason of an exception. Also, it avoids abrupt termination of a program.

What is need for exception handling?

When the exception is raised, the program gets terminated abruptly. Along with this, it also generates a technical message about the exception, which is difficult to understand by the user of a system. Also, because of this abrupt termination, the code segments after exception, which are not dependent on the exception, also get terminated.

So, we must take care of following things:

- Proper message should be displayed to the end user.

- Code after the exception (if it is not related to code that generates exception) should execute smoothly.

To achieve this, we can perform exception handling.

Explain hierarchy of an exception

The top most class in hierarchy of exception is **Throwable**. The **Throwable** class is further extended by two different classes, *Error* and *Exception*. Both Error and Exception classes have their further subclasses.

The following figure shows the hierarchy of exception in Java.

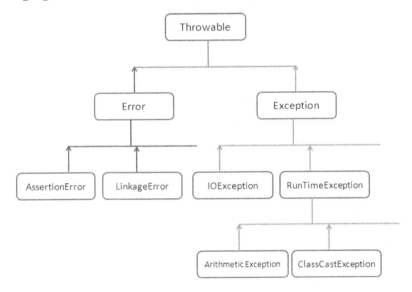

Figure 4.1: Hierarchy of Exception

Note: This figure is not complete, as it is not possible to show all the classes in a single glance. But, if you are able to explain even if these many classes this would be enough for interviewer.

Tell me something about the Throwable class

Throwable is the super class for the exception classes in Java. Only the objects of this class or subclass can be handled by Java. The **Throwable** class or its subclass contains two constructors, default constructor, and a parameterized constructor with a String argument. This String argument is used to return the complete information about the exception. If we want to get the message of the exception, we can use the **getMessage()** method of this class.

How do you classify exceptions?

Exceptions are classified in two different types:

- **Checked Exception**

  These types of exceptions are checked by the compiler. The compiler checks if the exception is handled. If it is not handled, then a compilation error is generated. Normally, such types of exceptions are generated when we communicate with resources from a Java program. Such exceptions need to be handled either by using try-catch block or by using the throws keyword at the method declaration. **IOException**, **SQLException** are types of such exceptions.

- **Unchecked Exception**

  These types of exceptions are checked at the runtime. Even if the exceptions are not handled, the compiler does not complain. But, the program may end abruptly if any exception occurs. Whether to handle such exception or not is entirely dependent on the programmer. Some of the examples of such exceptions are, **ArithmeticException**, **ArrayIndexOutOfBoundsException**, **NullPointerException**, **NumberFormatException**.

Can you list out different exceptions that you know and the scenarios when they are thrown?

Following are some of the common exceptions and the situations in which they are arise:

Exception	Description
ArithmeticException	This is RunTimeException and occurs when exceptional arithmetic operations are performed, which are not permitted.
ArrayIndexOutOfBoundsException	This exception occurs when an array element is accessed with an invalid index number.
NullPointerException	This exception occurs when the reference tries to invoke the methods or member of an object, though it is not referring to any object.
NumberFormatException	This exception occurs when a String is converted into number, but it is not convertible to a number.

ClassCastException	This exception occurs when we try to convert one type to another when it is not convertible.
CloneNotSupported	This exception occurs when we try to clone the object, but it does not implement a Cloneable interface.
InterruptedException	This exception is thrown when the Thread is in the waiting or sleeping mode.

Table 4.1: Types of exceptions

How to handle an exception?

To handle the exception, you need to first identify the block that may generate exception. Once you know which block generates an exception, you need to put that code in the try block. The try block will be followed by the catch block, where we handle the exception. The catch block in its argument contains the reference of the exception object, which may be generated by the try block. If the exception object, which is generated by the try block, matches with the type of the catch argument, then the catch block executes.

The following syntax shows how to use the **try-catch** block:

```
try{
  //code block
}
catch(Exception e){
  //exception handling block
}
```

Can you use the try block without the catch block?

Though it is not recommended, you can use the try block without catch. In that case, you need to compulsory use the finally block as an alternative to the catch block. The finally block always executes even if the exception occurs or not. But in absence of catch, if the exception occurs, the program will be terminated abruptly. This is very uncommon practice that overrides whole reason of exception handling concept.

Can we use a single try block to handle multiple types of exceptions?

We can use a single try block, which may raise multiple types of exceptions. This try block may be followed by a single catch block, which may handle all the exceptions generically, or multiple catch blocks matching with types of exception, which are generated within the try block.

Can a single catch block handle multiple types of exceptions?

Yes. We can use a single catch block to handle the multiple exceptions. In order to achieve this, the catch block must be generic. This means that instead of handling a specific exception, it should use the Exception object as an argument, which accepts all the types of exceptions that are thrown from try block. However, to handle the specific exception types, you need to check the type of exception, as shown in the following code snippet of the catch block:

```
catch(Exception e){

  if(e instanceof ArithmeticException){

    //handle the exception of type ArithmeticException

  }

  if(e instanceof NullPointerException){

    //handle the exception of type NullPointerException

  }

}
```

What is a difference between error and exception in Java?

Error and **Exception** are subtype of the **Throwable** class. So, both may cause the program to terminate abruptly if not handled. But, a point to remember is errors are not recoverable. That means there is no way by which you can handle the errors if they occurred at run time. The program will terminate abruptly. However, whenever you feel that the exception might cause the abrupt termination of your application, you can control the abrupt termination by providing the exception handling code.

What is cascading of an exception?

Cascading of an exception is propagation of an exception. When the exception is raised, it needs to be handled in the same method block. But, sometimes, if we do not handle that exception, the exception is carried forward to the other method from where the original method is called. Such approach of forwarding the exceptions to the next method is termed as cascading exceptions or propagation of exception.

What is a chained exception?

Chained exceptions were introduced in JDK 1.4. Chained exceptions allow you to re-throw a new exception when some exception is occurred. While doing so, you can still maintain the cause of earlier exception, which can be chained to the next exception. To achieve this, the **Throwable** class is modified with two additional methods and constructors listed as follows:

- **New methods**

  ```
  Throwable getCause()
  Throwable initCause(Throwable t)
  ```

- **New constructors**

  ```
  Throwable(String s, Throwable t)
  Throwable(Throwable t)
  ```

The following code snippet illustrates how we can use the chained exception:

```
try {
  //some code
} catch (IOException e) {
  throw new MyException("IOExceptionoccurred", e);
}
```

In the preceding example, the catch block handles the **IOException**, but instead of completing the handling, it re-throws another exception **MyException**..

How do you handle the exception in a generic way?

Normally, to handle an exception, we use the catch block. In the catch block, we use the specific type of **Exception** object as an argument. Once the exception object is thrown, it will be caught by the corresponding catch block. But, instead of handling the specific exception object, we can use the super class **Exception** as an argument. This is considered to be a polymorphic reference in which the super class reference can reference to its subtype. Because all the exception types are sub-type of the Exception super class, the **Exception** super class can refer to all types of exceptions.

The following catch block illustrates the use of a generic way of handling an exception:

```
catch(Exception e){
  //catch block to handle exception
}
```

When do you recommend of handling the exception in a generic way? What is the complexity of using this approach?

Typically, when we are not aware of what kind of exception might get generated, we can use the generic approach to handle an exception. One of the complexities of using this approach is the catch block will become generic because of which we need to take extra efforts to display the exception message according to the type of exception. We have already discussed how to achieve this in earlier questions.

Can we use generic approach of exception handlers along with other exception handlers?

Yes, we can definitely do so. But, you need to follow the important rule, which you combine the both. According to standards, your generic catch block must be at the end of all catch blocks.

The following code snippet will give a compilation error as the generic exception handler is written at the beginning:

```
catch(Exception e){
  //catch block to handle exception
}
catch(ArithmeticException ae){
  //catch block to ArithmeticException
}
catch(NullPointerException ne){
  //catch block to handle NullPointerException
}
```

This happens because if we add the generic exception handler at the beginning, then all exception objects thrown by the try block are caught by this catch block. This makes other catch blocks as duplicate catch blocks as the exception of that type is already handled.

The following code snippet shows the actual way to combine the generic and specific exception handler:

```
catch(ArithmeticException ae){
  //catch block to ArithmeticException
}
```

```
catch(NullPointerException ne){
    //catch block to handle NullPointerException
}
catch(Exception e){
    //catch block to handle exception
}
```

What is use of the finally block?

The finally block is used to write the code that we want to execute irrespective of whether an exception occurs or not. The finally block is normally used to close the resources that are opened during the *try-catch* block. Of course, we can close the resource within the try-catch block as well, but that is not recommended as we cannot guarantee the complete execution of either the try or catch block. If the exception occurs, then the try block is terminated, and JVM executes the catch block. But, if no exception occurs, then JVM never goes to catch block. Because of this, we need one block of code that is always confirmed to get executed, irrespective of the exception status. The finally block serves this purpose.

Can you use the finally block without using the catch block?

Yes, we can use the finally block after the try block without having the catch block. As we know, the finally block is always executed; it does not bother about the existence of the catch block.

If we use the finally block without the catch block, what happens if the exception is thrown by the try block?

In such case, the try block throws an exception, and a generic message will be generated. The actual exception is handled within the finally block even if finally block does not have any facility to catch the exception as a part of the argument:

Observe the following code snippet:

```
public class Exception1 {
  public static void main(String[] args) {
    int a, b, sum, div, mul;
    a=10;
```

```
  b=0;
  try {
   sum = a + b;
   System.out.println(sum);
   div = a / b;
   System.out.println(div);
   mul = a * b;
   System.out.println(mul);
  }
  finally {
   System.out.println("Finally called !!");
  }
 }
}
```

In the preceding code, the try block will generate **ArithmeticException**. But, we do not have the catch block to handle this exception. So, the try block will be terminated. But, while doing so, it will print that the exception is generated. JVM then executes the finally block, and the detailed exception trace will be returned back as shown:

```
10
Exception in thread "main" Finally called !!
java.lang.ArithmeticException: / by zero
     at Exception1.main(Exception1.java:11)
```

What is the difference between ClassNotFoundException and NoClassDefFoundError?

Both of these exceptions are related to searching of a class at runtime. If we are loading a class by using **Class.forName()** and if the said class is not found in classpath, then **ClassNotFoundException** is generated. On the other hand, **NoClassDefFoundError** occurs if the class is present at compile time, but it is not available at runtime.

How to create a user-defined exception?

To create a user-defined or custom exception, we need to create a class that is a type of exception. As an exception is a super class for this class, the object of this class can be thrown and catch similar to other exception types.

This class may also contain the constructor to initialize a String member, which will contain the information about the exception. Along with this, it should also implement the **toString()** method to return the String to the exception handler.

The following code snippet shows how to create a user-defined or custom exception:

```java
public class MyException extends Exception{
  String str;
  public MyException(String str) {
   this.str=str;
  }
  public String toString() {
   return "MyException occurred";
  }
}
```

How to use a user-defined exception?

User defined exceptions are not known to JVM, so it is not automatically thrown by JVM. It is a responsibility of the developer to throw the object of such exception based on the scenario for which such exceptions are created. We need make use of the "throw" keyword to throw the object of user-defined exception explicitly.

The following code snippet shows how we can throw and handle the exception of type **MyException,** which we have created earlier:

```java
public void doSomething() {
  int x=10;
  if(x<10)
   try {
    throw new MyException("Number not matching");
   } catch (MyException e) {
    // TODO Auto-generated catch block
    System.out.println(e);
   }
}
```

What is use of the throws keyword?

In some cases, we come across situation in which a method contains a code that may generate an exception. Normally, we need to handle such an exception by using the try-catch block within that method. But, if we do not want to handle that exception ourselves, we may use the throws keyword in the declaration of the method. This denotes that the method contains some code, which generates the exception. But, the method had not handled it, and it is the caller's responsibility to handle the exception.

The following code snippet shows how to use the throws keyword:

```
public static void displayContent(File f) throws IOException {
  FileInputStream fis;
  fis = new FileInputStream(f);
  while (fis.read() != -1) {
   // business logic to read the file
  }
}


public static void main(String[] args) {
  // TODO Auto-generated method stub
  File f = new File("d:\\sample.txt");
  try {
   displayContent(f);
  } catch (IOException io) {
   System.out.println("IO Exception occurred!!");
  }
}
```

The preceding code snippet declares a method **displayContent(File f),** which reads the content of the file. Reading of file generates **IOException,** which is a checked exception. But, the method does not put the code of the file reading in try catch; instead, the method declares itself as it throws **IOException**. This forces the invoker of method, to handle the exception. If you observe the invocation of **displayContent()** in the **main()** method, it is wrapped within the try-catch. This try-catch handles the **IOException,** which is thrown by the actual method.

Give a scenario where the throws keyword can be used

When the code snippet within a method generates any exception, we need to handle that an exception. If we handle the exception in the method itself, it will be a concrete way of handling the exception for all the other users who are calling that method. But, if the method does not handle that exception and it is delegated to the invoker, then the invoker gets more flexibility to handle the exception in that way he/she wants to handle.

What are the updates in exception handling provided by JDK 7?

JDK1.7 introduced 2 features in the exception handling mechanism as:

- Automatic resource management
- Multi-catch block statement

What is automatic resource management?

Automatic resource management or try-with-resources is a new mechanism introduced in JDK1.7, to implement a more robust and reliable way to handle the exception that deals with resources.

Normally, when we deal with resources in exception handling, we need to close the resources. To do this, we implement the finally block and close the resource inside that block. But, the problem is, as the resources are within the try block to close it outside the try block, the developer needs to take extra efforts that might make the code more bulky. Instead, JDK1.7 provides a way to open the resources in the arguments of the try itself, which can be closed automatically by JVM when we are done with the try block.

The following code block shows the **BufferedReader,** which is opened as a resource as an argument in the try, which will be closed automatically by JVM:

```
try (BufferedReader reader = new BufferedReader(

    new InputStreamReader(System.in)))
```

By this approach, we do not need to use the finally block to close the **BufferedReader**. **BufferedReader** is opened within the try argument as a resource that will be closed automatically by JVM after completion of the try block.

How are the resources closed automatically in the automatic resource management concept in Java?

From JDK 1.7 onward, the **AutoCloseable** interface is introduced. This class is implemented by different classes that can used as resources. Classes related to I/O, networking, RMI implement this interface. The interface exposes the *close()* method for all implementer classes. When such resources are used within the try block as resources, the close method is implicitly invoked by JVM. We do not need to close such resources explicitly in finally.

What is a multi-catch block statement?

This is another update in JDK1.7. Often, in an application, we come across a situation in which a single try block can generate more than one exception. To handle such multiple exceptions, we can earlier write multiple catch blocks one after another. We can make a ladder of the catch block. This approach is replaced in JDK1.7 by implementing a multi-catch block statement. In this case, we can club all the exception types in a single catch block separated by pipe (|). This is parallel to the OR block in the if statement. The following code snippet shows how we can use a multi-catch block to handle **ArithmeticException**, **ArrayIndexOutOfBoundsException** and **NullPointerException**:

```
catch(ArithmeticException | ArrayIndexOutOfBoundsException |
NullPointerException e){
  //exception handler code
}
```

You can also use the generic exception object inside this catch block, but you should use it at the end.

In some cases, we observed the main method throws an exception. What do you mean by that?

When you have a code that throws any exception, you need to handle it. There are a couple of alternatives to do that. Either you put the code in the try-catch block inside a method or declare the method with the throws clause. If you declare a method with the throws clause, the invoker must handle it. But, at times, even the invoker does not handle the exception. In such case, your code may get terminated abruptly.

To avoid this, you can declare the main method as it throws that exception. It means that the exception is not handled within main, but it is a propagator to the invoker of the main method. In other words, the exception is propagated to JVM, and it will handle that exception.

What is the use of the printstackTrace() method?

Normally, when we handle exception, in the try block, we print the information about that exception for the user. One of the ways to do that is to print the exception reference directly. But, a limitation of this approach is the user will get the reason of the exception, but he/she will not get the exact line because of which the exception occurred.

Consider the following code snippet:

```
1.  class ExcecptionDemo {
2.      public static void divideNumber() {
3.          try {
4.              int ans = 5/0;
5.          }
6.          catch (Exception e) {
7.              System.out.println(e);
8.          }
9.      }
10.
11.     public static void main( String args[] ) {
12.         divideNumber();
13.     }
14. }
```

Here, we know that the program is going to fail. When we execute the program, the program gives following information about the exception:

java.lang.ArithmeticException: **/ by zero**

So, instead of using the printing of the exception reference, we can invoke the **printStackTrace()** method of exception reference in catch as shown:

```
catch (Exception e) {
```

```
        e.printStackTrace();
            }
```

This will return us the output as:

java.lang.ArithmeticException: / by zero
        at ExcecptionDemo.divideNumber(ExcecptionDemo.java:4)
        at ExcecptionDemo.main(ExcecptionDemo.java:12)

Can we use the throw keyword for both the checked and unchecked exceptions?

The throw keyword is used to throw some exception explicitly. Though normally we use the throw keyword for custom exception, we can use this with a pre-defined exception as well. We can throw both the checked and unchecked exceptions.

Can we use the throws keyword for both the checked and unchecked exceptions?

We can use the throws keyword for both the checked and uncheck exceptions.

What happens to the finally block if the try block returns a value to the caller? Does it still execute?

The finally block works as a guarantor. No matter whatever happens to try, finally executes. So, even if try returns some value successfully to its invoker, finally still executes. In this case, finally will execute first, and then the value will be returned back to the invoker function.

What happens if the try and finally blocks execute different Boolean values?

Note: This is a tricky question. Because normally, when we implement the finally block, we write the resource closing code into it. So, the interviewer is expecting the common sense approach in your answer.

If you have a method that returns Boolean, then your try block must return a Boolean value. But, it not compulsory that try and finally should return the same value. That means, your try can return true, and finally can return false. In such a case, as the finally executes even before the return statement is generated by try, the method returns from finally itself and returns false to the invoker.

Is there any way by which you can avoid the execution of the finally block?

As we know, the finally block is always executed irrespective of the status of the try block. The only way to avoid the execution of the finally block is to use **System. exit(0)** in the try block, as shown in the following code:

```java
public class RejectFinally {
  public static void main(String[] args) {
   try {
    System.out.println("Hello world");
    System.exit(0);
   } finally { .
    System.out.println("Goodbye world");
   }
  }
}
```

The preceding code exits from try block because of **System.exit(0)**, which in fact exits the application. The code generates **Hello World** output as finally block is not executed.

What is the reason for OutOfMemory Error? Do you have any ways to solve it?

This error occurs whenever JVM goes out of memory. In other words, when JVM is not able to allocate a heap memory for a newly created object, then this error is generated. This is not handled at runtime, as to recover out of this error, we need to increase the heap memory of JVM.

If a method does not throws any checked exception, can we invoke such method in the try-catch block where the catch block handles the checked exception?

No, we cannot invoke any method in the try-catch block using the checked exception if the method does not throw that type of exception. However, if you do the same thing with an unchecked exception, it is permitted.

Conclusion

In this chapter, we discussed what an exception is and how to handle it. We also talked about the different types of exceptions and the situations that are responsible for such exceptions. We studied different keywords like try, catch, finally, throws, and throw that take an active part in different mechanisms of exception handling. During this chapter, we discussed different interview questions that you may face about exception handling. I am sure you must be in better position now to answer many of such interview questions. In the next chapter, we will discuss how to work with file handling and I/O in Java.

CHAPTER 5
I/O and File Handling

Introduction

Taking data from user and processing it is always a need of an application. It is a hardest thing in the universe to find an application that does not work with either taking data from user or writing data to some output. After all, applications are meant for that; they are meant to produce results based on some inputs. For all the traditional programming languages like C, taking the input and formatting output is the simplest task to do. But, often, I hear Java developers complaining about the complex I/O API to work with input/output. But often, one that is heard may not be actual facts. I/O in Java is rich in size, and it is specific to a specific need. It contains lot many classes to perform basic operations and also decorators on the top of it. If you do not know the ingredients of the dish, you will naturally find it difficult to cook that dish. So, as a developer, it is at most important to know about this rich API and how it helps to perform different I/O operations in different scenarios. We should know not only how to take input/output from console, but also it is equally important to understand how we can store this information in flat file as well.

Structure

We are going to cover the following concepts with the help of interview questions:

- Stream-based hierarchy and character-based hierarchy

- Taking input from the user
- How to read and write the file using different classes
- Filtering data
- Process of serialization and de-serialization
- New input/output API from Java – NIO

Objective

This chapter covers the rich set of Java I/O API in detail. During this entire chapter, we will study different classes that take active part in reading/writing data, which is one of the most important requirements of any application. In this chapter, you will learn different input and output operations that you perform. At the end of this chapter, you will able to work with different I/O statements and how perform read/write operations on a file.

List different types of I/O streams

There are two types of I/O streams:

- Byte-based I/O streams
- Character-based I/O streams

Explain hierarchy of byte-based classes

These classes directly work with streams. The main two classes of this API are **InputStream** and **OutputStream**. Both these are abstract classes that provide different implementations such as **BufferedInputStream**, **BufferedOutputStream**, **FileInputStream**, **FileOutputStream**, **DataInputStream**, **DataOutputStream**, **PipedInputStream**, **PipedOutputStream**.

Explain System.in, System.out, and System.err

A system normally represents console to JVM, on which the program is executing.

- **System.in**

  This is static filed of the predefined **java.lang.System** class and instance of **InputStream**. This is a standard instance that is used to take an input from the user. This provided a method **read()** to take the data from user.

- **System.out**

  This is a static field of predefined Java class **java.lang.System**. As a hierarchy, a system is an instance of the **PrintStream** class, and **PrintStream** is the subclass of **OutputStream**. This is used to print the output on the console.

- **System.err**

  This is almost similar to **System.out**;**System.err** is a static field of **java.lang.System**. This is also an instance of **PrintStream,** which is a subclass of the **OutputStream** class. Normally, this statement is used to print the error message on the console. Mostly, you would see this statement in a catch block of exception handlers.

Explain hierarchy of character-based classes

The reader and writer hierarchy is used to input/output the data in the character format. Though internally they are processed as bytes, they are exposed to a developer as character handlers. **Reader** and **Writer** are the top most abstract super classes for this hierarchy. **BufferedReader**, **BufferedWriter**, **FileReader**, **FileWriter**, **StringReader,** and **StringWriter** are some of the implementation classes of these super classes.

What is the necessity of two types of streams? Why do we need byte streams and character streams?

Byte streams help in operating on the files containing ASCII characters. Sometimes, files also contain Unicode characters. To read such resources, Java introduced **character-based streams**. The ASCII is a subset of Unicode, so to read the files with the English characters, one can use either byte streams or character streams.

In your opinion, which is better to use, byte streams or character streams?

I feel it is better to go with character streams. The character-based streams have more features than byte-based streams such as using **BufferedReader**. One can use **BufferedReader** instead of **BufferedInputStream** or **DataInputStream**. The **BufferedReader** has a **newLine()** method to go for the next line. If one wants to use a byte-based stream, they have to go for extra coding.

What are filter streams, and which are those?

The **filter streams** add an extra functionality to the existing streams such as giving line numbers to the destination, even though they do not exist in the source. The filter streams also help in increasing performance of the copying operations.

The filter stream classes are as follows:

- **LineNumberInputStream**: This class enables adding line numbers to the destination file.

- **DataInputStream**: The class offers methods such as **readInt()**, **readDouble()**, and **readLine()** using which one can read an **int**, a **double**, and a **String** at a time.

- **BufferedInputStream**: The class offers a buffering effect, which increases the performance to the peak.

- **PushbackInputStream**: The class enables pushing the required character back to the system.

What is PrintStream and PrintWriter? Are they same? What is the difference between them?

Both these classes offer functionality of displaying data using the **println()** method. However, both these classes belong to two different categories, byte streams and character streams.

Explain the File class?

The **File** class is a non-stream class. The class is used to find the properties of a file such as when the file was created or modified, whether the file has read and write permissions, what is the size of the file, and so on. This normally points to a file location, which can be used further to open the file in read or write mode. The **File** object does not assure that the file is present or not; when we use this reference with **FileWriter** or **FileOutputStream,** then only JVM checks the existence of the file.

What is FileInputStream?

The **FileInputStream** class is used to read the content of a file. It is a concrete implementation of **InputStream**. So, this provides the implementation for methods like **read()**, **available()**, **close()**, and so on. This class provides following constructors to open the file in the read mode:

- public FileInputStream(String fileName) throws FileNotFoundException

- public FileInputStream(File file) throws FileNotFoundException

- public FileInputStream(FileDescriptor fd)

What is FileOutputStream?

The **FileOutputStream** class is used to write into a file. It is a concrete implementation of **OutputStream**. So, this provides implementation for methods like **write()**, **flush()**, **close()**. The **write()** method can take the **int** or **byte[]** array, which can be passed to a file. This class provides the following constructors:

- public FileOutputStream(String filename) throws FileNotFoundException

- public FileOutputStream(File file) throws FileNotFoundException

- public FileOutputStream(FileDescriptor fd)

- public FileOutputStream(String name, boolean append) throws FileNotFoundException

Can we read the data from webpage?

Java provides the **java.net** package, which consists of different classes to communicate with the network. To communicate with the web page, we can make the use of the URL class, which takes into account URL in the format String as an argument to which we can connect. One we get connected with the specified URL, we can use the **openStream()** method of **InputStream,** which downloads the data from the server, and then using the **read()** method, we can read the data.

When is the Scanner class used?

The **Scanner** class was introduced in Java 1.5. It is used for reading data stream from the input. Before **Scanner** to read the input, one was using **DataInputStream,** then after reading the stream, one can convert it into the respective data type such as String, integer, or double, and so on. But, the **Scanner** class is a more flexible class that provides direct methods to scan the different data type like **nextFloat()**, **nextDouble()**, **nextInteger()**, and so on.

What is a Buffered stream?

Buffered streams are used to store the larger amount of data in buffer. To input the data, we can use **BufferedInputStream,** and to generate the output, we can use **BufferedOutputStream**. When the method **read()** is invoked on **BufferedInputStream**, the data is not removed from the stream, but it is removed from the buffer. Similarly, if we use **BufferedOutputStream**, the data is stored in the internal byte array, and instead of writing the data byte-by-byte, the entire array is pushed as an output. This approach is considered to be more efficient than the traditional I/O approach.

Explain BufferedWriter. Where are flush() and close() used?

The buffer is a temporary storage area where data is stored. The **BufferedWriter** class is an output stream class that creates a buffered character-output stream.

- The **flush()** method is used for clearing all the data characters stored in the buffer and make it empty.

- The **close()** method is used to close the opened character output stream.

Explain the hierarchy of data streams

These are the classes that are specialized to read different primitives like integers, floats, or even strings. The two important implementations are **DataInputStream** and **DataOutputStream**, which are subclasses of **FilterInputStream** and **FilterOutputStream**, respectively. Additionally, these also implement an interface. **DataInput** is implemented by **DataInputStream,** and **DataOutput** is implemented by **DataOutputStream**. These interfaces provide different methods like **readBoolean()**, **readInt()**, **readLine()**, **write()**, **writeInt()**, **writeDouble(),** and so on, which are implemented by these classes accordingly.

Can we read the data from multiple sources at the same time?

Yes, it is possible. Java provides **SequenceInputStream,** which can chain multiple input streams together to read the data from different sources. This is also a subclass of **InputStream**. **SequenceInputStream** reads all the bytes from the resources in a sequence, and at the end, the stream is closed.

The following are the two constructors of this class:

- `public SequenceInputStream(Enumeration en)`

- `public SequenceInputStream(InputStream ins1, InputStream ins2)`

Here, in the second constructor, the **InputStreams,ins1** and **ins2,**can be of type **SequenceInputStream**.

The following code snippets show you how you can open different streams to read the data from home page of websites **www.rediff.com** and **www.bpbonline.com**:

```
1. try {
2. URL u1 = new URL("http://www.rediff.com/");
3. URL u2 = new URL("http://www.bpbonline.com");
4. SequenceInputStream sin = new SequenceInputStream(u1.openStream(),
5. u2.openStream());
6. }
7. catch (IOException e) {
8. //exception handler block
9. }
```

How to create temporary files? How to delete temporary files?

When an application terminates, the created file can be deleted using the **deleteOnExit()** method. This file deletion will be attempted only if the virtual machine is terminated normally. In case of the abnormal termination of the application, the file may not be deleted. Also, once deletion is requested, it is not possible to cancel that request.

One can use the following code to create, and after use, delete the temporary file:

```
1. File tem = File.createTempFile("myfile", ".txt");
2. tem.deleteOnExit(); //This will delete when JVM exits
```

Did you work with properties files? How to create properties files dynamically?

Yes, I worked for JDBC connection properties. The property file is used to store the configuration-related data of application. An application can pull this data at runtime.

The file dynamically can be created as follows:

```
1. Properties props = new Properties();
```

```
2. //Populating the properties file
3. props.put("driver_class_name", "com.mysql.cj.jdbc.Driver");
4. props.put("username", "root");
5. props.put("password", "mypass");
6. FileOutputStream os= new FileOutputStream("D:\\mydir\\myfile.
   properties");
7. //Storing the properties in the file
8. props.store(os, "This is a sample properties file");
```

What is serialization and deserialization?

Serialization is the process of maintaining the state of an object in the form of a sequence of bytes for a longer duration. **Deserialization** is the opposite of serialization. It restores an object from these bytes. The **java.io** package offers API for the serialization and deserialization process. To serialize any object, the class representing that object must implement the **Serializable** interface.

Which methods are declared within the Serializable interface?

Serializable is a marker interface that does not have any method declared within it. This only makes the object of that class eligible for the process of serialization.

Did you work with serialization and deserialization? Please explain the process

Yes, I worked with these processes. We can serialize and deserialize the data as follows:

1. Let us consider we have Person as the POJO class.

2. We can serialize the data as follows:

   ```
   1. FileOutputStream fos= new FileOutputStream("persons.txt");
   2. ObjectOutputStream oos = new ObjectOutputStream(fos);
   3. // Method for serialization of object
   4. oos.writeObject(person);
   5. oos.close();
   6. fos.close();
   ```

3. Deserialization can be done as follows:

```
1. FileInputStream fis= new FileInputStream("persons.txt");
2. ObjectInputStream oin = new ObjectInputStream(fis);
3. // Method for deserialization of object
4. Person person = (Person)oin.readObject();
5. oin.close();
6. fis.close();
7. System.out.println("name = " + person.getName());
8. System.out.println("age = " + person.getAge());
```

What is SerialVersionUID?

A version number that is associated with each serializable class is called a **SerialVersionUID**. This number is used during the process of deserialization. The number is used to verify whether a serialized object has loaded for the classes that are compatible with respect to serialization. **InvalidClassException** will be thrown in case if the receiver loads a class of the object that has different UID than that of corresponding sender's class while deserialization.

Sometimes, even if you implement Serializable for a class, you cannot serialize an object. Can you explain why?

Yes, sometimes you may come across **NotSeriazableException,** even if the class implements the **Serializable** interface. This happens because of the following reasons:

- If you are using containment within that object, and the contained object is not serializable

- Superclass, of the class does not implement the **Serializable** interface, and it even does not have a default constructor

- If someone is deliberately throwing **NotSerializableException**, just to assure that object should not be serialized

How to customize the process of serialization?

To customize the process of serialization, instead of implementing the **Serializable** interface, we need to implement the **Externalizable** interface. Unlike the

Serializable interface, this interface is not a marker interface; it declares the methods **readExternal()** and **writeExternal(),** which must be overridden. By this way, instead of JVM taking the entire responsibility of serialization process, developers can write their custom logic to serialize an object.

How to protect the data from being serialized?

If you need any data member to get protected from the process of serialization, you can declare that data member with the **transient** keyword. Members declared with the **transient** keyword are not serialized even if the object is serialized.

Have you dealt with Random access files?

The **RandomAccessFile** class is designed to work with files offering random access to the contents of the file. Working with the **RandomAccessFile** class offers the functionality of **DataInputStream** and **DataOutputStream** combined together in one class. In addition to the functionalities offered by them, the class offers another method **seek()**. This method enables one to move to the specific position in the file and then change the value stored there.

We need to keep in mind the file structure while using the **RandomAccessFile** class. The **RandomAccessFile** class has methods for reading and writing primitives and UTF-8 strings.

If I want to create a directory, which class should I use?

We have the **File** class to create the files, but there is no Directory class. The **File** class itself is used is used to create file as well as directory.

One can create the directory having name as **mydir** using the following code:

```
1. File dir = new File("/path/mydir");
2. if (!dir.exists()){
3.     dir.mkdirs();
4. }
```

Explain the difference between InputStream and OutputStream?

InputStream is used to read data from source such as a file, a socket, or from the standard input.

OutputStream is used to write data to the destinations such as a file, a socket, or standard output.

Can you explain the difference between BufferedReader and FileReader?

FileReader is specifically used to read the data from the specified file if it exists. However, **BufferedReader** acts as a decorator. **BufferedReader** offers buffering for faster I/O.

The **FileReader** class offers a **read()** method to read the data from the file. One can use it to read data from the **myfile.txt** file as,

```
1.  FileReader fr=new FileReader("C:\\myfile.txt");
```

BufferedReader acts as decorator, which offers the **readLine()** method to read the data as follows:

```
1.  FileReader fr=new FileReader("C:\\myfile.txt");
2.  BufferedReader br=new BufferedReader(fr);
```

As **BufferedReader** is a decorator, it can also be used to read data from the standard input. We can use the following code to read the standard input:

```
1.  InputStreamReader isr=new InputStreamReader(System.in);
2.  BufferedReader br=new BufferedReader(isr);
```

Explain the use of the PrintStream class?

The **PrintStream** class is used to write data to the standard output. We all very frequently use **System.out.println()** to display something on the console. In this, out is an object of the **PrintStream** class on which we are invoking **println()** method.

Can we close the stream in a try block? Why one should close the streams in a finally block? What change happened in JDK 7 to close the stream?

One should close the stream in a finally block because the finally block is always executed irrespective of whether the exception occurred or not in a try block.

If we close stream in try, it can be closed only if the code gets executed without an exception.

From JDK 7 onward, we do not need to explicitly close the stream if we open it within try with resources. This is possible because now it implements the **Autoclosable** interface:

```
1. try (BufferedReader br = new BufferedReader(
2.                     new FileReader("C:\\myfile.txt"))) {
3. //code here
4. } catch (IOException e) {
5.             e.printStackTrace();
6. }
```

Can we convert a file into a string? Can you explain how?

The following code snippet shows how we can convert a file into a string:

```
1. FileInputStream fi = new FileInputStream(name_of_file);
2. byte[] buffer = new byte[10];
3. StringBuilder sb = new StringBuilder();
4. while (fi.read(buffer) != -1) {
5.   sb.append(new String(buffer));
6.   buffer = new byte[10];
7. }
8. String file_to_string = sb.toString();
```

Can we set permissions on a file? Which permissions can be set on a file? How to set permissions on a file?

The file permissions are required to be changed whenever the user wants to restrict the operations on a file. There are a number of methods that offer checking and setting the permission of a file. For example, a read-only file can be set to permit the permissions of writing data to it.

We can check the permission with methods such as:

- **canExecute()**: The function checks whether the application is allowed to execute the file. It will return true if the path name exists, and the application is allowed to execute the specified file.

- **canRead()**: The function checks whether the application is allowed to read the file or not. The method return true if it can be read by the application.

The following methods are used to change or set the permissions on a file:

- **setExecutable()**: The method allows to set the owner's execute permission for path name.

- **setReadable()**: The method is used to set the owner's read permission.

- **setWritable()**: The method is used to set the owner's write permission.

Have you ever got java. io.FileNotFoundException for Access is denied? Do you know how to fix that?

I got this exception while creating a file on the C drive where my OS is installed.

We can change its permission as follows:

- Go to **C:\Program Files**.

- Right click **Java** on the folder and click on **Properties**.

- Now select the **Security** tab.

- Click on the **Edit** button.

- A pop-up **PERMISSIONS FOR JAVA** window will open.

- Click on **Add**.

- One more popup will open. Here, in the **Enter object name** box, enter your user account name, and after that, click **OK**.

- In the **PERMISSIONS OF JAVA** window, you will find several clickable options such as **CREATOR, OWNER, SYSTEM,** and so on. One of them is your username. Select it, and check mark the **FULL CONTROL** option in **Permissions for** sub-window.

- Hit **Apply** and **OK**.

What is a memory-mapped file? Explain the advantages and disadvantages of a memory-mapped file

The **memory-mapped files** are the files in Java that allow an application to access contents directly from the memory. This is achieved by mapping the whole file, or some part of the file into memory. The operating system will take care of loading the page requested and then writing that into the file while the application deals with the memory. This allows very fast I/O operations. The memory used to load the memory-mapped file is from outside of the Java heap space. The `java.nio` package offers memory-mapped file operations. `MappedByteBuffer` can be used to read and write from the memory.

Advantages

- The performance is important to build a high-frequency electronic trading system. The memory-mapped file is a faster way than using a standard file access using normal I/O operations.

- The memory-mapped file allows the developers to load a potentially larger file, which is not accessible otherwise.

- Most of operating system supports memory-mapped I/O operations. Also, with the 64-bit architecture, it is possible to map almost any file into memory and also access it directly using the Java application.

- The file can be shared; it gives the developers shared memory between processes, and this can be more than 10x lower latency using a socket over loopback.

Disadvantage

As the operating system only loads a portion of the file into the memory, when the requested page is not present in the memory, then it will result in a page fault.

What is NIO? What is the difference between I/O and NIO?

- Java new input–output is known as NIO, which was introduced with JDK 1.4. The NIO offers high-speed, block-oriented I/O to the library.

- I/O is blocking I/O; however, NIO is non-blocking I/O. It means the thread will be blocked until it completes the IO operations. However, the thread can perform some other operation if the data is not available and does not block the process.

- The old I/O is stream based; however, the NIO is buffer oriented. It means the NIO first reads the data in a buffer and then makes it available for asynchronous processing. Also, it is possible to move back and forth in the buffer, but in older stream-based operations, it was not possible.

What are the fundamental components of NIO?

The following are the fundamental components of NIO:

- **Channel buffers:** In standard IO, operations are either character or stream based, but the NIO uses channels and buffers. It means the data is always written from a buffer to the channel and then read from the channel into the buffer.

- **Selectors:** The selector is an object that is used to monitor multiple channels for the events such as connection opened, data arrived, and so on. It makes possible the single thread to monitor multiple channels for the data.

- **Non-blocking I/O:** The application must have a mechanism to find when the data is ready so that the operation will not be blocking to wait till the data is arrived.

What are selectors?

Selectors are introduced in NIO, which enables a single thread to monitor multiple channels of the input. One can register multiple channels with the selector. After that, one can use a single thread to select the channels that have input available for processing. Also, one can select the channels that are ready for writing. The mechanism of a selector makes it very easy for a single thread to manage multiple channels.

What are channels?

The **channels** are used to perform NIO operations. They act as a tube though which the data will be transported between the buffer and the entity. The data is read from the entity via channels and placed in the buffer to consume. The best part of channels is they can be used for both read and write operations. It means the channels read the data from entity in the buffer and then write the data from the buffer to the destination asynchronously as well.

Explain the NIO channel classes

The following are the types of channels classes:

- `FileChannel`: This is a file-based channel used for reading as well as writing operations that cannot be placed on the non-blocking mode. One can get the instance of **FileChannel** by invoking the **getChannel()** method on the instance of the file.

- **SocketChannel:** These are the channels that can be used to operate in the non- blocking mode. **SocketChannel** is mainly divided into following three types of channels:
    - o **DatagramChannel:** This class can be used to perform read and write operations over the network using UDP.
    - o **SocketChannel:** The **SocketChannel** class can be used to read and write the data over the TCP network.
    - o **ServerSocketChannel:** This class is used to perform IO operations over the TCP connections.

How and when the buffer is cleared when using the BufferedWriter class?

Buffer is cleared in the following situations:

- Naturally when the buffer is filled completely
- Explicitly when the **flush()** method is called

One needs to call the **flush()** method once at the end of file writing operation so that all the residual content will be dumped to the file.

What is the output of the following code? Will the physical file will be available at the location after the execution of the following code?

File f = new File("myfile.txt");

The code will only be executed without an exception, but no physical file will be created. In case if the file needs to be created, one needs to execute the code as follows:

```
1. f.createNewFile();
```

How can you pull specific types of file for processing?

Java provides the **FilenameFilter** interface, which lets you to provide the information about which kind of files can be accepted. This interface, which is present in the **java.io** package, declares the **accept()** method as follows:

```
1. public abstract boolean accept(File directory, String name);
```

This method takes 2 arguments; the File object, which points to the directory, and file name. This method returns true if the file that you have declared has passed through this filter and matches the condition, else returns false.

Conclusion

In this chapter, we discussed about the different classes and interfaces that are used in an I/O operation. Java I/O API is vast in number, but we have tried to cover many classes and interfaces that play a vital role in the interview questions, which is the prime goal of this book. In this chapter, we have discussed many such questions that can be asked in a Java interview. In the next chapter, we will discuss how you can create multi-threaded applications and interview questions related with the same.

CHAPTER 6

Concurrency

Introduction

Right from the early days of programming, developers are writing sequential programs to develop an application. Often, such programs were executed on a system that has to perform a single task throughout its life. Though initially it was not a big concern, in the later stages of hardware development, when hardware and operating systems evolved to their next stages, such programming was considered to be inefficient as well as expensive. Sequential programs do not utilize the power of the operating system and hardware to their full extent. This gave rise to the concept of multithread or concurrent programming where different programs can run simultaneously on the operating system. To understand the concept of a multithreaded program, you can take real-time examples from your day-to-day life. While boiling water for tea, you can fetch a newspaper that is on your doormat, or while having a cup of tea, you can even read the newspaper; these tasks are typically asynchronous in nature. Similarly, there are many tasks in applications that do not depend on each other. Such tasks can be executed simultaneously by using the concepts of threads.

Structure

The concept of a thread is relatively new for a beginner Java programmer. If you do not understand the basics of multithreading, then understanding the advanced concurrent API will be a bit challenging. During this chapter, we will be discussing the following:

- What is a thread, and how to create it

- Different ways of create a thread and their significance

- Inter-communication between threads

- Life cycle methods of threads

- Concurrency API

- Interview questions and answers on multithreading

Objective

In this chapter, you will learn what is a thread and how to create it. We will also discuss about how different threads can communicate with each other to create an efficient application. In the later stages, we will discuss the concurrency API of Java, which makes the multithreaded programming way simpler than the traditional programming approach.

What is multithreading? Can you explain multithreading?

Multithreading is a situation in which multiple threads are executed simultaneously. Multithreading consumes less memory. As threads are lightweight, they enhance the performance of an application.

What is a thread?

A **thread** is a lightweight sub-process. It is a separate path of execution because each thread runs in a different stack frame. A process may contain multiple threads. Threads share the process resources, but still, they execute independently.

What are the advantages of multithreading?

The advantages are as follows:

- The thread is lightweight. So, it enhances the application performance.

- Multithreading reduces more servers, as one server can execute multiple threads at a time.

- Even though some background task is running, multithreading allows an application to be always reactive to accept an input.

- As multithreading includes execution of multiple threads independently, it allows the faster execution of tasks.

- The threads share the common memory resources. So, multithreading provides better utilization of cache memory.

What is a process? Can you differentiate between a process and a thread?

A program in the execution is called the **process**, and a **thread** is a subset of the process.

The differences between them are as follows:

- Processes are independent, but the threads are the subset of a process.

- The processes have different address space in the memory. However, the threads contain a shared address space of the process.

- The inter-thread communication is faster and easier than the inter-process communication.

- The context switching is faster between the threads as compared to the processes.

What is the difference between synchronous and asynchronous programming in multithreading?

The following are the differences between synchronous and asynchronous programming:

- **Synchronous programming**: It is a programming model. In synchronous programming, a thread is assigned to complete a task. Once the thread starts working on the task, it is only available for other tasks after the completion of the assigned task.

- **Asynchronous programming**: In asynchronous programming, one job can be completed by more than one threads. It enhances the application performance and hence provides maximum usability.

Is it possible to predict the thread behavior?

No one can predict the thread behavior. It is said so because it is the thread scheduler that does the execution of threads. The developer has no control on choosing the thread to execute. The thread scheduler may have different implementation on different platforms. So, it may happen that the same threading program may produce different outputs in subsequent executions on the same platform as well.

What do you understand by inter-thread communication?

Multithreaded applications essentially consist of different threads performing their task to achieve the business need. While achieving this, such multiple threads can communicate with each other. They may have data or method invocation, which is shared across them. This is normally required to make sure that the CPU always remains utilized, reducing its idle time. Such communication between threads generates the information exchange between them. This information exchange is sometimes complex as the information might get exchanged even before the business logic gets completed. To control this confusion, inter-thread communication is controlled by different methods like *wait()*, *notify()*, and *notifyAll()*.

What is the purpose of the wait() method in a thread?

The object class has the **wait()** method, which is used for inter-thread communication in Java. The method is used to pause the current thread, and it wait until another thread does not call the **notify()** or **notifyAll()** method.

Are you aware of the synchronized block? Why the wait() method is called from the synchronized block?

The **wait()** method comes in picture when one tries to perform inter-thread communication. The synchronized block provides the lock of the monitor to the respective thread. Once the thread has the lock, it becomes the owner of the monitor. If we do not use the synchronized block while invoking the **wait()** method, it will throw the **java.lang.IllegalMonitorStateException** exception.

How would you maintain the sequence of execution of a thread in Java? If you have multiple threads, how would you control that a particular thread executes first and other execute later?

This can be achieved by invoking the **join()** method on particular thread. Suppose if you have three threads: **thread1, thread2,** and **thread3**, and you want **thread1** to complete its task first, then you can invoke **join()** on **thread1**. Remember that you must have invoked the **start()** method on **thread1** before invoking the **join()** method.

What does the join() method do?

The **join()** method causes the currently running thread to pause its execution until the thread it joins completes its task.

The **join()** method comes with three overloaded versions as follows:

- **join()**: This method will put the current running thread on wait until the thread on which the method is called is dead. In case if the thread is interrupted, then it will throw **InterruptedException**.

- **join(long milliseconds)**: This method works similar to the join()method, but it waits for the specified time as denoted in arguments.

- *join*(**long milliseconds, int nanoseconds**):In this overloading method, along with the milliseconds, nanoseconds are also added to denote the waiting period for join.

Explain the thread life cycle. What are the states in the lifecycle of a thread?

Each thread goes through the following states during its lifetime:

- **A New Thread**: In this state, a new instance of the Thread class is created. However, the thread is not alive.

- **The Runnable Thread**: The thread becomes runnable once a **start()** method is called on the thread. It makes the thread ready to run. The thread is not in the running state as it is not yet selected by the thread scheduler.

- **The Running Thread**: When the thread scheduler selects the thread from the thread pool, its **run()** method is invoked. This method execution denotes that the thread is running.

- **The thread is Waiting or Blocked:** In this state, the thread is alive but is not running or it might be waiting for the other thread to finish.

- **The thread is Dead or Terminated:** This state is achieved when the execution of the **run()** method is complete. The thread is said to be dead or terminated after this.

What is context switching?

Whenever we work with multiple threads, we shift from one thread to another. In **context switching,** the states of the executing threads are stored. This stored state is restored, and the thread is resumed from that point onward when the thread gets a chance of execution again.

Differentiate between the Thread class and Runnable interface for creating a thread?

A thread can be created by two ways:

- By defining a class that extends the **Thread** class
- By defining a class that implements the **Runnable** interface

The differences between the two ways:

- When one uses an extension of the **Thread** class, the class cannot extend another class, as Java does not support multiple inheritances. However, when one uses implementation of the **Runnable** interface, the class can still extend another class to utilize its services.

- Once we write a class extended from the **Thread** class, each of thread creates the unique object and associates with it. However, if one uses implementation of the Runnable interface, multiple threads share the same object.

- The Thread class has inbuilt methods such as **getPriority()**, **isAlive()**. But, the **Runnable** interface has a single method **run()**.

What is the relationship between Thread and Runnable?

The **Thread** class implements the **Runnable** interface. As the **Runnable** interface declares the **run()** method, the **Thread** class implements empty implementation of the **run()** method.

What are different overloaded constructors Thread provides?

The Thread class provides the following types of constructors:

Constructor	Description
`Thread()`	Creates a new Thread object
`Thread(Runnable r)`	Creates a new Thread object for Runnable target object
`Thread(String s)`	Creates a new thread with a title
`Thread(Runnable r,String s)`	Creates a new thread for Runnable target object and also adds a title to it
`Thread(ThreadGroup t, Runnable r)`	Creates a new thread for Runnable target object, which belongs to a particular thread group
`Thread(ThreadGroup t, Runnable r,String s)`	Creates a new thread for Runnable target object, which belongs to a particular thread group and with a title for the thread

Table 6.1: Constructors of a thread

Can we start a thread twice? What happens if the *start()* method is invoked twice on a thread?

No, it is not possible to restart the thread multiple times. Once a thread is started, it is executed by the thread scheduler, and it completes the **run()** method. After this, it enters the dead state. If one still tries to start a thread, it will give a **java.lang. IllegalThreadStateException**, which is a type of **RuntimeException**.

Is it possible to invoke the run() method instead of start() directly?

The **run()** method is a valid public method. So obviously, it is possible to invoke the **run()** method directly. But, we need to understand the difference between invoking **start()** and **run()**. When one invokes the **run()** method directly, it does not work as a thread. It will be considered as a normal object invoking the **run()** method. Because of this, a new stack will not be created. When one calls the **start()** method, it internally calls the **run()** method. This creates a new stack for the thread.

Is it compulsory to override the run() method? What will happen if we do not override the run method?

The **Thread** class is a concrete class, so when one extends a class from Thread, there is no compulsion on overriding the **run()** method. As we are not overriding the method, no custom code is available to the newly created thread to execute, and nothing will happen.

However, if we are writing a class that is implementing the **Runnable** interface, then we do not have a choice, and we must override the **run()** method of the **Runnable** interface.

Can we override the start() method? What will happen if we override it?

The **Thread** class has the **start()** method, which is not final. So, it is legal to override this method. But, when in the code we call the in-built **start()** method on the thread, it internally calls the **run()** method where our custom code has been written for the newly created thread. If we override the **start()** method, then the **run()** method will not be invoked internally. Hence, we need to explicitly invoke the **run()** method. Otherwise, it will never be invoked.

Why are the suspend() and resume() methods deprecated?

The **suspend()** method is deadlock-prone. When the target thread holds the lock on an object, when it is in suspended state no other thread can lock that object until the target thread is resumed. The new thread which tries to owe the lock on an object or monitor which is already owned by the target thread, must invoke the resume() on target thread method, else it will result in deadlock condition. Such a deadlock is also called as **frozen processes**. The **suspend()** method puts the thread from the running state to the waiting state. Now, the thread can go from the wait state to the runnable state only when the deprecated **resume()** method is called on the thread. The **resume()** method is used only with the **suspend()** method, and that is the reason it is also deprecated.

Why the destroy() method is deprecated?

The **destroy()** method is also deadlock-prone. When the target thread holds a lock on an object that is destroyed, no thread can lock this object. It is very similar to the deadlock formed when the **suspend()** and **resume()** methods are used improperly. Once the deadlock is formed, one must call the **destroy()** method. When the destroy method is called on Threads, it will throw a runtime exception, and the **destroy()** method puts the thread from running to the dead state.

Explain the difference between the wait() and sleep() method. What is the difference between the wait() and sleep() method?

One of the most important differences is the hierarchy of these methods. The **wait()** method is defined in the Object class, and the **sleep()** method is defined in the **Thread** class. The **wait()** method releases the lock acquired by a thread; however, the **sleep()** method does not release the lock.

How threads communicate with each other? Which methods the developer can use to achieve inter-thread communication?

More than one threads can communicate with each other with the help of the **wait()**, **notify()**, and **notifyAll()** methods. The **wait()** method can be used to wait for the result from another thread. The **notify()** and **notifyAll()** methods are used to send the notifications to the threads that are in the wait state.

Why wait(), notify(), and notifyAll() are in the Object class and not in the Thread class?

The Object class has monitors, and multiple threads can access one object. Only one thread can hold the object monitor at a time to have synchronized methods or blocks. The **wait()**, **notify()**, and **notifyAll()** methods being supplied by the Object class allow all the threads created on that object to communicate with each other easily.

In case if the **Thread** class provides the **wait()**, **notify()**, and **notifyAll()** methods, then the thread communication will be a problem. The synchronization on the object will not be possible. If each thread will have its monitor, then there will not be a way of achieving synchronization, which will lead to inconsistency in the state of the object.

What is thread starvation?

Thread starvation happens when the thread does not have enough CPU time for its execution. It may be caused due to different reasons such as:

- Low-priority threads get less CPU time for execution compared to high-priority threads. So, the lower-priority thread may starve away waiting to get enough CPU to perform the task.

- In the deadlock situation, two or more threads wait for each other to release the lock. So, both the threads starve away to get CPU.

- The thread might be waiting for a long time for the lock on an object's monitor as no other thread is calling the **notify()** or **notifAll()** methods.

Explain the daemon thread. What are daemon threads?

Daemon threads are low-priority threads. The daemon threads provide the background support and services to the user threads. The JVM terminates the daemon thread automatically if the program remains with the daemon thread only. The following two methods from the Thread class are available for the daemon threads:

- **setDaemon(boolean status)**: The method is used to mark the thread as a daemon thread or a user thread.

- **isDaemon()**: The method does a check for the thread whether it is a daemon or not.

How to create a daemon thread? Can we make the user thread a daemon thread if the thread is started?

If a thread is already started and after that one tries to make that as daemon, it will throw **IllegalThreadStateException**. One can only create a daemon thread before starting that thread.

The following code snippet demonstrates how to create the daemon thread:

```
public class DaemonThread extends Thread {
  public DaemonThread(String name) {
   super(name);
  }
```

```java
public void run() {
 // Checking the thread is Daemon or not
 if (Thread.currentThread().isDaemon()) {
  System.out.println("The " + getName() + " is Daemon thread");
 } else {
  System.out.println("The" + getName() + " is User thread");
 }
}
public static void main(String[] args) {
 DaemonThread thread1 = new DaemonThread("thread1");
 // Set user thread to Daemon
 thread1.setDaemon(true);
 thread1.start();
}
}
```

What is a shutdown hook?

The **shutdown hook** is a thread that is invoked implicitly before JVM shuts down. One can use it to perform cleaning up of the resource to save the state when JVM shuts down either normally or abruptly. The shutdown hooks can only be started only when JVM shutdown occurs. The shutdown hooks are more reliable than the **finalize()**method, as there are very less chances that shutdown hooks will not run. The **halt(int status)** method of the **Runtime** class can be called to stop the shutdown hook.

When should we interrupt a thread?

A thread is paused once a **wait()** or **sleep()** method is called on it. One can interrupt a thread when we want to break the sleep or wait state of that thread by calling the **interrupt()**method.

What is synchronization? How to achieve synchronization?

Sometimes, the application has some shared resources that can be accessed by multiple threads. **Synchronization** is the capability of controlling the access of multiple threads to such shared resources. Synchronization is used to prevent thread interference and to prevent the consistency problem. Whenever multiple threads try to do the same task, there is a high possibility of obtaining wrong results. To avoid such a scenario, the process of synchronization can be used. In synchronization, only one thread is allowed to be executed at a time.

Synchronization can be achieved by using:

- Synchronized method
- Synchronized block
- Static synchronized method

Can you give any real-time example of synchronization in an application?

One common example could be reading and writing a file concurrently. Imagine a scenario in which one user is trying to read from the file and another user is trying to update the file. So, if the file is accessed by both users simultaneously, then the end result would be very complicated and weird. In such cases, you can control the entry of the second user to update the file while the first user is still reading the file using the concept of synchronization.

What is the purpose of the synchronized block?

Synchronization allows a single thread to execute the code written in the function to avoid the side-effects. But sometimes, only a couple of lines of code may cause the side-effect and not the entire function. This means it is unnecessary to make the entire function synchronized. The synchronized block can be used under such conditions to lock an object for any shared resource. Only one thread at a time can execute on a particular resource written inside the synchronized block, and all other threads that attempt to enter are blocked.

Can we declare a constructor as synchronized?

No, we cannot declare the constructor as synchronized. A constructor is used for creating an instance of an object. It means that when the constructor is called, the process of object creation is ongoing. So, until an object is not created, it does not need any synchronization. If we try to declare the constructor as synchronized. it will show a compilation error.

Note : One needs to remember that a constructor cannot be synchronized; however, it is possible to write the synchronized block inside the constructor.

Can you explain an intrinsic lock?

When synchronization is built around an entity, it is called as the **intrinsic lock** or **monitor lock**. The intrinsic locks play a vital role in enforcing exclusive access to an object's state as well as establishing the relationships that are essential for the visibility. A **lock** is associated with every object. When a thread needs an exclusive and consistent access to an object's members before accessing them, then the object should acquire the object's intrinsic lock.

Note that after the completion of the task, the lock should be released. The thread owns the intrinsic lock only between the time it has acquired the lock and released the lock. Once a thread owns an intrinsic lock, no other thread can acquire the same lock. It means the other thread will be blocked when it attempts to acquire the lock. Once the thread releases an intrinsic lock, another thread can acquire it.

What is reentrant synchronization?

When a thread has a lock, another thread cannot acquire a lock, but a thread can acquire a lock that it already owns. **Reentrant synchronization** is a situation of allowing a thread to acquire the same lock more than once. Reentrant synchronization describes a situation in which the synchronized code, directly or indirectly, invokes a method that also contains synchronized code, and more importantly, both the sets of code use the same lock. In case no reentrant synchronization is used, then the synchronized code takes many additional precautions to avoid thread blocking.

What is a deadlock?

In multithreaded applications, it is quite normal to have an inter-thread communication. **Deadlock** is a situation in which all the threads are waiting for a resource and the resource is held by some other thread, which is also in the waiting state. That means, none of the thread is executing or getting a chance to execute. So, all the threads are universally in the waiting state. Deadlock is a very complicated situation, and while writing a multithreaded application, one should always take care of avoiding it.

How to detect a deadlock condition? How can it be avoided?

We can detect a deadlock condition by running the code on the command prompt and collecting the thread dump. In case any deadlock is present in the code, then a message will appear on the command prompt. There are certain ways to avoid the deadlock condition as:

- Avoid the use of nested lock.

- The nested lock is one of the common reasons of coming across the deadlock. The deadlock occurs when one provides the locks to various threads, so make sure one should give one lock to only one thread at any particular time.

- Avoid the use of unnecessary locks.

- If not required, one must avoid the locks.

- Using thread join.

- The thread join enables to wait for a thread until some other thread does not finish its execution. The maximum use of the join method can help in avoiding a deadlock.

Explain the thread scheduler

A developer creates the threads. Then, they are under the supervision of a **thread scheduler**. The thread scheduler, which is the part of JVM, schedules the thread and decides which thread to execute. The thread scheduler uses preemptive and time slicing as two mechanisms to perform this scheduling of the threads. The thread scheduler decides which thread to choose depending upon the priority of a thread. The scheduler is also responsible for determining the waiting time of the thread.

What is the preemptive, non-preemptive scheduling and time slicing? Explain the advantages of preemptive, non-preemptive scheduling

The following are the different algorithms used for thread scheduling:

1. **Preemptive scheduling**

   Preemptive scheduling is a scheduling method in which the tasks are mostly assigned with their priorities. Under certain scenarios, it is important to run a task with a higher priority before any other lower-priority task. Sometimes, the thread with lower-priority task is running; however, we still want the higher-priority task to be executed. In preemptive scheduling, the tasks that have the highest priority task execute until they enter the waiting state or dead state, or any other higher-priority task comes into existence.

   Advantages of preemptive scheduling

   - The preemptive scheduling method is a more robust approach, as no single process cannot monopolize the CPU.

- The choice of running task reconsidered after it is interrupted.

- Every event causes the interruption of running tasks.

- In this method, the operating system makes sure that the CPU usage is the same by all running processes.

- The preemptive scheduling is beneficial when we use it for the multi-programming environment.

2. **Non-preemptive scheduling**

In the non-preemptive scheduling method, the CPU has been allocated to a specific process. The process that keeps the CPU busy will release the CPU either by switching context or terminating. It does not need any specialized hardware, so this type of scheduling is used for various hardware platforms. The non-preemptive scheduling occurs after the process voluntarily enters the wait state or terminates.

Advantages of non-preemptive scheduling

- The scheduling offers low scheduling overhead.

- It is conceptually a very simple method.

- It tends to offer high throughput.

- It needs less computational resources for scheduling.

3. **Time slicing**

In time slicing, a particular task executes for a predefined slice of time, and after that, it re-enters the thread pool of ready tasks. The thread scheduler then determines which task should execute next depending on the priority or some other factors.

What is thread priority?

Thread priority is a number associated with the thread from 1 to 10. The number 1 denotes the minimum priority, and 10 denotes the maximum priority. The Thread class also provides variables of final static int type for setting thread priority. The thread having **MAX_PRIORITY** is likely to get more CPU as compared to the low-priority threads. The **setPriority(int priority)** method is used for changing the priority of the thread, and the method returns the priority that the thread has.

What is race condition?

Under multithreaded scenarios, more than one thread might need to access the same resource. The **race condition** is actually a problem that occurs when various threads that are executing simultaneously are trying to access a shared resource at the same time. One can properly use synchronization to avoid the race condition.

What is the volatile keyword in Java?

The **volatile** is a keyword that is used to achieve the thread safety in multithreaded programming. The change in one volatile variable is visible to all other threads, so one variable can be used by one thread at a time.

What is ThreadLocal?

When an application uses multithreading or the concurrency code, it comes with the cost of synchronization or locking. But, it all comes with a great effect on the scalability of the application. When multiple threads share an object, synchronization is a way to achieve safety. **ThreadLocal** is another way to achieve thread safety. It does not require synchronization; instead, it eliminates sharing by providing explicitly a copy of an object to each thread. An object is no more shared, so there is no requirement of synchronization. Automatically, it improves scalability and performance of the application.

What is a thread pool?

A **thread pool** is a group of worker threads that are waiting for the task to be allocated. The threads in the thread pool are supervised by the scheduler that pulls one thread from the pool and assigns a task to it. Once the assigned task to the thread is complete, the thread again returns to the thread pool. The size of the thread pool depends on the total number of threads that are kept at reserve for execution.

What is atomic action in concurrency in Java?

A**tomic action** is an operation that can be performed in a single unit of a task without any interference from any other operation. The atomic methods are available in the `java.util.concurrent` package. It is not possible to stop the atomic action in between the ongoing task. It will stop only after the completion of the task. All the read and write operations for the primitive variable are the atomic operation, except long and double. All the read and write operations for the volatile variable are the atomic operation.

What is a lock interface in the concurrency API in Java?

The `java.util.concurrent.locks.Lock` interface is used as the synchronization mechanism. It works similar to the synchronized block. There are a few differences between the lock and synchronized block that are discussed as follows:

- The **Lock** interface provides the guarantee of a sequence in which the waiting thread will be given the access, whereas the synchronized block does not guarantee it.

- The **Lock** interface provides the option of timeout if the lock is not granted access, whereas the synchronized block does not provide that.

The methods of the Lock interface, that is, **Lock()** and **Unlock(),** can be called in different methods, whereas a single synchronized block must be fully contained in a single method.

Did you use concurrency APIs? Which concurrency APIs have you worked with? Which are the main components of a concurrency API?

The concurrency API is available in the **java.util.concurrent** package. We can find the following classes and interfaces in the package:

- `Executor`
- `ForkJoinPool`
- `ExecutorService`
- `ScheduledExecutorService`
- `Future`
- `TimeUnit(Enum)`
- `CountDownLatch`
- `CyclicBarrier`
- `Semaphore`
- `ThreadFactory`
- `BlockingQueue`
- `DelayQueue`
- `Locks`
- `Phaser`

What is the Executor interface in a concurrency API?

The **Executor** interface is provided by the package **java.util.concurrent,** which can be used to execute a new task with the help of the *execute()* method. This is an automotive way to achieve multithreading without developer taking extra efforts to create and manage threads.

Explain the ExecutorService interface from the concurrency API

ExecutorServiceinterface is the child interface of the **Executor** interface, and it adds the features to manage the lifecycle.

Explain the difference between the ScheduledExecutorService and ExecutorService interface?

The **java.util.concurrent** package includes both **ExecutorService** and **ScheduledExecutorService** interfaces. **ExecutorService** enables a asynchronous execution of the task in the background. The **ScheduledExecutorService** interface has some additional methods than its parent **ExecutorService**. The methods enable to execute the **Runnable** and **Callable** tasks with some delay or repeatedly after fixed time period.

What is the difference between Callable, Runnable, and Future interface?

Both the **Callable** and **Runnable** interfaces are used by the classes that are interested in the execution of multiple threads with the following differences:

- The **Callable** interface can be used only after Java 5, whereas the **Runnable** interface can be used from very first version of Java. So, **Callable** is the improved version of *Runnable*.

- The **Callable** interface can return a result, but the **Runnable** interface cannot return any result.

- The **Callable** interface can throw a checked exception, but the **Runnable** interface cannot.

On the other hand, the **Future** interface is used to provide the result of a concurrent process, and it is returned by the **Callable** interface. The interface has following methods for implementation:

- **cancel(boolean status)**: This method is used to cancel the execution of the assigned task.

- **get()**: The method waits for the time till the execution is completed, and after that, the result is retrieved.

- **isCancelled()**: The method returns a Boolean value. The method returns true when the task was canceled before its completion.

- **isDone()**: The method also return a Boolean value. The method returns true if the job is completed successfully; otherwise, it returns false.

What is the difference between traditional multithreading and parallel programming?

Multithreading was designed to work with single CPU and also to utilize idle time of the CPU. Unfortunately, even though the system has multi cores, multithreading will not be able to take advantage. The fork-join framework uses parallel programming, and it can utilize multiple processors available in a computer, which enhances the application performance.

What is the fork-join framework in Java?

The **fork-join framework** is introduced in JDK 7 under the **java.util.concurrent** package. The fork and join framework is used to achieve parallel programming. The framework uses the **divide-and-conquer** strategy to divide a big task into smaller manageable tasks.

What is a divide-and-conquer algorithm in the ForkJoin framework?

One big task is divided into smaller tasks in a such a way that the subtask is small enough to be solved independently. The **divide-and-conquer** strategy recursively divides a task into smaller subtasks until the subtask is not small enough to be solved independently.

State the ForkJoinPool features. Why is it necessary to explicitly shutdown the ForkJoinPool?

The **ForkJoinPool** is a special thread pool that is designed to work with the *fork-join* task splitting. The pool uses work the stealing approach to manage the threads. A queue of the tasks is maintained for each thread in the *fork-join*Pool. When the queue of one thread is empty, it can take tasks from another thread, which improves the application performance. One needs to shutdown the pool explicitly because the pool uses a low-priority daemon, which runs intermittently in the background and dies after all other user threads die. One can use the **shutdown()** method for shutting a pool, if required. Also, one can set the level of parallelism; however, setting the level does not guarantee those many number of tasks will be managed simultaneously. So, it is possible to execute more tasks than the level of parallelism of the *fork-join*pool.

Can you explain the real-world application of the fork-join framework

Let us assume we have an array of 100,000 or more elements. One wants to calculate the sum of the array elements. It will be time consuming to perform the calculation task one by one. Instead, one can use *the fork-join* framework for the calculation. The framework uses the *divide-and-conquer* strategy for parallel programming. The strategy recursively divides an array into smaller sub-arrays until the sub-array is not small enough to be added independently. In case one of the threads is taking more time or busy, the pool uses the work stealing approach for managing threads.

What are the Executors in the Executor framework?

Executors area part of the concurrency API. Executors area factory that supply the methods to return **ExecutorService**, **ScheduledExecutorService,** and **ThreadFactory**. Executors have the following methods:

- **newFixedThreadPool()**: The method returns the pool having fixed number of threads. One needs to pass a number to the method to manage that many number of threads. When concurrently submitted tasks are more than the maintained pool size, then the rest of tasks need to wait in queue. The method has **ExecutorService** as a return type.

- **newScheduledThreadPool()**: The method is also used to create a fixed size pool with an extra facility to schedule the thread, which can run after some defined delay. The method is useful to schedule the task. The method has **ScheduledExecutorService** as a return type.

- **newCachedThreadPool()**:It creates a pool without any fixed number of threads. The thread will be created at runtime. When there is no task to execute, the thread will be alive for 60 seconds, and eventually, it will die. The method is best to create a thread pool with short-lived threads. The method has a return type as **ExecutorService**.

Explain FutureTask

The **FutureTask** class is an implementation of the *Future* interface. The result generated from it can only be obtained if the execution of one task is completed. In case the computation is not yet completed, then the **get()** method will be blocked. However, if the execution is completed, then it cannot be re-started or even canceled.

What is difference between shutdownNow() and shutdown() in the Executor framework in Java?

Both the methods **shutdown()** and **shutdownNow()** belong to **ExecutorService**. The **shutdown()** method enables the stopping of the thread after completion of the current task and does not accept a new task to execute. The **shutdownNow()** method also tries to stop the running threads. This is a forceful way to half all the tasks that are running or scheduled to run. It will not execute any task that has been submitted but not yet started. This returns a list of all the tasks that are in the waiting state for execution.

How to terminate a thread in the Executor framework?

ExecutorService has a method **awaitTermination(long timeout, TimeUnit unit)**, which takes the time and unit of time as arguments. After the specified time, the thread pool is terminated. In case one needs to terminate a task immediately, then we can use the same method by passing zero seconds as timeout.

What are the different policies in the Executor framework?

The following are the different policies of the Executor framework:

- **ThreadPoolExecutor.AbortPolicy**: This policy is a handler for rejected tasks. It handles the tasks that have been rejected.

- **ThreadPoolExecutor.CallerRunsPolicy**: This policy handles the rejected task, but it runs the rejected task directly.

- **ThreadPoolExecutor.DiscardOldestPolicy**: This policy handles the rejected tasks that are the oldest and unhandled. It discards the tasks that are the oldest.

- **ThreadPoolExecutor.DiscardPolicy**: This policy handles the rejected tasks that are rejected silently.

How one can get a value returned from the Callable thread in the Executor framework?

We can use Future to get the return value of the callable thread, as shown in the following code:

```
ExecutorServiceservice = Executors.newCachedThreadPool();

Future<Integer> future=service.submit(new CallableThread());

int val=future.get();
```

Which classes in collection provide concurrency?

The following classes in collection provide the concurrency mechanism:

- **BlockingQueue**:

  The package **java.util.concurrent** provides the interface **BlockingQueue**, which is the child of the **Queue** interface. It provides the functionalities such as waiting for the queue to become non-empty before retrieving an element, or waiting for the space to become available in the queue before storing another element.

- **ConcurrentMap**:

  The package **java.util.concurrent** provides the interface as a child of the **Map** interface, which ensures thread safety and atomicity guarantees. The interface supports atomic operations on the underlying map variable. It has the **get()** and **set()** methods that work for reading and writing operations on the volatile variables.

- ConcurrentNavigableMap:

  ConcurrentNavigableMapinterface is included in the **java.util. concurrent** package as a child of the **ConcurrentMap** interface. It supports **NavigableMap** operations such as **lowerKey**, **floorKey**, **ceilingKey**, **higherKey,** and so on.

How can you solve the consumer–producer pattern by using BlockingQueue?

The consumer–producer problem can be solved using the **wait()** and **notify()** methods. The consumer–producer pattern can be optimized using the **BlockingQueue** interface. The **BlockingQueue** interface has the **put()** and **take()** methods for solving the consumer–producer pattern. The **put(i)** method is used by the producer to produce in the shared queue, and the *take()* method is used by the consumer to consume from the shared queue.

What care should be taken while writing a thread-safe code? What are the most important points one must keep in mind while writing a multithreaded application?

The thread-unsafe code may cause various issues to the application. And, that is the reason utmost care should be taken while writing a thread-safe healthy code and avoid deadlocks. Some of the things that we can follow are as follows:

- Use the immutable **String** in place of **StringBuffer,** as whenever a change happens in the value of a string, it produces a new String.

- The unsynchronized method with a multithreaded code may lead to race condition. So, try to use the synchronized block or synchronized methods.

- The final variables are thread-safe as once a value is assigned, it cannot be altered. If possible, try to use final variables.

- The static variables are also not thread-safe. If such static variables are used in the unsynchronized static methods, then multiple threads may enter the method concurrently, which leads to an issue. One must declare the static methods as synchronized.

- When a field is declared as volatile, all threads can see a consistent value for that variable. The volatile variables can be considered as an alternative to synchronized methods. So, whenever possible, use volatile variables.

- Using thread-safe collections, for example, in place of using `HashMap`, use `ConcurrentHashMap` or `HashTable`; instead of using `ArrayList,` use `Vector`.

What happens when the object that has the lock calls the sleep() or wait() method?

When the `sleep()` method is called, the thread does not leave the object locked, thought it goes from the running state to the waiting state. Now, the thread waits for the specified sleep time to be complete, and once it is completed, the thread continues the runnable state.

When the `wait()` method is called, then the thread leaves the object's lock, and it goes from the running state to the waiting state. Now, the thread waits for other threads on the same object to call either the `notify()` or `notifyAll()` method. When any one of the `notify()` or `notifyAll()`method is called, the thread leaves the waiting state and goes to the runnable state. Once a thread is in runnable state, it acquires the object's lock again.

Conclusion

In this chapter, we discussed about the concurrency mechanism of Java. There are many tasks in an application that can be executed simultaneously, which will improve the performance of the application. We studied how to achieve this by using the concepts of multithreading. But, while running this multithreading application, sometimes, there might be problems of cross-functioning of threads, which will create unwanted or undesirable outputs, as multiple threads are accessing common data. To avoid this, we must know how to implement synchronization, which we studied through different interview questions during this entire chapter. At the end of this chapter, we talked about the update in the concurrency API introduced in Java. In the next chapter, we will discuss about Java database connectivity.

CHAPTER 7

Java Database Connectivity

Introduction

Data, data, and data! The world is full of data. This data can be in different formats. Even our brain consists of huge data. Every day, in and out (even at night), our brain receives lot of data, and to our surprise, we can recall that data as and when we require it. On the similar lines, our application deals with lot of data. This data could be generated by application or entered by user. But, this data is not immortal. The data dies when an application exits. At times, it is still acceptable. But, imagine a scenario that you deposit some amount in your bank account through an application. Obviously, when you restart you application, you would like to see the reflection of that amount in your bank. But, that cannot happen as data is erased automatically when an application is terminated. So, there must be a way to store this data somewhere permanently even if the application is terminated. And, the application should able to pull that data whenever it restarts. Another example would be the identity proof that you provide at account opening. You would expect that once you provide such information to bank, the bank authorities should never ask for your identity proof for each transaction. You can store such data either in the flat files or in database. We have already discussed how to store the data in file in *Chapter 5, File Handling*. But, file lacks storing the data in a structured format, which makes it more difficult to find the data based on some condition. In order to achieve this, Java had introduced the JDBC API, which can communicate with the database to store, retrieve, or update the data in the structured format.

Structure

In this chapter, we will discuss:

- What is persistency
- How to connect with the database using JDBC API
- Different interfaces, which are part of the JDBC API
- What is connected and disconnected architecture of JDBC
- How to implement transaction management
- How to answer different interview questions on JDBC effectively

Objective

At the end of this chapter, you will able to learn different interview questions based on **Java Database Connectivity (JDBC)**. Working with JDBC is always complex, as one needs to remember many interfaces and their sequence, so as to achieve the desired result. In this chapter, we will start our journey from very basic concepts. We will begin with understanding the concept of persistency, and then we will learn how to achieve the same using the JDBC API. We are not targeting any specific database to explain JDBC, but in few code snippets, we have used MySQL as the underlying database. But, you are free to change those database-specific code snippets as per your choice of database. Understanding JDBC is very important when you will study Hibernate in future topics.

Persistency is one of most important segments of any application. So, an interviewer is always keen to know whether you know the basics of persistency. Let us discuss some of the very basic questions that you might come across in an interview related to JDBC.

What is persistency?

Persistency is storing data for a longer duration.

What are the ways for persistency?

Java provides various ways to store the data.

- The very initial way to store the data is file handling. Java objects can be saved in a file using serialization.
- Java objects can be stored in **XML** files, and using **JAXB APIs,** developers can deal within Java applications.

- **Java Database Connectivity (JDBC API)** enables persisting data in databases.
- **Object Relational Mapping (ORM)** provides a mechanism to perform CRUD operations with data in database.

What is JDBC?

JDBC is a **Java API for Database Connectivity**. The API developed by Sun Microsystems, now part of Oracle, is used to deal with a database. JDBC API facilitates a mechanism for the connection to the DB. It also provides the methods to execute the CRUD queries on the database.

Can you explain the architecture of JDBC?

Figure 7.1 represents the architecture of JDBC:

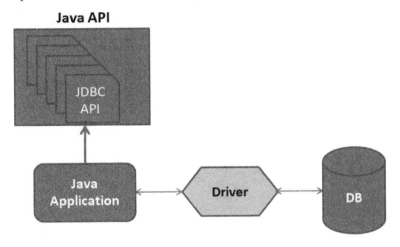

Figure 7.1: *JDBC architecture*

As you can observe from *Figure 7.1*, the Java application communicates with the JDBC API to establish connectivity with database. However, Java application cannot communicate with the database directly. We need to have a JDBC driver layer between the Java application and database. This driver converts the Java API to the corresponding database API and vice-versa.

What is a driver in JDBC? Why it is required?

The **JDBC driver** is a component of software that enables a Java application to interact with the underlying database. It provides the implementation of different interfaces provided by the Java API. Normally, this driver is provided in the format of a jar file like, `mongo.jar`, `mysql-connector-XXX.jar`.

Why is a JDBC driver required? What is the use of the JDBC driver?

JDBC drivers are client-side adapters that are installed on the client machine. The drivers help to convert requests from Java programs to a protocol that the DB can understand. It also transfers the results generated from the database vendors to the Java application.

How many types of drivers are available? Which drivers have you worked with? What is a Type 4 driver?

There are 4 types of JDBC drivers.

Types of drivers:

- Type 1 or JDBC-ODBC bridge driver
- Type 2 or native API driver or partial Java driver
- Type 3 or network protocol driver
- Type 4 or pure Java driver

Explain in detail types of drivers

Following are the different types of drivers:

- **Type 1 or JDBC-ODBC bridge driver**

  Type 1 driver uses the ODBC driver installed on each client machine to connect to the database. One needs to configure **Data Source Name (DSN)** on the system to use ODBC. The JDBC-ODBC bridge driver converts the JDBC method calls into the ODBC function calls. The conversion of data takes place from JDBC to ODBC, making it slower. As no extra download or installation is required, it is easy to use. But, we cannot overlook a thing of configuring DSN on every system, which makes it tedious to migrate from system to system.

- **Type 2 or native API driver or partial Java driver**

  Type 2 driver uses the client-side libraries of the database. In Type 2 driver, the JDBC API calls are converted into native C/C++ API calls, which are unique to the database. Whenever one changes the database, he/she has to change the native API, as it is specific to a database. Its performance is better than the JDBC-ODBC bridge driver. These drivers are provided by the database vendors and must be installed on each client machine.

- **Type 3 or network protocol driver**

  Type 3 driver is extremely flexible and uses a three-tier approach to access databases. The network protocol driver uses middleware, which converts JDBC calls into the vendor-specific database protocol. The driver is entirely written in Java and does not require any client-side library.

  JDBC clients use standard network sockets to communicate with a middleware application server. Now, the socket information is translated by the middleware application server into the call format required by the DBMS and forwarded to the database server. As no code is installed on the client and a single driver can actually provide access to multiple databases, it is very flexible.

- **Type 4 or pure Java driver**

  Type 4 or pure Java-based driver communicates directly with the database through a socket connection. It directly converts JDBC calls into the vendor-specific database protocol, hence provides the highest performance driver available for the database. It is entirely written in Java and usually provided by the vendor. As the driver is DB-specific, we need to remember to add a new driver definition every time we change the DB.

Can you explain the procedure to connect to a DB? What are the steps to connect to a database?

The following steps are to be followed to connect to a database:

- Register the driver
- Get the connections to the DB
- Create a statement instance
- Perform CRUD operations
- Close the opened connection

What are the ways to register the driver?

There are different ways to register the driver as follows:

- The **forName()** method of **Class** enables registering the driver class. The method loads the driver class dynamically. The driver to load depends on which DB you want to connect with.

  ```
  Class.forName("oracle.jdbc.driver.OracleDriver");
  ```

- We also can use the **newInstance()** method to work around with noncompliant JVMs as follows:

  ```
  Class.forName("oracle.jdbc.driver.OracleDriver").
  newInstance();
  ```

- We can use the static **DriverManager.registerDriver()** method to register the driver. You can use the **registerDriver()** method if you are using a non-JDK-compliant JVM.

  ```
  Driver driver = new oracle.jdbc.driver.OracleDriver();

  DriverManager.registerDriver( driver );
  ```

Note: If the driver that you are specifying is not available, then JVM will generate `ClassNotFoundException`. For `TypeIV` driver, you can add the corresponding jar file in your project.

Explain the difference between Class.forName() and DriverManager.registerDriver()

This question can be re-framed as:

Why developers always use Class.forName() to register the driver?

Why is it recommended not to use DriverManager.registerDriver() for driver registration?

The JDBC specification requires a driver to get register itself when the class is loaded. The class is loaded using the **Class.forName()** method. In JDBC 4, the drivers are able to load automatically just by keeping them the class path.

On the other hand, **DriverManager.registerDriver()** is manual. It is potentially dangerous, as it causes the driver to be registered twice. When the code requires deregistration of a driver to prevent memory leak, then we only end up deregistering it once and leave a second instance registered.

JDBC API

Java provides the **JDBC API**, using which we can connect to the underlying database. It contains many interfaces, and as a developer, you must be aware of that. You can expect a few questions related to different interfaces, which are discussed in the further section.

If JDBC is an API, who provides the implementation?

The vendors implement the JDBC API and provide it in a JAR file. For example, *MySQL* provides the `mysql-connector-**.jar` file as a driver; we can add this JAR file to communicate with **MySQL DB**. This jar contains the implementations for different interfaces.

Can you list different interfaces of JDBC API?

JDBC provides different interfaces such as **Connection**, **Statement**, **PreparedStatement**, **CallableStatement**, **ResultSet**, and so on.

What is the standard process to obtain a DB connection? How to obtain JDBC?

We can obtain the **Connection** as given in the following steps:

- Load the selected driver to communicate to the DB:

```
Class.forName("oracle.jdbc.driver.OracleDriver");
```

Or

```
Class.forName("oracle.jdbc.driver.OracleDriver").newInstance();
```

Note: in the same way, you can connect to MySQL or PostgreSQL databases.

- Obtain the connection as follows:

```
Connection conn = DriverManager.getConnection(URL, USER, PASS);
```

Note: You might get the question about how JVM connects to the DB by retrieving a URL. So, make sure that you know how to configure a URL in the preceding argument.

Now, the **Connection** is ready to use. Once the DB operations are done, we can close the connection as follows:

```
conn.close();
```

How to obtain a generated Primary Key (PK) from a DB?

Whenever one inserts record into a table, either application sends a Primary Key (PK) of that row to the DB or asks the DB to generate the PK for the row such as an auto-incremented column.

We can retrieve the values of that particular column using the **getGeneratedKeys()** method **if** statement as follows:

```
stmt.executeUpdate(INSERT_QUERY,Statement.RETURN_GENERATED_KEYS);
ResultSet rs = stmt.getGeneratedKeys();
```

Which interfaces are used to fire queries that perform CRUD operations on a database?

This question can be re-framed as:

What is the difference between Statement, PreparedStatement, CallableStatement?

Whenever we want to perform CRUD operations on a DB, we can use **Statement**, PreparedStatement or **CallableStatement** under different scenarios.

- **Statement**

  Statement is a general-purpose method to communicate with a table. It is used to fire up the static queries.

- **PreparedStatement**

  PreparedStatement is a very useful way to fire the same SQL queries again and again with different parameter values at runtime. It is useful to execute dynamic or parameterized queries. **PreparedStatement** is a precompiled query, and the firing of query happens only once, which saves time. Thus, it increases the performance of application.

- **CallableStatement**

  CallableStatement is used to execute the stored procedures. We can pass three types of parameters to **CallableStatement** as follows:

  - **IN parameter:** The IN parameter is used to pass values to the stored procedure.

  - **OUT parameter:** The OUT parameters are used to hold the result that is returned from the procedure.

  - **INOUT parameter:** The INOUT parameter holds both IN and OUT parameters.

How to use CallableStatement? How to call a procedure using CallableStatement?

Working with **CallableStatement** comprises the following steps:

- Creating **CallableStatement** object.
- Use the **setter()** methods to pass **IN** parameters.

- Use the **registerOutParameter()** method to register the **OUT** parameters.
- Executing **CallableStatement**.
- Use the **getter()** methods to retrieve the result returned by the stored procedure.

Let us understand how to code for **CallableStatement** to call **procedure1** in different cases:

Case 1: Without *IN* or *OUT* parameter

```
CallableStatement callstmt = con.prepareCall("{call procedure1}");
callstmt.execute();
```

Case 2: With *IN* parameter but no *OUT* parameter

```
CallableStatement callstmt = con.
prepareCall("{call procedure1(?,?)}");
callstmt.setInt(1,10);
callstmt.setString(2,"name1");
callstmt.execute();
```

Case 3: With both *IN* and *OUT* parameters

```
CallableStatement callstmt =
                    con.prepareCall("{call procedure1(?,?,?)}");
callstmt.setInt(1,10);
callstmt.setString(2, "name1");
callstmt.registerOutParameter(3, Types.VARCHAR);
callstmt.execute();
String address = cstmt.getString(3);
```

Case 4: With *IN* and *INOUT* parameters

```
CallableStatement callstmt = con.
      prepareCall("{call procedure1(?,?)}");
callstmt.setInt(1,10);
callstmt.setString(2, "name1");
callstmt.registerOutParameter(2, Types.VARCHAR);
callstmt.execute();
String address = cstmt.getString(2);
```

What is ResultSet? How to obtain ResultSet?

The **ResultSet** refers to the data in the form of a row and column, which is achieved as a result of query execution.

One can obtain **ResultSet** by firing select query with *Statement* as follows:

```
Statement st=con.createStatement();
ResultSet rs=st.executeQuery("select * from employee") ;
```

We can also use parameterized query, or **PreparedStatement** to obtain the **ResultSet** object.

What functionalities ResultSet provides? Which of the functionalities of ResultSet have you worked with?

ResultSet provides the methods to obtain the data, navigation through the data, and to update the data. Following are some of the methods of **ResultSet**:

- **getXXX(int)**: Returns a data from the column, the index of which is declared in the method. XXX represents the type of data that you are interested to retrieve. For example, if you wish to retrieve the String data from the second column, the method will be invoked as **getString(2)**.

- **getXXX(String)**: This method is exactly similar to the earlier method. The only difference is, instead of the column index number, you need to provide the column name as an argument. For example, if you wish to retrieve the String data from the **first_name** column, the method will be invoked as **getString("first_name")**.

- **next()**: Moves the cursor to the next row of **ResultSet**.

- **previous()**: Moves the cursor to the previous row of **ResultSet**.

- **first()**: Move the cursor to the first row of **ResultSet**.

Note: These are not all the methods, but considering the scope of the question, these are enough. The interviewer will make up his/her mind about your knowledge even if you can enlist these many methods.

How to find ResultSet has a data or it is empty?

The cursor returned by the **ResultSet** cursor always points to the beginning of **ResultSet**. It means the cursor points before the first row. Even if we do not have any records based on our query, **ResultSet** is still generated. But, it is empty. But, when one calls the **next()** method in such a case, the application throws an exception. In order to avoid this, we need to check what the **next()** method returns before we process it. The **next()** method returns **false** if there is no next record available in **ResultSet**.

The following code snippet shows how we can achieve that:

```
Statement st = con.createStatement();
ResultSet rs = stmt.executeQuery("select * from Employee");
if (rs.next() == false) {
    System.out.println("ResultSet in empty");
} else {
  do {
    String name = rs.getString(1);
    System.out.println(name);
  } while (rs.next());
}
```

What is scrollable ResultSet?

This can be re-framed as:

What is ResultSet.TYPE_SCROLL_INSENSITIVE and ResultSet.TYPE_SCROLL_SENSITIVE?

ResultSet holds the data. By default, **ResultSet** is not updatable. The cursor moves in the forward direction only. Also, the data in the **ResultSet** cannot be changed. However, the scrollable **ResultSet** is more flexible, and it is scrollable as well as updatable.

The **ResultSet** is scrollable, which means one can traverse through records in the forward as well as backward direction. The scrollable **ResultSet** has the ability to read the first record, last record, next record, and the previous record.

To generate the scrollable **ResultSet**, the **Statement** object must be provided by the scroll type constants as follows:

- **ResultSet.TYPE_FORWARD_ONLY**: The default type of **ResultSet,** which allows **ResultSet** to move only in the forward direction.

- **ResultSet.TYPE_SCROLL_INSENSITIVE**: This constant enables scrolling of data in both the forward and backward direction, but it is insensitive to **ResultSet** updates.

- **ResultSet.TYPE_SCROLL_SENSITIVE**: This constant enables scrolling of data in both the forward and backward direction. Opposite to **ResultSet.TYPE_SCROLL_INSENSITIVE**, the data is sensitive to **ResultSet** updates.

In updatable **ResultSet**, the changes will be immediately persisted in the database and reflected by the **ResultSet** object in real time.

The **ResultSet** concurrency type helps in finding whether the **ResultSet** is updatable or only readable. **ResultSet** has two concurrency levels as:

- **ResultSet.CONCUR_READ_ONLY**: **ResultSet** is not updatable.
- **ResultSet.CONCUR_UPDATABLE**: **ResultSet** is readable as well as updatable.

The following code snippet shows how to create a scrollable **ResultSet,** which is insensitive and only readable:

```
Statement st = con.createStatement(ResultSet.TYPE_SCROLL_INSENSITIVE,
               ResultSet.CONCUR_READ_ONLY);
```

We can also use **PreparedStatement** instead of **Statement**. As mentioned earlier, to create updatable **ResultSet**, you need to change the second argument of the **createStatement()** method as **ResultSet.CONCUR_UPDATABLE**.

One can fire a query using the Statement instance, is it possible to insert a row to a DB without using statement or firing query?

The updatable **ResultSet** can be used to insert rows in the table using **insertRow()** of **ResultSet**.

We need to keep in mind that each column in the inserted row, which does not allow null as a value and also does not have a default value, must be given a value. Before you invoke **insertRow()**, you must invoke the **updateXXX()** method, to modify the column data.

```
Statement st = con.createStatement(ResultSet.TYPE_FORWARD_ONLY,
                                ResultSet.CONCUR_UPDATABLE);
ResultSet rs = stmt.executeQuery("SELECT  * FROM employee");
rs.moveToInsertRow();
rs.updateString("first_name", "Value of name");
rs.updateString("last_name", "Value of Last name");
rs.updateInt("emp_id", 123);
rs.insertRow();
rs.moveToCurrentRow();
```

If ResultSet is with a default working mechanism and one tries to update the data, what will happen?

This will generate exception, `com.mysql.jdbc.NotUpdatable`. It means that the `ResultSet` must come from a `Statement,` which is created from the scrollable and updatable `ResultSet` type.

Which kind of an exception would normally occur in JDBC, and how to handle it?

`java.sql.SQLException` is the most common exception that needs to be handled in a JDBC program. There is no difference in handling the traditional exception and an exception in JDBC. We can use the `try-catch`, `try-multi catch,` and even, `finally` block. Along with this, we can also use the `AutoClosable` interface to get rid of the `finally` block.

Along with `SQLException,` one can also come across other exceptions like `SQL NonTransientException`, `SQLTransientException`, `SQLRecoverableException`, `BatchUpdateException`, `SQLClientInfoException`.

What is transaction management in JDBC?

Transaction represents a single unit of work to be performed on a DB. In other words, transaction can also be considered as a group of operations that are used to perform a task.

When more than operations are going to be performed as a unit of work, the transaction management is more important. If all operations are completed successfully, then the transaction becomes success. If any one of the operations fails, all the remaining operations get terminated and leads the transaction to reach to a failure state.

What do you mean by ACID properties of transaction management?

ACID properties define properties of transaction management. It is an acronym for **Atomicity, Consistency, Isolation, and Durability**.

- **Atomicity**: Atomicity means either all fired queries will be successful or none of them.

- **Consistency**: Consistency ensures the consistent state of data.

- **Isolation**: Isolation makes sure one transaction is isolated from other transaction.

- **Durability**: Durability ensures, once the transaction is committed, it will remain committed, even if an event of errors occur.

Why the application needs transaction management?

In JDBC, a transaction is auto-committed. This default behavior is acceptable in small applications. However, in the enterprise Java application, we may need to customize the behavior for the following reasons:

- It increases the application performance

- It allows maintaining the integrity of business processes

- Transaction management allows us to use distributed transactions

Can you explain how transaction management increases the speed or performance of an application?

Sometimes, an application needs to perform bulky operations. It may happen that the user is inserting hundreds of rows in a database. Such insertions, if performed independently, can cause a performance hit. But, using a transaction, you will able to commit all these insertions in a single go, which is obviously beneficial for the performance of the application.

What are the types of transaction?

Transactions can be categorized as:

- **Local transaction**

  The **local transaction** specifies the statements are executed on single transactional resources such as JDBC. Local transactions are easier to implement, which is useful in a centralized computing environment. In a local transaction, the application components and resources are located at a single site, and it involves a local data manager running on a single machine.

- **Distributed transaction**

  The **distributed transactions** are span through multiple transactional resources. In distributed transaction management, the transaction manager is responsible for all database-specific operations. One needs to keep in mind, the distributed transaction must be synchronized and available at different locations.

- **Nested transaction**

    The **nested transaction** occurs within the reference of some other transaction. Any changes made by nested transaction are not visible to the existing or host transaction. All the changes occurred in the nested transaction can be notified to the host transaction once it is committed. A nested transaction helps in managing isolation of the transaction mechanism.

How to provide transaction management in JDBC?

By default, JDBC is auto-committed. To take the control of transaction management, we need to perform following steps:

- Disable auto commit:

    ```
    con.setAutoCommit(false);
    ```

- Perform CRUD operations using the **execute()** or **executeUpdate()** methods and then invoke the **commit()** method:

    ```
    con.commit();
    ```

- In case any operation in a transaction is not executed or an exception occurs, then the invoke **rollback()** method:

    ```
    catch(SQLException se){
    // Whenever exception occur
      con.rollback();
    }
    ```

What are commit() and rollback() methods?

The transaction we begin can be either successful or fail. Based on that, we can decide if we want the changes of already executed tasks to be permanently reflected or would like to undo them. To achieve this, transaction management provides two methods, which are as follows:

- **commit()**: Once the CRUD operation is performed and we want those changes to be reflected in a DB permanently, we call the **commit()** method.

- **rollback()**: Whenever the CRUD operations are performed, there is a chance of getting an exception while executing one of the steps. This might be already executed steps as well. So, to maintain consistency of the data, whatever changes are made till that point need to be roll backed. To undo these changes, one needs to invoke the **rollback()** method.

What is Savepoint? How to use Savepoint?

Transaction is a concept of performing more than one operation one after the other. While performing these multiple operations, we may need an intermediate mark within the current transaction, which can be achieved by **Savepoint**. Once we set **Savepoint**, the transaction can be rolled back to that **Savepoint** without affecting the preceding work. The following code snippet elaborates how to create and use **Savepoint**:

```
1. Savepoint savepoint = con.setSavepoint();

2. //intermediate operations

3. con.rollback(savepoint);  // rolling back till 'savepoint'
```

What is metadata? What is DatabaseMeta Data and ResultSetMetaData?

Metadata is the data that provides a structured description about another data. JDBC provides different objects to provide information about the information such as follows:

- **DatabaseMetaData**: It provides the information about the underlying database with which the application is communicating.

  We can use **DatabaseMetaData** to obtain database information such as follows:
  - o Database users, tables, views, and stored procedures
  - o Database schema and catalog information
  - o Information about PK, foreign key of a table

- **ResultSetMetaData**: It provides the information about **ResultSet** that is generated by the query.

  We can use **ResultSetMetaData** to obtain database information such as follows:
  - o Number of columns, name, type, and length
  - o Is the column is readable/writable, searchable

What is BatchUpdate? How to perform batch processing?

In **batch update,** a batch of updates is grouped together and sent to the database in one batch instead of sending the updates one after one. The following are the advantages of batch update:

- Using a batch of updates helps to perform updates in one go, which is faster than sending the data one by one, and then to wait for each one to finish.

- Batch update helps in reducing the network traffic.

- The speed is comparatively more than executing the updates one by one.

- We can use batch updates for SQL inserts, updates, as well as deletes.

The following code snippet describes how to use batch updates:

```
Statement st = null;
try{
    st = con.createStatement();
    st.addBatch("update employee set firstname='ABC' where id=1");
    st.addBatch("update employee set firstname='Eric' where id=4");
    st.addBatch("update employee set firstname='May'  where id=7");
    int[] affected = st.executeBatch();
} finally {
    if(st != null) st.close();
}
```

Note: We can also use `PreparedStatement` instead of `Statement` in the preceding code. **What is a cursor in JDBC?**

A cursor is pointer maintained by the **ResultSet** object that points to the current row in **ResultSet**.

What is connected and disconnected architecture?

Java provides different architectures to retrieve data from a database such as:

- **Connected architecture**

  The connection must be opened to access the data retrieved from the database.

- **Disconnected architecture**

  The data retrieved from database can be accessed even when the connection to the database was closed.

JDBC by default uses connected architecture. However, disconnected **RowSet** supports disconnected architecture to deal with the DB.

What is RowSet?

The instance of **RowSet** is a Java bean component introduced in JDK 1.5. It is a wrapper of **ResultSet,** which holds tabular data in an easier and flexible way than **ResultSet**. The **RowSet** object is scrollable and updatable by default.

What are different types of RowSet?

A *RowSet* is of two types:

- **Connected RowSet**: A connected **RowSet** object establishes a connection with the database to carry out the CRUD operations. The connection is maintained until the **RowSet** object is closed.

- **Disconnected RowSet**: In a disconnected **RowSet** object, the connection is established to the database only while reading and writing the data to the DB. It does not hold a connection while processing the data.

Both connected and disconnected **RowSet** objects are almost same, except the following:

- Disconnected **RowSet** is lighter in weight compared to connected **RowSet** objects.

- Disconnected **RowSet** is by default **Serializable**.

- Disconnected **RowSet** can be used to send data to lightweight clients such as mobiles, and so on.

RowSet is an interface. So, what are its types and implementation classes?

The following are the different types of **RowSet**:

- **JdbcRowSet**

  One of the extended interfaces of **RowSet** is **JdbcRowSet,** which is a wrapper around a **ResultSet** object. This enables to use the **ResultSet** as a **JavaBean** component. **JdbcRowSet** is a connected **RowSet,** which maintains its connection to a database using a JDBC technology-enabled driver. An instance of **JdbcRowSet** can simply take calls invoked on it, and then in turn, that is called on its **ResultSet** object. The **JdbcRowSet** object is by default scrollable and updatable. When the driver and database do not support scrollable or updatable **ResultSet**, the application can populate a **JdbcRowSet** object with the data of a **ResultSet** object, and then, we can operate on the **JdbcRowSet** object.

The concrete implementation of **JbdcRowSet** is **JdbcRowSetImpl**.

The following code snippet illustrates the usage of **JdbcRowSetImpl**:

```
JdbcRowSetImpl jdbcRowset= new JdbcRowSetImpl();

jdbcRowset.setCommand("SELECT * FROM employee WHERE empid = ?");

jdbcRowset.setURL("jdbc:mysql:mydb");

jdbcRowset.setUsername("mysql");

jdbcRowset.setPassword("mysql");

jdbcRowset.setInt(1, 100);

jdbcRowset.execute();

JdbcRowSetImpl jdbcRowset= new JdbcRowSetImpl();

jdbcRowset.setCommand("SELECT * FROM employee WHERE empid = ?");

jdbcRowset.setURL("jdbc:mysql:mydb");

jdbcRowset.setUsername("mysql");

jdbcRowset.setPassword("mysql");

jdbcRowset.setInt(1, 100);

jdbcRowset.execute();
```

- **CachedRowSet**

  A **CachedRowSet** object is a disconnected **RowSet**. It is a container for rows of data, which caches its rows in memory, enabling to operate without always being connected to a data source. A **CachedRowSet** object contains rows from **ResultSet**. However, it can also contain rows from any file with a tabular format like a spreadsheet. Whenever the data in **CachedRowSet** is modified, those modifications can be propagated to the source of the data. The implementation of this is **CachedRowSetImpl**.

- **WebRowSet**

  WebRowSet is better for platform-independent communication. **WebRowSet** is an extension of **CachedRowSet**. Using this, **RowSet** provides the facility for reading and writing database query results into an XML file. The implementation of this is **WebRowSetImpl**.

- **JoinRowSet**

  A **JoinRowSet** is an extension of **WebRowSet,** which consists of related data from different **RowSets**. **JoinRowSet** facilitates a standard way to establish an SQL JOIN between disconnected **RowSets** without connecting to the data source. Any number of **RowSet** objects, which implement the **Joinable** interface, can be added to a **JoinRowSet** object. The **Joinable** interface provides methods for specifying the columns based on which the JOIN action will be performed.

- **FilteredRowSet**

  Sometimes, a **RowSet** object has to provide a degree of filtering to its contents. Here, one can provide a query language for all standard **RowSet** implementations. But, it is a complex and impractical approach for lightweight components. The **FilteredRowSet** supplies a lightweight solution for filtering the data.

What is SQLTimeoutException?

JDBC provides the **setQueryTimeout(int seconds)** method to set up the waiting time to capture the result from the statements. If the query does not return the result in the specified time given in the argument, **SQLTimeoutException** is fired.

Conclusion

In this chapter, we discussed what type of questions based on JDBC can be asked during your Java interview. While discussing this, we learned many things about how to connect with a database and how to retrieve information or data from a database to application. We also talked about different interfaces and their implementation, which forms the core part of JDBC. We are still on first floor of the tower; there are many things to learn and understand as far as a Java interview is concern. In the next chapter. we will discuss *Collections* in detail.

CHAPTER 8
Collections

Introduction

Java is an object-oriented programming language. Software created using Java comprises of a number of objects that communicate with each other. It is always essential to group these objects together so as to perform some common operations on these objects. Normally, such operations need to be performed manually by a developer repetitively. To reduce such effort, Java introduced the collection framework, which consists of predefined data structures and algorithm, which can be applied on an object. **The collection framework** is essentially a group of different interfaces and their implementation classes using which one can group the objects based on different scenarios. Every interface on its own facilitates different functionalities to a group of objects based on which objects are arranged or traversed. Such functionalities give flexibility to the developers to use objects in an application to their full capacity to achieve the desired result. Sometimes, the developers are in a need of objects that are ordered; sometimes, they want the same object group without duplicates, or sometimes, the same object group in some sorted order. The collection framework provides all such solutions to the developers.

Structure

Understanding the collection framework is often assumed to be complex. It consists of a number of interfaces, sub-interfaces, and their implementation classes. In this chapter, we will cover the different aspects of the Collection framework as:

- What is the need for the Collection framework?
- Different Collection interfaces:
    - o List
    - o Set
    - o Queue
    - o Map
- Utility classes like Collections and Arrays

Objective

Every interface in Collection is defined to achieve a specific functionality. To remember such a big API is not an easy task. And, because of its importance in real-time projects, Collection is one of the most favorite topics in the Java interview process. As mentioned, the Collection Framework API is huge. So, covering each and every class is not possible or, in fact, not required as far as the interview process is concerned. But, for sure, in this chapter, you will learn how to answer almost every important question, right from the concept to implementation so that you will succeed in an interview. You will able to master the different collection types like List, Set, Queue, and Map, and their implementations.

Explain the Collection framework. What is the Collection framework?

JDK 1.2 introduced the Collections Framework in which a group of all the collections interfaces, implementations, and algorithms is added. These APIs, which are a collection of classes and interface, are used to store, find, add, and manipulate the objects. The framework offers interfaces such as has **List**, **Set**, **Map**, **Queue,** and their implementation classes like **ArrayList**, **Vector**, **HashMap**, **Stack**, and **HashSet**, and so on for this purpose.

List the benefits of the Collections framework

Java Collections is now equipped with Generics and Concurrent Collection classes for thread-safe operations. It includes blocking interfaces along with their implementations in the Java concurrent package.

The following are some of the benefits of the collections framework:

- The framework reduced the development effort with the help of core collection classes instead of implementing our own version of collection classes.

- The code quality is enhanced by the use of well-tested collections classes.

- It reduces the effort for maintaining the code by using the collection classes offered in JDK.

- It helps in reusability and interoperability.

Explain the difference between an array and collection. What are the main differences between an array and collection?

The array and collection both support storing of the data. There are some differences between them, which are stated as follows:

- Arrays are always of a fixed size. It means once the size of an array is defined, it cannot be changed at runtime, but the collection is dynamic in size. It means the size of a collection can be changed dynamically at runtime.

- Arrays can store only one type of objects or homogeneous elements, but a collection can hold heterogeneous objects.

- Arrays do not have predefined methods for data manipulation, and the user needs to provide logic for sorting and searching of elements. However, the collection offers predefined methods for data manipulation.

What are legacy classes?

The Collection framework is not part of JDK from the beginning. It was added from JDK 2 onward. So, instead of the collection framework, JDK relied on some classes and interfaces for storing and manipulating the collection of data. The following are the legacy classes:

- **Vector**:

   Vector is similar to **ArrayList,** except the methods of **Vector** are synchronized, while those of **ArrayList** are non-synchronized.

- HashTable:

   HashTable works on the execution of the *Map* interface. Each entry in **HashTable** is a key-value pair.

- **Dictionary**:

  Dictionary is an abstract class that holds each element as the key-value pair. **Hashtable** is a sub-type of the **Dictionary** class.

- **Properties**:

  It is an extension to the **Hashtable** class. **Properties** is thread-safe, so it does not need any manual sync to hold the values in the key pair.

- **Stack**:

  Stack is referred to as LIFO, which allows popping of elements only from one end. It is an extension to the **Vector** class.

What are the interfaces available in the collection framework? Explain the various interfaces used in the Collection framework

The **java.util** package offers various interfaces and classes as a part of the collection framework. The following is the list of interfaces of offered by the framework:

- **Collection interface**: **java.util.Collection** is the primary interface offered by the framework. The interface is extended from the **Iterable** interface. All the interfaces and classes must implement this interface.

- **List interface**: The **java.util.List** interface extends the Collection interface. The list interface is an ordered collection of objects, which not necessarily be sorted naturally. It allows the duplicate elements. The interface also allows random access of elements.

- **Set interface**: The **java.util.Set** interface is a collection of objects that does not allow duplicate elements. The elements are unordered and unsorted. The interface offers inherited methods of the Collection interface.

- **Queue interface**: The **java.util.Queue** interface defines a queue data structure. A queue offers storing the elements in the form **First In First Out (FIFO)**.

- **Map interface**: **java.util.Map** stores elements in a key-value fashion. The Map interface does not implement the Collection interface. It allows a unique key, but the elements can be duplicate elements. The elements are stored in an unordered, unsorted manner.

What is the advantage of the generic collection?

The following are the advantages of using the generic collection:

- While fetching or iterating the elements, typecasting is not required if one uses the generic class.

- The generic is type-safe and checked at compile time.

- The generic collection makes sure to offer stability of the code by making it bug-detectable at compilation.

What is type erasure?

By default, the collection API allows to hold heterogeneous elements. This heterogeneity may create a problem while processing the data of the collection. To avoid such processing issue, generics has introduced in JDK 1.5. The use of generics assures type safety; it means the collection is allowed to hold the elements only of the same type, and heterogeneous elements cannot be allowed inside.

Though generic is powerful, it only enforces the type constraints only at compile time, and the information about the type is not available at runtime. This process of erasing the type information at runtime is called as **type erasure**.

What is the difference between Collection and Collections?

The following are the differences between the Collection and Collections:

- **Collection** is an interface, and **Collections** is a class.

- The **Collection** interface offers standard functionalities of data structure to List, Set, and Queue. The **Collections** class offers methods to sort and synchronize the collection elements.

- **Collection** is the root interface, and **Collections** is a general utility class.

- The **Collection** interface provides the methods that can be used to manipulate the elements stored in the respective data structure. The **Collections** class provides the static methods for various utility methods for collection objects.

What are the advantages of the Collection framework?

The following are the advantages of the Collection framework:

- The framework reduces the programming effort as it provides predefined methods.

- Use of the framework increases the performance, as it offers use of high-performance implementations of data structures and algorithms.

- It offers interoperability between unrelated APIs so that the collection can be changed from one to other.

- The framework is very easy to learn and implement functionalities.

State the difference between ArrayList and Vector

Both **ArrayList** and **Vector** has **List** as the parent interface. It means both of these classes are an indexed, ordered, unsorted collection. However, there are some major differences between them, which are stated as follows:

- **ArrayList** is not synchronized; however, **Vector** is synchronized.

- **ArrayList** is not a legacy class, but **Vector** is a legacy class.

- **ArrayList** increases its size by 50% of the array size. **Vector** increases its size by doubling the array size.

What are the similarities between ArrayList and Vector?

Both, ArrayList and Vector possess following similarities:

- Both the classes are indexed collection.

- Both are backed up by an array internally.

- Both the classes are an ordered collection. It means the order in which we insert the elements is always maintained.

- The iterator implementation of both the classes is fail-fast by design.

- Both the collections allow null values.

- Both allow random access to element with the help of index number.

What is the difference between ArrayList and LinkedList?

The following are the differences between ArrayList and LinkedList:

- **ArrayList** uses a dynamic array, and **LinkedList** uses a doubly linked list.

- **ArrayList** is not efficient for manipulation, but **LinkedList** is.

- **ArrayList** is better when one wants to store and fetch the data. However, **LinkedList** is the best option for manipulating the data.

- **ArrayList** provides random access, but **LinkedList** does not.

- As **ArrayList** stores only object, it takes less memory overhead, but **LinkedList** stores the object as well as the address of that object, so it takes more memory overhead.

What are the differences between Array and ArrayList?

Both array and ArrayList are index collections with the following differences:

- The array is always of fixed size, and it cannot be resized at runtime, while the size of **ArrayList** can be changed dynamically.

- The array is of the static type, and **ArrayList** is of dynamic size.

- The array allows storing primitive as well as objects; however, in **ArrayList,** one can store only objects primitive data type, which cannot be stored in **ArrayList**.

Explain the difference between the length of an array and size of ArrayList?

One can obtain the length of an array using the property length, but **ArrayList** does not support length property. **ArrayList** offers the **size()** method, which can be used to find the number of elements in the list.

Can array and ArrayList be inter-convertible? How to convert ArrayList to an array and an array to ArrayList?

Yes, we can.

- One can convert an array to ArrayList with the help of the **asList()** method of the Arrays class. The **asList()** method is the static method offered by the Arrays class that accepts the List object.

- In the same way, one can convert ArrayList to an array using the **toArray()** method of the **ArrayList** class.

How would you create an array of primitives from a list?

The **toArray()** method discussed in the earlier question creates an array of wrappers. If you try to generate an array of primitives using this method, it will throw an exception. So, the only option to create such array is to copy the elements from the list to the array explicitly using the **get()** method of list.

ArrayList can be modified at runtime. What if we want a read-only ArrayList?

By default, ArrayList can be modified at runtime. It means one can access, remove, or update the elements using the **add()**, **remove()**, or **set()** methods, respectively.

But, one can obtain a read-only ArrayList by calling the **Collections. unmodifiableList()** method. When **ArrayList** is read-only, one cannot modify the collection using the **add()**, **remove()**, or **set()** methods.

The following code snippet shows how to use this method:

```
List<Integer> list = new ArrayList<Integer>();
        // populate the list
        list.add(10);
        list.add(20);

        // printing the list
        System.out.println("Initial list: " + list);

        // getting unmodifiable list
        // using unmodifiableList() method
        List<Integer> nonModifiableList = Collections
                                        .unmodifiableList(list);

        // Adding element to new list
        System.out.println("Trying to modify the list");
        nonModifiableList.add(30);
```

If you try to execute the preceding code, you will end up with exception **UnsupportedOperationException** shown as follows:

```
Initial list: [10, 20]
Trying to modify the list
Exception in thread "main" java.lang.UnsupportedOperationException
        at java.util.Collections$UnmodifiableCollection.add(Unknown Source)
```

Can ArrayList contain duplicate elements? What are the ways to remove duplicates from ArrayList?

By default, ArrayList can contain duplicate elements. Using the following two ways, one can remove duplicates from ArrayList:

- **Using HashSet**

  One can remove the duplicates from ArrayList using HashSet. This means, you need to convert ArrayList to HashSet. However, in that case, it will not preserve the insertion order.

- **Using LinkedHashSet**

  The use of **LinkedHashSet** maintains the insertion order while removing the duplicates. It can be done using the following steps:

  - First, copy all the elements of ArrayList to **LinkedHashSet**.

  - Now, empty ArrayList with the help of the **clear()** method. The **clear()** method will remove all the elements from the list and make it empty.

  - Finally, copy all the elements of **LinkedHashset** to **ArrayList**.

By default, ArrayList is ordered. Is there any way by which you can reverse or sort the elements in ArrayList?

By default, ArrayList does not provide any such functionality. But, using the utility class, we can achieve this. The following code snippet shows how to achieve the same:

```
List<Integer> list = new ArrayList<Integer>();
// populate the list
```

```
list.add(10);
list.add(6);
list.add(20);
list.add(4);
list.add(15);
// printing the list
System.out.println("Initial list: " + list);
Collections.reverse(list);
System.out.println("Reversed list: "+list);
Collections.sort(list);
System.out.println("Sorted list: "+list);
```

The output of the preceding snippet would be as follows:

```
Initial list: [10, 6, 20, 4, 15]
Reversed list: [15, 4, 20, 6, 10]
Sorted list: [4, 6, 10, 15, 20]
```

What are the ways to synchronize ArrayList?

ArrayList can be synchronized using the following two ways:

- **Using the Collections.synchronizedList() method**

    o The method accepts a list and returns a synchronized list.

    o The method is useful when one does not want to synchronize the traversal, but needs to prevent interference among concurrent threads.

    o This is costly, as it needs a separate array copy with every write operation.

    o This mechanism is very efficient when one has a list and we only need to traverse over its elements without modifying them frequently.

- **Using the CopyOnWriteArrayList() method**

    While iterating over **CopyOnWriteArrayList()**, even if one tries to modify the data while iterating over it, it does not throw **ConcurrentModificationException** because the iterator iterates over the separate copy of **ArrayList**. Also, the write operations will perform on the copy of **ArrayList**.

Explain the difference between the List and Set interfaces

Both the List and Set interfaces are extended from the Collection interface. They have the following differences:

- List can contain duplicate elements, but Set can contain only unique elements.

- List is an ordered collection. It means it maintains the insertion order. However, Set is an unordered collection.

- The List interface allows any number of null values, but the Set interface only allows a single null value.

- The List interface contains Vector as a single legacy class. But, the Set interface does not have any legacy class.

What is the difference between HashSet and TreeSet?

Both **HashSet** and **TreeSet** classes are the implementation of the **Set** interface. But, they have the following differences:

- **HashSet** is unordered, but **TreeSet** maintains ascending order.

- **HashSet** is impended by hash table, whereas **TreeSet** is a tree structure.

- **HashSet** is faster than **TreeSet**.

- **HashSet** is backed by **HashMap,** and **TreeSet** is backed by **TreeMap**.

What is the difference between HashMap and HashTable?

- **HashMap** is non-synchronized, meaning it cannot be used to share between threads directly, and it needs to implement a proper synchronization code. But, **Hashtable** is synchronized, and it can be safely shared with many threads.

- **Hashtable** does not allow any null key as well as null value, but **HashMap** allows one null key and multiple null values.

- **HashMap** is generally preferred over **Hashtable** if one does not need synchronization.

Does HashTable allow null? Can you explain the reason why HashTable does not allow null? Can you explain the reason why HashMap allows null?

- Each entry in the **HashTable** is in the form of a key-value pair. If one wants to successfully store elements to and retrieve the stored objects from it, the objects that are used as keys must implement the **hashCode()** and **equals()** methods. But, if we use null, then it is a problem as null is not an object. As it is not an object, it cannot implement both the **hashCode()** and **equals()** methods.

- **HashMap** is an advanced version with improvement on **Hashtable**. **HashMap** was created in later versions. When one puts a null key to **HashMap,** the **hashcode()** method is not called on the null values; instead, it puts the key in bucket having value equal to 0. **LinkedList** is used to manage multiple objects in that bucket. So, if there are already objects in a bucket having value equal to 0, the null object will be appended to **LinkedList** in that bucket. When one tries to retrieve the value at null key from **HashMap**, the searching is done for value at null key in bucket 0.

Remember there can be only one null key in Java HashMap.

What is WeakHashMap?

This is also implementation of **Map** similar to **HashMap,** with one of the most important change. In case of **HashMap**, if the key that we declared is of object type, then it is connected to the garbage collector. It means the **HashMap** takes over the garbage collector, because of which garbage collection cannot delete the key. In case of **WeakHashMap**, the same **HashMap** gives up the power of deleting the used keys of type objects to the garbage collector, which makes **HashMap** weak; thus, the reason it is termed as **WeakHashMap**.

Can you explain the concept of WeakHashMap with the help of some code?

Sure. The following code snippet shows how the garbage collector can take an active role in deleting the unused keys that are of the object type:

```
Map hashMap= new HashMap();
Map weakHashMap = new WeakHashMap();
```

```
String keyHashMap = new String("HashMapKey");
String keyWeakHashMap = new String("WeakHashMapKey");

hashMap.put(keyHashMap, "MyHashMap");
weakHashMap.put(keyWeakHashMap, "MyWeakHashMap");
System.out.println("Values before GC :");
System.out.println(hashMap.get("HashMapKey")+"          "+weakHashMap.
get("WeakHashMapKey"));

keyHashMap = null;
keyWeakHashMap = null;

System.gc();
System.out.println("Values after GC :");
System.out.println(hashMap.get("HashMapKey")+" "
                                +weakHashMap.get("WeakHashMapKey"));
```

As shown, the keys associated with the objects are set to null. But, even after that, the **HashMap** key survives and points to the actual object, which is not the case with **WeakHashMap**.

The following is the output of this code snippet:

```
Values before GC :
MyHashMap MyWeakHashMap
Values after GC :
MyHashMap null
```

Note: You can also use a user-defined object as a key instead of a String and implement the finalize() method to prove that the garbage collector is actually working in WeakHashMap.

Explain the differences between Iterator and ListIterator?

The following are the differences between **Iterator** and **ListIterator**:

- **Iterator** is useful for traversing the elements in the forward direction only. But, **ListIterator** is useful for traversing the elements both in the forward and backward directions.

- **Iterator** can be used in most of the collections such as **List**, **Set**, and **Queue**. But the **ListIterator** use is limited to **List** only.

- **Iterator** offers only removal operation while traversing the collection. But, **ListIterator** offers adding, updating, and removing the elements while traversing the collection.

State the differences between Iterator and Enumeration?

The following are the differences between **Iterator** and **Enumeration**:

- **Iterator** can traverse through both legacy and non-legacy elements. But, *Enumeration* can traverse only legacy elements.

- **Iterator** is fail-fast, and **Enumeration** is not.

- **Iterator** is slower than **Enumeration**.

- **Iterator** offers removal operation while traversing the collection. However, **Enumeration** can only traverse through the collection.

Explain the difference between the List and Set interfaces?

The differences between **Set** and **List** are as follows:

- **List** is an ordered collection. However, **Set** is an unordered collection.

- **Set** contains unique values, but **List** can contain duplicate values.

- **List** is not sorted by default. Set provides a sorted version as **TreeSet**.

Explain the differences between the Set and Map interfaces?

The differences between the **Set** and **Map** interfaces are as follows:

- **Set** contains only values, but **Map** contains key and values both.

- **Set** contains all unique values. However, **Map** can contain duplicate values associated with the unique key.

- **Set** can have a single null value, but **Map** allows a single null key but can have any number of null values.

What are the differences between HashMap and HashSet?

The differences between **HashSet** and **HashMap** are as follows:

- **HashSet** implements the Set interface, and **HashMap** implements the Map interface.

- **HashSet** contains only values, whereas **HashMap** includes key and value as one entry.

- **HashSet** can be iterated directly. However, to iterate over **HashMap,** one needs to convert it into *Set* first.

- **HashSet** cannot contain duplicate values. But, **HashMap** can contain duplicate, which will be associated with unique keys.

- **HashSet** can contain a single null value, but **HashMap** can have only a single null key. **HashMap** allows any number of null values.

Explain the differences between HashMap and TreeMap?

The differences between **HashMap** and **TreeMap** are as follows:

- **HashMap** is unordered. However, **TreeMap** is sorted in ascending order.

- **HashMap** implements a hash table by default, and **TreeMap** implements a tree structure.

- One can sort **HashMap** using key or value, but **TreeMap** can be sorted by keys only.

- **HashMap** allows a null key with multiple null values, but **TreeMap** does not allow any null key but can contain multiple null values.

- Search operation is faster in **HashMap** as compared to **TreeMap**.

It is often said that HashMap is sorted by keys. How can you sort it by values?

We can perform the following steps to sort **HashMap** by its values:

1. Convert **HashMap** to **LinkedList** by invoking the **entrySet()** method.

2. Use the `Collections.sort(arg1, arg2)` method and pass `LinkedList` as the first parameter. The second parameter of this invocation would be the *Comparator* implementation.

3. Convert `LinkedList` to `HashMap`.

What are the differences between HashMap and Hashtable?

The following are the differences between `HashMap` and `HashTable`:

*   `HashMap` is unsynchronized, but `HashTable` is synchronized.

*   `HashMap` allows one null key and multiple null values. However, `HashTable` does not allow any null key or null value.

*   `HashMap` is not read-safe and can be useful for non-threaded applications. But, `HashTable` is thread-safe, and it can be shared between various threads.

*   `HashMap` inherited from the `AbstractMap` class and `HashTable` is inherited from the `Dictionary` class.

What does Comparable do?

The `Comparable` interface is used to sort the objects of the POJO class using `compareTo(Object)`. But, it offers a single way by which one can sort the sequence.

Set allows only unique elements; then, why are we getting the size equal to three and not two? What do we need to do so that Set will only have unique elements?

Yes, as per theory, Set allows only unique elements. When we add instances of the user-defined classes, Set does not have any way to equalize two instances. The one which is in Set and the one which the user wants to add can be checked for their equality using the `equals()` method implicitly. However, in the Employee class, the developer has not defined one. It means the `equals()` method of the class object, which is the default parent of the Employee class, is getting invoked. By default, the `equals()` method compares two references and not content of the two instances. Obviously, two instance references are not equal, which means two instances though have the same content or values of the properties, Set treats them as two unique instances and allows them to add.

What will be the output of the following code?

```
class Employee{
    private int empId;
    private String name;
    //default and parameterised constructor
    //getters and setters
    //compareTo method
    }
Class Test{
    public static void main(String[] args){
    Set<Employee> employees =new TreeSet<>();
    employees.add(new Employee(1,"abc"));
    employees.add(new Employee(2,"abc1"));
    employees.add(new Employee(1,"abc"));
    System.out.println("elements of set:-"+ employees);
    }
}
```

The preceding code will generate exception **java.lang.ClassCastException**.

Why are we getting an exception? What to do to get rid of the exception?

Here, we will get **java.lang.ClassCastException**.

Reason:

TreeSet is by default sorted collection. It means all the elements one will insert into a sorted set must implement the **Comparable** interface as we are not implementing the **Comparable** interface, and if we violate the restriction, we will get **ClassCastException**.

Solution:

Implement the **Comparable** interface in the **Employee** class and override the **compareTo()** method.

What is the difference between Comparable and Comparator?

Both the **Comparable** and **Comparator** interfaces are used for sorting the elements in a collection, but there are few differences as follows:

- The **Comparable** interface allows sorting of collection only in a single way. But, **Comparator** allows a collection to be sorted in multiple ways.

- **Comparable** is included in the **java.lang** package, and **Comparator** is included in the **java.util** package.

- **Comparable** provides **compareTo()** for comparing the data, and **Comparator** provides the **compare()** method for sorting.

- The POJO class needs to implement the **Comparable** interface for sorting the data of the collection. But, there is no compulsion to implement **Comparator**.

What do you understand by BlockingQueue?

The **BlockingQueue** is an interface that extends the Queue. It offers concurrency in the operations such as retrieving, inserting, and deleting the data. While retrieving any element, it waits for the queue to be non-empty. While storing the collection, it waits for the available space. It is a thread-safe collection that cannot contain null elements.

Why to use Properties file?

Sometimes, while writing the code, one may need some values to be used, which can be changed in future or as per the client requirements. If one hardcodes these values, the change in values needs to recompile the class along with redeployment. The properties file can contain the entries in the key and value pair. Instead of hardcoding, if these values are fetched from the properties, file recompilation of the class is not required, even though the values in the properties files are changed at runtime. Using the properties file makes the application easy to manage. The values such as driver name, username, and password for database connectivity are a very common way to store the values in the properties file.

What does the hashCode() method do? Explain the hashcode() method?

The **hashCode()** method returns an integer value called as the hash code value. The **hashCode()** method returns the same integer number if two keys are identical. But, it is possible that two hash code numbers can have different or may be same keys.

If two objects do not have an equal result by using the **equals()** method, then the **hashcode()** method will provide different results for both the objects.

What will be the output of the following code?

```
class Employee{
    private int empId;
    private String name;
    //default and parameterised constructor
    //getters and setters


}
Class Test{
    public static void main(String[] args){
    Set<Employee> employees =new HashSet<>();
    employees.add(new Employee(1,"abc"));
    employees.add(new Employee(2,"abc1"));
    employees.add(new Employee(1,"abc"));
    System.out.println("initial size:-"+ employees.size());
    employees.remove(new Employee(2,"abc1"));
    System.out.println(" after removal the size:-"+ employees.size());
    }
}
```

Even after calling the **remove()** method, the object will not be removed, and the initial size and size after removal remain the same.

The instance of an employee exists in the set; then, why the initial and final size is same? What to do so that the code will work fine?

Yes, the instance is available in the **HashSet** collection. When we try to remove the existing instance, we must decrease the size of the set. However, practically, we get the opposite result, and the initial size is equal to the final size.

Reason:

When we invoke the **remove()** method, the **remove()** method first of all tries to find whether two instances are equal or not. Yes, the equals() **method** comes in picture when equalization of instances is required. But, here, we are using **HashSet**. When we use **HashSet,** first of all, the hash code of two instances must be equal before checking the properties are equal or not. But, the employee does not has the **hashCode()** method. Being the child of the object, the object class's **hashcode()** method will be invoked. It means both instances have different hash code values, and if the hash code of two instances is different, the **equals()** method will not be invoked for comparing the properties. And that is why, though the content is the same, the instance will not be removed.

Solution:

Add the **hashCode()** implementation in the Employee class.

Why do we override the equals() method?

The **equals()** method is used for checking the equality of two objects. One overrides the methods if they want to check the objects based on the property.

What will be the output of the following code?

```java
class Employee{
    private int empId;
    private String name;
    //default and parameterised constructor
    //getters and setters
    //getters and setters
    }
Class Test{
    public static void main(String[] args){
    List<Employee> employees =new ArrayList<>();
    employees.add(new Employee(1,"abc"));
    employees.add(new Employee(2,"abc1"));
    employees.add(new Employee(5,"abc3"));
    System.out.println("initial size:-"+ employees.size());
    Employees.remove(new Employee(1,"abc"));
    System.out.println("size of list after removing an element:-
                    "+ employees.size());
    }
}
```

As an output, you would expect the element getting removed from list. But surprisingly, the element will not be removed, and the size of the list before and after removal is observed to be the same.

Though the instance is available, why the employee instance is not getting eliminated? What do we need to do so that the remove method will work?

Yes, the instance is available in the list, so it must be removed, but practically, it is not removed.

Reason:

When we try to remove an instance of the user-defined classes, the **remove()** method internally crosschecks first of all the equality of the instances. If instances are equal, it will be removed; otherwise, that will not be removed. Now, to check the equality of the instances, the **equals()** method will be invoked implicitly. However, in the Employee class, the developer has not defined one. It means the **equals()** method of the class Object, which is default parent of Employee class, is getting invoked. By default the **equals()** method compares two references and not the content of the two instances. Obviously, two instance references are not equal. As instances are not equals, the remove method does not work and the size remains same.

Solution:

Add the **equals()** method in Employee class and define how we want two instances to be treated for equality. For example, if two instances have the same **empId**, they will be treated as equal.

Can we synchronize the collection interfaces? What are the ways by which one can synchronize the List, Set, and Map elements?

Yes, there are some ways by which the collection interfaces can be synchronized. The **Collections** class offers the following methods to make the *List*, *Set* or *Map* elements as synchronized:

- `public static List synchronizedList(List l)`
- `public static Set synchronizedSet(Set s)`
- `public static SortedSet synchronizedSortedSet(SortedSet s)`
- `public static Map synchronizedMap(Map m){}`

- `public static SortedMap synchronizedSortedMap(SortedMap m)`

What is hash-collision in the hashtable, and how to handle it?

When we have two different keys with the same hash value, the scenario is called as hash-collision. When two different entries have the same hash value, then both of them are kept in a single hash bucket so as to avoid the collision.

We have following two ways to avoid hash-collision:

- **Separate chaining:** Separate chaining is simple to implement. In this, the arrangement is made in such a way that each cell of hash table will point to a linked list of records that have same hash function value.

- **Open addressing:** In open addressing, all elements are stored in the hash table itself. It means the size of the table must be greater than or equal to the total number of keys. Open addressing is done by performing linear probing, quadratic probing, or double hashing.

Explain the purpose of the initial capacity and load factor parameters of a HashMap? What are their default values?

- **Initial capacity:**
  - One can pass the value for the initial capacity as an argument to the constructor while creating an instance of **HashMap**. The initial capacity affects the size of the internal data structure of **HashMap**. **HashMap** maintains the internal data structure as an array. This array has power of two. It means the initial capacity argument value is increased to the next power of two.
  - The initial capacity is 16 by default.

- **Load factor:**
  - The load factor of **HashMap** is the ratio of the number of elements divided by the number of buckets.
  - For example, if we have 16 buckets containing 12 elements, then its load factor is $12/16 = 0.75$. A higher load factor denotes multiple collisions. When the load factor is high, the map should be resized to the next power of two. It means the load factor argument is a maximum value of the load factor of a map. When the map achieves this load factor value, it will resize its internal array to the next power of two value.

o The default load factor value is 0.75; it means one can put 12 elements in **HashMap** when the initial capacity is not mentioned.

o The same is true for goes for **HashSet**, as it is internally backed by **HashMap**.

What is the default size of load factor in any collection on which hashing is based? How is it calculated?

- The default size of load factor is 0.75.

- The default capacity can be computed as the initial capacity multiplied by the load factor.

- *For example*, 16 * 0.75 = 12, which means 12 is the default capacity of Map.

What is the meaning of fail-fast?

Whenever one tries to modify the internal structure while iterating through the elements in the collection, it will throw the **ConcurrentmodificationException** exception. This is called as **fail-fast**. All the implementations of **Iterator** in the collection classes are fail-fast, except the concurrent collection classes, such as **ConcurrentHashMap** and **CopyOnWriteArrayList**.

Explain the differences between fail-fast and fail-safe?

- **Fail-safe:**

  The classes in **java.util.concurrent** are fail-safe. It means it is not affected by any modification in the collection. While iterating through the fail-safe collection, Iterator never throws **ConcurrentModificationException**. The Iterator fail-safe property works with the clone of the underlying collection. But, of course, to achieve this, there is a requirement of extra memory.

- **Fail-fast:**

  By default, all the collection classes in the **java.util** package are fail-fast. This does not allow collection modification while iterating. When we try to modify the element while iteration, the fail-fast iterator throws **ConcurrentModificationException**. It uses the original collection to traverse the elements. There is no requirement of extra memory.

Which features are added to collection in JDK 8? What are the Collection-related features in Java 8?

The following features have been added to Java 8 Collection API:

- The Stream API has been added to collection classes for processing the data sequentially as well as parallelly.

- The **Iterable** interface is now extended with **forEach()** as a default method, which one can use to iterate over the elements in the collection.

- The **forEach()** method is very helpful using lambda expressions for the Consumer interface as an argument.

- The Collection API is also improved by adding the **forEach Remaining(Consumer action)** method to the Iterator interface.

Explain why Collection does not extend the Cloneable and Serializable interfaces?

Collection is an interface that specifies a group of objects, which is known as elements.

As it is an interface, the choice of how these elements are maintained is left up to the concrete implementations of the Collection interface.

For example, **List** is extended from the Collection interface, which allows duplicate elements, but Set, which is another extension of Collection, does not allow duplicates. Adding **clone()** in collection does not make sense as Collection, being an interface, is an abstract representation, so it is all up to the implementation of the **clone()** method and not the declaration. The concrete implementation should decide how it should be cloned or serialized.

So, making the cloning or serialization implementation compulsory by adding it to the interface is less flexible and more restrictive. So, it has to be the choice of the specific implementation class to decide as to whether it can be cloned or serialized or both.

Why the Map interface does not extend the Collection interface?

The **Map** interface and all of its implementations are the part of the Collections framework. However, **Map** does not extend Collection because all of the interfaces that extend Collection support only values. However, **Map** contains every entry in it as a key and value pair. Collection offers the methods to retrieve the elements. However, the **Map** methods offer retrieving the list of keys or list of values that do not fit in handling the elements paradigm.

Explain an Iterator. What is an Iterator?

Iterator is an interface that offers the methods for iterating over collection. One can get the **Iterator** instance using the **iterator()** method of that respective collection. Using the iterator, one can remove the elements from the underlying collection during iterating over it. **Iterator** implements the iterator design pattern to offer a generic way for traversing through the elements of the collection.

Why Iterator does not offer a method for adding elements to the collection?

The contract by which the iteration over the elements happens is unclear. So, if in case one tries to add the element in list, which is an ordered collection, due to unclear semantics of iterator, it will not guarantee the addition of the element to the last position. Another special iterator **ListIterator** provides an operation to add the elements, as it guarantees the order of the iteration.

Can we directly use the next() method to fetch the element without moving the cursor using the Iterator? Why the Iterator does not offer a method to get the next element directly without moving the cursor?

The object is stored in the memory, which has a reference address. Now, to get the value of any object, you need to provide this reference information. According to the API, the cursor in the **Iterator** always points to the middle, so it is important to move that cursor to the current position. The call to the **next()** method will move the cursor to the current position.

State the differences between the Iterator and ListIterator?

Both **Iterator** and **ListIterator** are used for iteration, with the following differences:

- **Iterator** can be used to traverse over the List and Set collections. On the other hand, **ListIterator** can be used for traversing over the List only.

- **Iterator** can traverse in the forward direction only. However, **ListIterator** can be used to traverse in both the forward and reverse directions.

- **ListIterator** is inherited from the **Iterator** interface. It offers extra functionalities such as adding, replacing, and fetching using the index position for both previous and next elements.

What are different ways available to iterate over a list?

One can use *Iterator* and/or for-each loop for iterating over the list. The use of **Iterator** is more thread-safe as it assures whenever the underlying list elements are modified, it will throw **ConcurrentModificationException**. Both these ways can be used as shown in the following code snippet:

- **Using the Iterator:**

```
List<String>list = new ArrayList<>();
Iterator<String> it = list.iterator();
while(it.hasNext()){
    String data = it.next();
    System.out.println(data);
}
```

- **Using the for-each loop:**

```
List<String> list = new ArrayList<>();
for(String data : list){
    System.out.println(data);
}
```

What is UnsupportedOperationException? When does the UnsupportedException occur in the execution?

UnsupportedOperationException is an exception that is used to indicate that the operation is not supported. It is used extensively in JDK classes of the collections framework. **java.util.Collections.UnmodifiableCollection** throws this exception for all add and remove operations.

For example, let us consider we have an array, and we obtain a list from it as:

```
List<String> fruits= Arrays.asList("Mango", "Kiwi", "Orange", "Papaya");
```

Now, if we try to add another fruit to the list as:

```
Fruits.add("Strawberry");
```

We will get **UnsupportedException**.

The same exception will occur while removing the elements from the obtained list.

What is the difference between the following two statements

```
List<String>  fruits=  Arrays.asList("Mango",  "Kiwi",  "Orange",
"Papaya");
```

And

```
String [] fruits= {"Mango", "Kiwi", "Orange", "Papaya"};

List<String> fruitList= new ArrayList<>(Arrays.asList(fruits));
```

The first statement provides a non-mutable list. If one tries to add or remove the element from the list, we will get **UnsupportedException**.

The second set of statements provide a mutable list, which means one can add as well as remove the elements from it.

How HashMap works in Java?

HashMap stores every entry as a pair of key and value in the **Map.Entry** static nested class implementation. It works on the hashing algorithm. It uses the **hashCode()** and **equals()** method while putting or getting the elements using respective put or get methods. When one calls the **put()** method by passing an entry as key and value pair, the **HashMap** uses the key **hashCode()** with hashing to find out the index where to store the key and value pair. The entry is stored in **LinkedList**. So, in case of having an already existing entry, it uses the **equals()** method to check whether the passed key already exists or not. If it exists, then it overwrites the value, and if it does not, then it creates a new entry and stores this key and value entry.

When one calls the **get()** method by passing the key, **HashMap** again uses **hashCode()** to find the index in the array, and after that, it uses the **equals()** method to find the correct entry and return its value.

HashMap has capacity, load factor, threshold resizing as properties. The initial default capacity of **HashMap** is 16, and the load factor is 0.75. The threshold is calculated by multiplying the capacity with the load factor. Whenever one tries to add an entry, the map size is checked. If the map size is greater than the threshold, then the **HashMap** rehashes the contents of the map into a new array having the larger capacity. The capacity is always the power of 2, so if we know that we need to store a large number of key and value pairs, then it is a good idea to initialize **HashMap** having the correct capacity and load factor.

Can we use instance of any class as Map key?

Yes, we can use an instance of the class as key of the map. But, we need to consider the following points before using the instance as **a**:

- If that class overrides the **equals()** method, it should also override the **hashCode()** method.

- The class should follow the rules associated with **equals()** and **hashCode()** for all instances.

- The class field if is not used in **equals()**, you should not use it in the **hashCode()** method as well.

- The best practice for a user-defined key class is to make it immutable so that the **hashCode()** value can be cached, thus providing fast performance. If we make the class immutable, it makes sure that **hashCode()** and **equals()** will not change in future, which will solve any issue with mutability.

How one can visit each entry in the collection of type Map? What are different Collection views provided by the Map interface?

The Map interface provides the following ways or methods to access the elements:

- **Set<K> keySet():**
  - The **keyset()** method returns a **Set** that contains the keys in the map. This set is backed by map. This means any changes to the map are reflected in the set, or if changes happen in the set, they will be reflected to map.
  - If the map is modified in the process of iteration over the set, the result of the iteration is undefined.
  - The set supports element removal, which removes the corresponding mapping from the map. This removal can be done via the **remove()**,

  `Set.remove()`, `removeAll()`, `retainAll()`, and `clear()` operations of **Iterator**. It does not support the **add()** or **addAll()** operations.

- **Collection<V> values():**
  - The method returns a collection that contains the values from the map.

  - The collection is backed by the map, and any changes to the map are reflected in the collection or vice-versa.

  - If the map is modified in the process of iteration over the collection is in progress, the results of the iteration are undefined.

  - The collection supports removal of an element that removes the corresponding mapping from the map via the **remove()**, **Collection.remove()**, **removeAll()**, **retainAll()**, and **clear()** methods of Iterator. It does not support the **add()** or **addAll()** operations.

- **Set<Map.Entry<K, V>> entrySet():**
  - The method returns a set of the mappings contained in the map.

  - The set is backed by the map, so changes to the map are reflected in the set or vice-versa.

  - If the map is modified while iteration over the set, the results of the iteration are undefined.

  - The set allows removal of an element that actually removes the corresponding mapping from the map via the **Iterator.remove()**, **Set.remove()**, **removeAll()**, **retainAll()**, and **clear()** operations, but it does not support the **add()** or **addAll()** operations.

Which collection classes from the framework are thread-safe?

The classes such as **Vector, Hashtable, Properties,** and **Stack** are synchronized; it means they are thread-safe and safe to use in a multi-threaded environment. In JDK 1.5, some concurrent APIs are included, which allows the modification during the process of iteration. It is possible because they work on the clone of the collection, making them safe to use in a multi-threaded environment. These classes are available in the **java.util.concurrent** package. These classes are **CopyOnWriteArrayList, ConcurrentHashMap, CopyOnWriteArraySet,** which allow modifying the collection while iterating.

Can you explain more about CopyOnWriteArraySet?

Introduced in JDK 1.5, it is a thread-safe version of Set. Internally, it uses `CopyOnWriteArrayList` for all the operations that are performed on the elements. Interestingly, this is backed by an immutable array. That means if you change any of the element of `CopyOnWriteArraySet`, it entirely creates a new array behind the scene. So, this Set implementation of Set is costlier if you are in a situation in which you want to modify the elements often.

What is Queue and Stack, list their differences?

`Queue` and `Stack` are used to store data before processing the data with following differences:

- `java.util.Queue` is an interface whose implementation classes are present in Java concurrent package.

- `Queue` is an interface; however, `Stack` is a class that is extended from *Vector*

- `Queue` allows retrieval of element in the First In First Out (FIFO) order, and *Stack* allows elements to be retrieved in the Last In First Out (LIFO) order.

- `Stack` offers the `push()` and `pop()` operations, and `Queue` offers the `offer()` and `poll()` methods.

- The `Stack` data structure is naturally a recursive data structure, which has well-suited well-recursive operations such as implementing pre-order, post-order, and in-order traversal of the binary tree. `Queue,` on the other hand, is a sequential data structure that can be used to process the data in order.

What are the best practices related to the Java Collections framework?

We can make the right choice of the collection based on the needs of size. For example, if we need a fixed size, we might use an array over `ArrayList`. If we need uniqueness, we will go with Set. If we need to maintain the object in the sorted way, we need to use `TreeSet`. If we want to achieve uniqueness even for duplicate objects, we can make use of Map implementation. Some collections allow specifying the initial capacity, so if we can estimate the number of elements that we want to store, we can use it to avoid rehashing or resizing.

Along with this, we need to also keep the following things in mind:

- Always write the application in terms of interfaces, not implementations so that we will have the flexibility to change the implementation easily in future.

- Always use generics that offer type safety, and also, it will avoid **ClassCastException** at runtime.

- Use the immutable classes provided by JDK as keys in *Map* so that we do not need to implement the **hashCode()** and **equals()** method for a custom class. It avoids coding overhead.

- Try to use **Collections**, utility class as much as possible for algorithms or to get read-only, synchronized, or empty collections, instead of writing own implementation. Own implementation means rigorous testing.

- The use of predefined classes will reduce code reuse. Also, they have low maintainability.

Can a null element be added to TreeSet or HashSet?

A null value can be added in *Set* if the set contains only one null element. This is because when we try to add the second element, Set tries to first do the check to find out duplicate values, and when the check is done against null, obviously, it will throw **NullpointerException**. **HashSet** is based on **HashMap,** so it can also contain null elements.

What are the differences between Collection and Collections?

The following are the differences between **Collection** and **Collections**:

- **Collection** is an interface, and **Collections** is a class.

- The **Collection** interface provides the standard functionality of data structure to **List**, **Set**, and **Queue**. And, the **Collections** class offers methods to sort and synchronize the collection elements.

- The **Collection** interface offers the methods that are used for data structure. However, the **Collections** class offers the static methods to be used for various operations on a collection.

What are the additional features provided by NavigableSet than SortedSet?

NavigableSet was introduced in JDK 1.6, which is extended from the **SortedSet** interface. It provides more functionalities than **SortedSet**. For instance, you can also navigate in reverse direction by using **NavigableSet,** which was not possible in **SortedSet**. Apart from this, it contains some more methods like **headset()**, **tailSet()**, **subset()**, **ceiling()**, **floor()**, **pollFirst()**, **pollLast()**, and so on.

What is PriorityQueue, and how it works?

PriorityQueue is the implementation of **Queue,** and as the name indicates, it works on the basis of priorities of elements. It pushes the sorted element to the head, which can be pooled out. Internally, it also uses the **Comparator** and **Comparable** interfaces for sorting to decide the priority of the elements.

How PriorityQueue is different than TreeSet or TreeMap if it uses the same Comparator and Comparable interfaces for sorting?

Though **TreeSet**, **TreeMap,** and **PriorityQueue** all use the **Comparator** or **Comparable** interface, there is a fundamental difference between them. Both **TreeSet** and **TreeMap** provide sorting and iteration over the elements. However, in case of **PriorityQueue**, the elements are not traversed. Only thing that is achieved is to find of the priority and push that element to the head according to priority.

What is Dequeue? Can you explain its working?

On a very simpler note, **Dequeue** is a double-ended **Queue**. In Queue, the elements are inserted at the tail and removed from the head. But, in **Dequeue**, you can perform these operations from both the ends. It is in fact a combination of Queue and Stack. It means it works on both the FIFO and LIFO algorithms. The classes **ArrayDeque** and **LinkedList** are implementation classes of the **Dequeue** interface. To facilitate addition and removal of elements from both sides, it provides different methods from **Queue** like **addFirst()**, **addLast()**, **offerFirst()**, **removeFirst()**, **removeLast(),** and so on.

Out of different Queue implementations, how do you decide which to use?

It is often confusing as to which implementation of **Queue** is to be used. But, if you are sure about your functional requirement along with the need for concurrency, your selection will be easier.

If you are interested to get the elements in the FIFO order, then the obvious choice is **ArrayDeque,** but if you are more interested in elements as per the priority, you need to choose **PriorityQueue**. This selection is based on the assumption that you do not expect the concurrent access for elements. If you intend to get concurrent access, then you can go for **PriorityBlockingQueue** or **DelayQueue**. In the situation in which you do not want to go for blocking approach for the **Queue,** then you can go for **ConcurrentLinkedQueue**.

What is IdentityHashMap? How is it different than normal HashMap?

IdentityHashMap was added in Java 1.4 version. This class is also implementation of Map, but it does not use internally the **equals()** and **hashCode()** method for object comparison. Instead of that, it uses the equality (==) operator to check the equality of object. So, this Map implementation is faster than the *HashMap*. Another difference is in terms of key, which is stored in **HashMap** and **IdentityHashMap**. In **HashMap,** the key has to be immutable, but in case of **IdentityHashMap,** the key is not required to be immutable.

Which are the most common methods from the Collections class that can be used to perform operations on List?

The following methods of the Collections class can be invoked to perform operations on List specifically:

- `void reverse(List<?> list)`
- `void rotate(List<?>, int distance)`
- `void shuffle(List<?> list)`
- `void sort(List<T> list)`
- `void sort(List<T> list, comparator<? Super T> c)`
- `void swap(List<?> list, int i, int j)`
- `void copy(List<?> dest, List<?> src)`

- `void fill(List<? super T> list, T obj)`
- `void replaceAll(List<T> list, T oldVal, T newVal)`

Conclusion

You have just completed one of the most important and complicated chapters for a Java interview. In this chapter, we discussed about the Collection framework in Java. We discussed in detail different interfaces and classes from this powerful API. We talked about the different types of collections like List, Set, Queue, and Map along with their significance. During this, we covered different implementation classes from this interface. Along with these classes, we also discussed the utility classes like Arrays and Collections and how they enhance the behavior of collections.

In the next chapter, we will discuss some miscellaneous concepts of Java like String, StringBuffer, Inner classes, Reflection, and so on.

CHAPTER 9
Miscellaneous

Introduction

Till now, we have seen many concepts in Java that will help you to crack a Java interview. We started right from the architecture of Java and discussed how Java is internally built. We also discussed in detail how to implement the object-oriented approach and also how to work with exceptions, concurrency, file handling, JDBC, and so on. But, Java is vast. Apart from all these, there are many other components that really makes application development more flexible and maintainable. In this chapter, we will talk about such miscellaneous terms, and we will discuss it via different interview questions.

Structure

This chapter covers following concepts:

- String and StringBuffer
- Inner classes
- Reflection API
- Unit testing
- Internationalization

Objective

At the end of this chapter, you will be able to answer interview questions based on different concepts like **String**, **StringBuffer**, inner classes, unit testing, and so on. This chapter will also give you some basic knowledge about how to implement all these concepts through some code snippets.

Are the following two same or different?

```
String emptyLiteral = "";
String emptyNewString = new String("");
```

emptyLiteral will be added to the String pool, while **emptyNewString** will go directly onto the heap.

```
String nullValue = null; and
String emptyLiteral = "";
```

Are the preceding to statements same or different?

These are different statements. If we tried to invoke any method on String having a null value, we will get **NullPointerException**. However, the first will not raise **NullPointerException**.

What are the differences between StringBuffer and StringBuilder?

The following are the differences between **StringBuffer** and **StringBuilder**:

- **StringBuffer** is synchronized, and **StringBuilder** is non-synchronized.
- **StringBuffer** is less efficient than **StringBuilder**.

What are the differences between StringBuffer and String?

The following are the differences between **StringBuffer** and **String**:

- **String** class is immutable, **StringBuffer** is mutable.

- **String** consumes more memory, and too many instances will be created on each operation performed on it. **StringBuffer** consumes less memory when you update strings.

- **StringBuffer** is faster than **String**.

- The **String** class overrides the **equals()** method of the **Object** class, but the **StringBuffer** class does not override the **equals()** method of the object.

What do you mean by reflection?

Reflection is a process that enables examining the class, modifying the behavior of the class at runtime. Using this, we can also examine the different components of a Java application like interfaces, fields, and methods at runtime.

Can you explain how to use reflection?

The class **java.lang.Class** offers various methods that can be used to get metadata of a class, examining and changing the runtime behavior of a class. The following code shows one of the ways to achieve reflection:

```
Class c=Class.forName("Employee");

System.out.println(c.getName());
```

The preceding code snippet will print **Employee**, which is the class name identified by process of reflection.

How to get an object of a class without using the new operator?

There are three ways to generate an object of a class as shown:

- **forName()** method of the **Class** class
  - o The method is used to load the class dynamically.
  - o It should be used if you know the fully qualified name of class. This cannot be used for primitive types.

  The code snippet of this is already shown in the earlier question.

- **getClass()** method of the **Object** class
  - o The method returns the instance of a **Class** class. It should be used if one knows the type. It can be used with primitives as well.

```
Simple s=new Simple();

Class c=s.getClass();

System.out.println(c.getName());
```

- The *.class* syntax
  - o If there is no instance but we know the type, then it is possible to obtain a class by appending **.class** to name of the type. The syntax can be used for primitive data type as well:

```
Class c = MyClass.class;
System.out.println(c.getName());
```

List out the different methods of reflection API with their usage

The following table lists some of the important methods of the reflection API:

Method	Description
public String getName()	Returns the class name
public Class getSuperclass()	Returns the super class
public Class[] getInterfaces	Returns the array for different interfaces implemented by the class
public Method[] getDeclaredMethods()	Returns the array of methods declared in the class
public Field[] getDeclaredFields()	Returns the array of the field declared in the class
public Constructor[] getDeclaredConstructors()	Returns the array of constructors declared in the class

Table 9.1: Important methods of the reflection API

Can we access the private field of another class using reflection?

Private field members are normally not accessed outside of a class. But, using reflection, we can do so. The reflection API provides a method **getDeclareField()**, using which you can get reference of that field, and then, you can access that field in your class. The following code snippet shows how to access the private field **personId** declared in the **Person** class from some other class:

```
Field personData= Person.class.getDeclaredField("personId");
personData.setAccessible(true);
String personValue= (String) personData.get(Person);
System.out.println("personValue= " + personValue);
```

What is an Inner class and their types?

The **Inner class** is a class nested inside another class. We have four flavors as follows:

- A class inside another class
- A class declared inside the function of a class
- An anonymous class
- Static inner class

What is the need for inner classes, or why do we use inner classes?

Inner classes are used when we want to group the classes together logically. More specifically, if we want only one class to utilize the services of another class, then instead of creating the class separately, we would create it as an inner class.

Can a static nested class have access to any other members from an enclosing class?

The static nested class does not have access to any other members of the enclosing class. This ensures the data, which is common to all the objects, is being accessed by the static nested class.

Can an inner class be declared as private?

Yes, the nested class can be declared with any specifier. As the outer classes has restriction of using the access specification, the inner classes do not have such restriction and can be even declared as private. This offers the flexibility for the nested class and also allows to be used only by the enclosed class.

What is shadowing?

When a declaration of a member in the inner class has the same name as that in the outer class, the inner class will have more preference for its local members than that of the enclosed members. It means it will shadow the member of the enclosed class. This process is known as **shadowing**.

What is JUnit?

JUnit is the testing framework that is used for unit testing of Java code.

What is unit testing?

The process of testing individual functionality (known as a unit) of the application is called **unit testing**.

Can you explain how do you test a unit of your application?

JUnit provides different annotations using which you can test your application. One of the important annotations we can use is **@Test**. This annotation can be applied on the method that is under test. The method under test can use methods like **assertEquals()** to check the expected result against the generated result. Depending upon this, the test is said to be succeeded or failed.

What are the useful JUnit extensions?

The following are some of the extensions of JUnit:

- JWebUnit
- XMLUnit
- Cactus
- MockObject

What are the important JUnit annotations?

The following are some of the important annotations used in JUnit:

- @Test
- @BeforeClass
- @Before
- @After
- @AfterClass

What is use of @Before and @After annotations?

When we execute any test case, we might need to execute some business logic before and after that test. The **@Before** annotation is applied on method to inform that before every test, the method should get executed. On the similar lines, the **@After** annotation is used to inform that the method will be executed after each test case.

What is use of the JUnitCore class?

Using the **@Test** annotation, we can test different methods individually. But, if we want to test multiple methods of application at the same time, we can make the use of the **JUnitCore** class. This class has a method **runClasses()**, which will run all the test cases and return the information in a bundle.

What is the difference between manual testing and automated testing?

Manual testing is performed by humans, so it is time-consuming and costly. **Automated testing** is performed by testing tools or programs, so it is fast and less costly.

How is the testing of "private" method done?

There is no direct way for testing of the private method; hence, manual testing is to be performed, or the method is changed to "protected" method.

What are the methods in fixtures?

Fixtures contains the following methods:

- setup
- teardown

What is internationalization?

Internationalization, which is also termed as i18N, is a concept where we create an application that can be adapted globally and display the messages or currencies and so on in the language corresponding to specific country or region.

What is localization?

Localization is a process of adding a resource to an application so that the application can support a particular language. To achieve this, we can take help of the Locale class, which represents languages and other settings like time-zone and so on for that region. The object of the Locale class can be created by passing the language and the country as argument.

How to change the format of a number using the Locale class?

The following code snippet shows how to change the format of a number using the **Locale** class:

```
double d=123.456

NumberFormat nf=NumberFormat.getInstance(Locale.ITALY);

System.out.println(" number in ITALY format is :"+nf.format(d));
```

Conclusion

In this chapter, you studied miscellaneous APIs from Java like **String**, **StringBuffer**, and **StringBuilder**. We also discussed the concepts like inner classes, reflection, and internationalization. We also had a small visit to the approach of unit testing to know how to test application. In the next chapter, we will discuss about *functional programming*, which is one of the most important enhancements in Java API recently.

CHAPTER 10

Functional Programming

Introduction

Interfaces always provide the loose coupling or flexibility to your application. They facilitate the subclasses to implement their own version of business logic as and when required. But often, when interfaces contain only one method, the developer feels that the implementation code they are writing is getting messy unnecessarily. For implementing a single method, they may have to write a complete class, which sometimes is bulkier than actual business logic, which is written in the overridden method from the interface. To overcome this complexity, Java had introduced a concept of closure in the format of anonymous inner class. Though anonymous inner class avoids the usage of a class, it still lacks in reducing the bulkiness of the code. Normally, it is said that the anonymous inner classes have "vertical problem," as we need to stack some lines of code to just incorporate a single line of business logic. The main objective of functional programming is to avoid such ceremonial code, which replaces a block of structural code in the declarative approach. This has certainly improved the approach of developers to handle the functional interfaces and collections.

Structure

In this chapter, we will discuss about different design patterns in software development. We are going to cover:

- What is functional programming?
- What is lambda?
- What is a stream and different ways to create it?
- What are different operations from the Stream API?
- What are predicates and their uses?

Objective

Though functional programming adds significant flexibility to developers in understanding how to implement, it is always a challenge for a beginner. Though it is not difficult, but shifting the mindset of a developer from traditional programming to functional programming is a point of concern. In this chapter, you will not only learn about how to implement functional programming, but also about different concepts like lambdas, streams, and so on. We will walk through the basics of lambda and streams. We will discuss different interview questions based on lambdas and streams, which form a very important part of your Java interview, if the interview is based on Java 8.

What are the new features introduced in Java 8?

The following new features are introduced in Java 8:

- Lambda expressions
- Method references
- Optional class
- Functional interface
- Default methods
- Nashorn, JavaScript Engine
- Stream API
- Date API

Note: Though this question looks very basic, it is an important question. Often when the interviewee mentions Java 8 as a skillset in the resume, he/she is not aware whether he/she uses Java 8 compiler or uses the features of Java 8. Because of backward compatibility of Java compilers, even if you do not use any new features of Java 8, you can still compile your pre-Java 8 programs on Java 8 compilers, which will make you feel that you are aware of the Java 8 API. Obviously, being an expert, the interviewer knows this, and he/she would be interested to know if you really worked with Java 8 or not.

What are functional interfaces, and how to create them? Is it necessary to declare a functional interface by the @ FunctionInterface annotation?

Java 8 introduced functional interfaces. The functional interface is an interface having only one abstract method. Java 8 provides many functional interfaces such as Supplier, Consumer, Function, and so on. It is also possible to declare a user-defined functional interface whenever required. One can develop the functional interface either by declaring an interface with a single abstract method. We can also annotate such interface by **@FunctionalInterface,** which contains a single abstract method. It is not compulsory to annotate the interface using **@FunctionInterface**. However, it is a preferred way, as the annotation makes sure that the interface will not contain any other abstract method, and if one tries to add, an error will occur.

Do we have any functional interfaces prior to Java 8 as well?

Yes. In pre-Java 8.0 versions, we do have some interfaces that behave like functional interfaces. In other words, they have only single abstract method to implement. The only difference is they are not annotated with **@FunctionalInterface**. The following are the examples of such interfaces:

- `java.lang.Runnable`
- `java.util.Comparator`
- `java.util.concurrent.Callable`
- `java.io.FileFilter`
- `java.nio.file.PathMatcher`
- `java.lang.reflect.InvocationHandler`
- `java.awt.event.ActionListener`
- `javax.swing.event.ChangeListener`

What is an SAM Interface?

Java 8 has introduced the functional interface, an interface that can have only one abstract method. As these interface contain only one abstract method, they are also called as SAM interfaces. **SAM** means **Single Abstract Method** interface.

Which guidelines are to be followed while defining a functional interface?

The following guidelines should be followed while defining a functional interface:

- A functional interface should contain only one abstract method.

- More than one abstract cannot be defined in the interface.

- To make sure that interface should not contain more than one abstract method, the interface must be annotated by **@Functionalinterface**. However, the use of annotation is not compulsory.

What are the default methods?

Default methods are the methods of the interface that has a body. These methods, as the name suggests, use the default keywords. The use of these default methods is "Backward Compatibility," which means if JDK modifies any interface (without default method), then the classes that implement this interface will break.

On the other hand, if you add the default method in an interface, then you will be able to provide the default implementation. This will not affect the implementing classes, as the class does not have the responsibility to implement its own version of that method.

What are the different characteristics of the lambda function?

The main characteristics of the lambda function are as follows:

- The method that is defined as a lambda expression can be passed as a parameter to another function.

- A function exist standalone without belonging to a class.

- One can skip declaring the parameter type as the compiler can fetch the type from the parameter's value.

- One can skip writing parenthesis if the function has no parameters or single parameter.

- The parentheses required for using multiple parameters

- Whenever the body of expression has a single statement, one can skip the use of curly braces to declare the function body.

Can you explain the different parts of a lambda expression, or how to write a lambda expression?

A typical lambda expression can take a form as follows:

(value1, value2) → body of function

It contains the following parts:

- Function calling, which may or may not consist of parameters to be passed to that function depending upon declaration of function.

- Arrow operator, which points to the function body.

- Function body, which may contain one or more than one lines of code

Can you show how can you implement a lambda expression by some real code?

A lambda expression is essentially connected with the functional interface and anonymous inner class concept. Let us consider the following functional interface:

MyInterface.java

```
@FunctionalInterface
interface MyInterface{
    public void doSomething();
}
```

The **@FunctionalInterface** annotation in the preceding code is absolutely optional.

Traditionally, to implement this interface, we can either write a concrete class that overrides the abstract method. But, instead of that, we can also go for the following lambda expression:

TestLambda.java

```
public class TestLambda {
    public static void main(String[] args) {
        MyInterface m=()->{
            System.out.println("Task is done");
        };
        m.doSomething();
    }
}
```

Did you work with Collection? Did you use the Stream API? Can you explain us the difference between the Collection API and Stream API?

The following points give an idea about what are the differences between collection API and stream API:

- The Stream API is introduced in Java 8 Standard Edition, the collection API is introduced in Java 1.2.

- The stream API is used to compute data. However, the Collection API can be used to store as well as compute the data.

- Stream API do not make use of **Iterator** and **Spliterators**. To iterate through the different elements, it simple uses **forEach**.

- Using the stream API, one can consume and iterate through the elements only once; however, using the collection API, it can be done as and when required.

What is method reference?

Method reference is one more feature introduced in Java 8. Method reference refers to the method of functional interface. A method reference can be used to replace a lambda expression while referring to a method.

The following line denotes the lambda expression:

```
name ->System.out.println(name)
```

The same expression can be converted to method reference as:

```
System.out::println
```

Here, **::** is an operator used to distinguish between the name of the class and the method name.

Explain the meaning of String::valueOf

It is an example of method reference or, more precisely, it is a static method reference. The expression creates a static method reference to the **valueOf** method of the **String** class. The expression can be used to return string representation of the argument that is passed of type Character, Integer, Boolean, and so on.

What is a Stream API? Why do we require the Stream API?

The **Stream API** has been added in Java 8, which includes the APIs for processing objects from a source such as collection.

It facilitates:

- Functional-style programming
- Aggregate operations making simplified processing
- Faster processing leading to better performance
- Parallel operations taking advantage of multithreading

What is the difference between limit() and skip()?

The **limit()** method is used to specify the number of elements to be returned. For example, when one says **limit(10)**, then the output will contain 10 elements. The following code snippet illustrates the working of the **limit()** method:

Stream.of(1,2,3,4,5,6,7,8,9,10,11,12,13,14,15,16).limit(10)

Here, we are setting the limit equal to 6. Hence, it will return the first 10 numbers.

The **skip()** method skips the number of elements till the specified index number. For example, if we invoke **skip(5)**, it will skip the elements till the fifth index and return rest of the elements.

The following code snippet illustrates the working of the **skip()** method:

Stream.of(1,2,3,4,5,6,7,8,9,10,11,12,13,14,15,16).skip(5)

This will skip till the fifth index and will return all the elements from Index 6.

Write a program to print 5 random numbers using forEach in Java 8?

The following code will generate 5 random numbers and print the generated values with the help of the **forEach** function.:

```
Random random = new Random();
random.ints().forEach(System.out::println);
```

What are intermediate and terminal operations? What is the difference between intermediate and terminal operations in Stream?

All Stream operations are categorized into terminal and intermediate operations.

- **Intermediate operations**: These are the operations that return the Stream on which some other operations can be carried out. The **intermediate operations** are called as **lazy operations,** as they do not process the Stream unless any terminal operation is carried on it. Some of the intermediate operational functions are `map()`, `filter()`, `distinct()`, `sorted()`, `limit()`, and `skip()`.

- **Terminal operations**: The terminal operations initiate processing of the Stream. When a **terminal operation** is called, then the Stream undergoes all the intermediate operations. Some of the terminal operational functions are `forEach()`, `toArray()`, `reduce()`, `collect()`, `min()`, `max()`, and `count()`.

Can you explain about the reduce operation in Stream?

Often when we work with group of data, that is collection, we need to perform different operations. Some of these operations may require generating the single value based on the elements present in that stream. It may be counting the elements or calculating the average or sum. In such cases, we can use the **reduce()** function of streams.

The following is the syntax of the reduce() function:

```
T reduce(T identity, BinaryOperator<T> accumulator);
```

Where,

- T is identity of initial value

- Accumulator is the function or process that we would like to perform on elements

For example, the following code snippet uses the **reduce()** function, which calculates the total of all elements from stream:

```
int total= data.stream().reduce(0,
                    (value1, value2) -> value1+ value2);
```

What is stream pipelining?

The **stream pipelining** is the concept of chaining operations together to produce the desired result. The stream operations are categorized as intermediate operations and terminal operations. Each of the intermediate operation returns an instance of Stream itself when it runs. One can perform any number of intermediate operations to process data. All these operations form a processing pipeline.

The pipeline must have a terminal operation, which terminates the pipeline and returns a final value.

What is meant by Stream is lazy?

Stream is lazy, because no action in the chain of intermediate operations will take place unless the terminal operation is used. Usually, when one uses the function, the movement, the flow control comes on that line, the function will be invoked, and action will take place. But, in Stream, that is not true. The intermediate operation will work only when a call to terminal method on the Stream is given.

Please list and explain different intermediate and terminal operations

The following table lists different intermediate operations:

Method	Description
filter()	Returns a stream of elements, which satisfies the given condition via the predicate
map()	Returns a stream that consists of result after applying some function on each element of the stream
sorted()	Returns a stream that consists of elements in a naturally sorted order
distinct()	Returns a Stream of unique elements
forEach()	Performs the given action on all the elements of a stream
limit()	Returns stream with first n elements of the collection
skip()	Returns a stream by skipping first *n* elements

Table 10.1: Intermediate operations

The following table lists different terminal operations:

Method	Description
toArray	An array containing array of a stream
Reduce	Performs a reduction operation on the elements of a stream using some initial value and a binary operation
Collect	Return a mutable result as a container of a List or a Set
Min	Returns a minimum element in a steam wrapped in an element of type Optional
Max	Returns a maximum element in a stream wrapped in an element of type Optional
Count	The total number of elements in a stream
anyMatch	Returns true if any one of the elements of the stream matches the given predicate
allMatch	Returns true if all of the elements of the stream matches the given predicate
noneMatch	Returns true if all of the elements of the stream do not match the given predicate
findFirst	Returns the first element of the stream wrapped in an object of type Optional
findAny	Returns any one of the element of the stream

Table 10.2: Terminal operations

What is the difference between the findFirst() and findAny() method? Can you explain the difference between the findFirst() and findAny() method

- The **findFirst()** method returns the first element meeting the specified condition using the predicate.

- The **findAny()** method returns any element matching the specified condition. The **findAny()** method is very useful while working with a parallel stream.

Can you show how the streams are lazy?

Let us consider the following code snippet where we would like to search the first occurrence of element whose value is greater than 5:

```
List<Integer> data= Arrays.asList(1,2,15,2,2);

Integer a = data.stream()
            .peek(num -> System.out.println("Filtered element: " + num))
            .filter(x -> x > 5)
            .findFirst()
            .orElse(null);

System.out.println(a);
```

The output of the preceding code snippet is as follows:

```
Filtered element: 1

Filtered element: 2

Filtered element: 15

15
```

As we can observe, we have used the **findFirst()** method of streams, and the moment the first matched element is found, the further elements are not checked. This approach makes the streams as *lazy streams*.

What is the difference between Iterator and Spliterator?

- **Iterator** is introduced in JDK 1.2, and **Spliterator** is introduced between JDK 1.8

- Iterators are used for iterating the Collection API. However, **Spliterator** used for the Stream API.

- **Iterator** has the methods **next()** and **hasNext()** for the iteration of the elements. **Spliterator** has method **tryAdvance()**.

- One needs to call the **iterator()** method on collection object for the iteration. But, for spliterate, we need to call the **spliterator()** method on the Stream Object.

- **Iterator** can iterate only in the sequential order. However, **SplitIterator** iterates in parallel and sequential order too.

Explain an Optional class?

Or

How can we avoid NullPointerException while performing operations on an object?

The `Optional` class is a class introduced in Java 8 used to avoid `NullPointerExceptions` under the `java.util` package. It acts as a container that is used to contain not-null objects. It contains many methods; some frequently used methods are `isPresent()` and `get()`.

- The method `isPresent()` makes sure whether the container contains values.

- The method `get()` returns the value if present otherwise it throws `NoSuchElementException`.

What is a predicate? Explain the difference between a predicate and function?

- `Predicate` and `Function` are pre-defined functional interfaces in Java 8 under the `java.util.function` package.

- `Predicate` returns a Boolean; however, Function returns an object.

- `Predicate` is written in the form of `Predicate<T>,` which accepts a single argument. However, `Function` is written in the form of `Function<T, R>,` accepting a single argument of type `T` and returns a result of type `R`.

- `Predicate` is used to verify a condition. However, `Function` is used to perform some action on the argument and then return the modified value.

What is the Consumer functional interface?

`Consumer` is a functional interface that accepts a single argument and processes it to produce a result without returning the generated result.

What is the Supplier functional interface?

`Supplier` is a functional interface. It does not accept any input parameters, but supplies the elements. The returned value from `Supplier` can be grabbed using the `get()` method.

What does the map() function do? Why do you use it?

The **map()** function of Stream performs a mapping operation. It allows the transformation of one type of object to other by applying some logic. It means one can take a List of String and transform it to a List containing the length of each String using map.

This is used when one wants to convert one object to another.

What does the flatmap() function do? Why do you need it?

The **flatmap()** function is an extension of the **map()**. It not only allows the transformation of one object into another, but it also can flatten it.

Explain the difference between map() and flatMap()?

When one uses the Stream function **map()**, it gives one output value per input value. However, when we use the **flatMap()** operation, it gives zero or more output value per input value.

Let us take an example.

Using **map(),** we will create a list as follows:

```
List<String>fruits =
        Arrays.asList("orange", "banana", "papaya", "mango");
List<String>fruits_updates =
        fruits.stream()
        .map(String::toUpperCase).collect(Collectors.toList());
```

Let us use **flatMap()**:

```
List<List<Integer>>listOfList=
    Arrays.asList(Arrays.asList(1, 2, 3),Arrays.asList(4, 5),
    Arrays.asList(6, 7, 8) );
List<Integer>list_flatten =
    listOfList.flatMap(list ->list.stream())
    .collect(Collectors.toList());
```

What does the filter() method do? When to use it?

The **filter()** method of the Stream is used to filter elements. The filtering condition is specified using a **Predicate** function.

For example, if you have a list of integers and want the only the integers that are divisible by 3, then we can use the **filter()** function. We will supply a function to check if a number is divisible by 3 or not using a *Predicate*, and **filter()** will apply this to each element of the stream.

Why to use the peek() function? What does the peek() method do? When should you use it?

The **peek()** method of Stream class enables to see through a stream pipeline. Here, we can peek through each step of the processing done and then print meaningful messages on the console. The main purpose of **peek()** is debugging the issues related to the lambda expression and the Stream processing.

What are the ways to create a Stream? Can you convert an array to Stream? How?

The following are the different ways to create a stream:

- **Using collection**: The Collection API has a stream method that enables the creation of a stream from a collection as:

  ```
  Stream<String> stream= list.stream();
  ```

- **From specified values:** We can create a stream from some specified values as:

  ```
  Stream<String> stream= Stream.of("mango","papaya","banana");
  ```

- **Creating empty stream:** The **empty()** method allows the creation of stream to avoid returning null for streams with no element.

  ```
  Stream<String> stream= Stream.empty();
  ```

- **Create a stream from an array:** The Stream has an **of()** method, and the **stream()** method of arrays also can be used to get the stream sequential stream from a specified array. Both these methods returns a Stream when called with a non-primitive type T as:

  ```
  String[]fruits ={ ("mango","papaya","banana"};
  ```

  ```
  Stream<T>stream  =Arrays.stream(fruits);
  ```

And,

```
Stream<T> stream = Stream.of(fruits);
```

Can you create a stream for primitives? What are its different types?

Yes, we can also create streams from a group of primitives. The Stream API provides different types of Streams to deal with the primitives like **int**, **long,** and **double**. **IntStream** handles **int**, **DoubleStream** handles double, and **LongStream** handles long type of data. The following code snippet shows how to handle the **int** data type with **IntStream** and print it:

```
IntStream.range(1, 5)
    .forEach(System.out::println);
```

Can you re-use the stream once the terminal operation is invoked? Can you give any real-time example?

As the word itself explains, the terminal operation terminates the stream. You cannot perform any action further once the terminal operation is performed as the stream is closed after that.

Consider the following code snippet:

```
Stream<String> mystream =
    Stream.of("d", "a2", "ab1", "ab3", "dce")
        .filter(s -> s.startsWith("ab"));
mystream.anyMatch(s -> true);     // ok
mystream.noneMatch(s -> true);    // exception
```

In the preceding code, after **anyMatch(),** the stream is closed because of which we cannot use any other methods on stream. So, invoking of **noneMatch()** after than will generate an exception.

Is there any way to re-use the stream after the terminal operation?

Though there is no direct method available for this, we can make the use of Supplier stream. This type of streams can store the original stream, which processes all the intermediate operations.

Consider the following code snippet:

```
Supplier<Stream<String>> mystreamSupplier =
    () -> Stream.of"d", "a2", "ab1", "ab3", "dce")
            .filter(s -> s.startsWith("ab"));
mystreamSupplier.get().anyMatch(s -> true);    // ok
mystreamSupplier.get().noneMatch(s -> true);   // ok
```

Can you explain how would you use streams to collect the object of Students, whose name starts with an "S"?

Assume that we have a **Student** class with data members as name and age. It also has a **toString()** method that returns a name.

The following code snippet uses the list, *students,* to create a stream and perform the operations to generate list **studentList,** which starts with **S**:

```
List<Student> studentList=
    students
        .stream()
        .filter(s -> s.name.startsWith("S"))
        .collect(Collectors.toList());
System.out.println(studentList);
```

How would you group students with their age?

The following code snippet can group the students with their age:

```
Map<Integer, List<Person>> studentsByAge= students
    .stream()
    .collect(Collectors.groupingBy(s -> s.age));
```

Can you explain Stateless and Stateful operations in Java streams?

Intermediate operations of streams are classified as:

- **Stateless operation**

  Some of the intermediate operations do not require to retain the information about the previous elements. It is processed independently of earlier elements. Some examples of stateless operations are **map()** and **filter()**.

- **Stateful operation**

  Some operations do require the reference of earlier elements, or the state of earlier elements. Such operations are termed as stateful operations. Some of examples of stateful operations are **sorted()**, **distinct()**.

What is the parallel stream?

A **parallel stream** can execute parallelly for processing tasks. It enables the faster processing of the elements, which lead to the enhancement of application performance.

For example, if you have a parallel stream of 1 million elements and you want to filter it according to some condition, then you can use a filter to do that.

The parallel stream launches multiple threads to perform the task and then may also combine the result.

For example, after filtering the elements, the parallel stream combines the result.

Can you explain how to create a parallel stream?

The following code snippet shows how to create parallel streams for list:

```
List<Integer> data= Arrays.asList(1,2,15,2,2,7,12);
data.parallelStream().forEach(System.out::println);
```

The output of this program is shown as follows:

2 12 2 2 1 15 7

As you can observe, the sequence of list is not maintained, though we know that the list is ordered. This is because of the fact that the parallel stream creates multiple threads to do the task of iteration and printing. So, where you are keen to keep the sequence of elements maintained, it is not advisable to use parallel streams.

Can we define the number of threads to generate parallel streams?

Yes, we can. Though there is no direct API in stream to do that, we can take the help of the fork and join framework to achieve this. You can create the fork and join object and wrap your stream operations within that. The following code snippet shows how you can achieve that:

```
List<Integer> data= Arrays.asList(1,2,15,2,2,7,12);
ForkJoinPool customThreadPool = new ForkJoinPool(4);
```

```
int actualTotal = customThreadPool.submit(() ->
                    data.parallelStream().reduce(0, Integer::sum)).get();
System.out.println(actualTotal);
```

The preceding code creates 4 threads using the fork and join framework, which takes up the job of adding the elements from the list that is converted to a stream.

Conclusion

Throughout this chapter, we have discussed some updates in Java 8. Specifically, we talked about functional programming. We discussed the implementations of lambda and streams. We discussed what is lambda and how to form lambda expressions. We also discussed streams, which give more flexibility to iterate and operate on a collection of data. During this, we also talked about the different methods that are provided by the stream API, like intermediate and terminal operations. At the end, we also discussed about parallel streams. In the next chapter, we will cover different the design patterns that play a vital role in a software architecture.

CHAPTER 11
Design Patterns

Introduction

How many times have we reiterated the statement *software designing is complex*? Every time when you design software, you need to remember this *not-so-favorite* phrase. But, the question is what makes software complex? That too, when we talk about the object-oriented programming, it is more complex. When we design software, we need to think about different objects for which we design different classes and interfaces. The behavior of objects is dependent on how effectively the developer had defined the classes and interfaces. Many times, we need to change the initial design of a class so as to achieve more flexibility and extensibility of system. Sometimes, the client changes the requirement in terms of the process or structure of software because of which we might have to design the complete structure from scratch. If you want to achieve that, design pattern is for your rescue. A design pattern provides you a way to design your classes and interface in a more flexible way.

Structure

We will learn the following key concepts during this chapter:

- Why and what is a design pattern?
- Different design patterns like:

o   Creational design patterns

o   Structural design patterns

o   Behavior design patterns

o   J2EE design patterns

• Implementations of design patterns in Java API

Objective

This chapter will cover most of the important design patterns that are useful to create applications more effectively. Along with this, the chapter also aims to make you aware of different interview questions that can be asked based on design patterns and how Java implements those.

Can you tell us what a design pattern is?

A **design pattern** is the extension code, which are language-independent strategies to solve common object-oriented design problems, solutions to repetitive coding, or writing code from the scratch. They define the techniques for making the application more flexible and reducing the coupling. The design pattern describes how to structure the classes to meet a given requirement of the systems to save the time and efforts and increase the efficiency.

What are the different categories of Java design patterns?

Based on the problem analysis, one can categorize the design patterns as:

• **Creational patterns:** These patterns are used to define and describe the ways of creating the objects. They describe in depth on how objects are created at class instantiation time.

o   Factory method

o   Abstract factory

o   Builder

o   Prototype

o   Singleton

• **Structural patterns:** The structural design patterns are concerned about how the classes and objects can be composed together to form a larger structure. They offer an efficient solution for the class compositions and object structures. The patterns are dependent on the concept of inheritance, which allows multiple classes or objects to work together as a single working unit. They simplify the structure by identifying the relationships in between them. These patterns focus on how the classes are inherited from each other and how they are composed from other classes.

- o   Adapter
- o   Bridge
- o   Filter
- o   Composite
- o   Decorator
- o   Facade
- o   Flyweight
- o   Proxy

- **Behavioral patterns:** The behavioral design patterns care about the interaction and responsibility of objects. The patterns focus around the ease in the interaction between the objects. However, the patterns make sure the communicating objects will be loosely coupled in order to avoid hardcoding.

  - o   Interpreter
  - o   Template method/pattern
  - o   Chain of responsibility
  - o   Command pattern
  - o   Iterator pattern
  - o   Strategy pattern
  - o   Visitor pattern

- **J2EE patterns:** The patterns used in designing J2EE applications.

  - o   MVC pattern
  - o   Data access object pattern
  - o   Front controller pattern
  - o   Intercepting filter pattern
  - o   Transfer object pattern

Explain the advantages of the Java design pattern?

The following are the advantages of the Java design pattern:

- The design patterns provide a templated, reusable solution that can be used in multiple projects.

- The design pattern helps in defining a solution that helps in defining the system architecture and customizing it, instead of coding everything manually.

- The design pattern is a way of capturing the reflection of the expert and experienced software engineers or developers. They provide a well-proved solution.

- The design patterns enable the transparency in the application design.

Explain the disadvantages of design patterns?

The following are the disadvantages of design patterns:

- The patterns do not lead to any direct code re-use.

- The patterns are deceptively simple.

- The teams using patterns in the application may suffer from patterns overload.

- When the teams are working together, integrating patterns into an application development needs highly intense human activity.

Which design pattern can be used to sequentially access the elements of a collection object easily?

The iterator pattern is used to sequentially access the elements of a collection object easily.

When is the service locator pattern used?

One can use the service locator design pattern to locate various services. Normally, this pattern uses the central registry, which is responsible to return the necessary service to the invoker. You may consider this central registry as JNDI. The important point to note here is, this pattern does not instantiate the services directly, so it is not tightly coupled. But, it registers the services with some servers and provides a way to locate them.

Which technologies use the Service Locator pattern?

EJB and JMS are the two examples that use the service locator pattern internally.

Which pattern can be used to decouple an abstraction from its implementation in the code?

To decouple an abstraction from its implementation, one can use the **bridge pattern**. Here, the implementation can vary independently. To achieve this independent modification, an interface is used as a bridge between abstraction and implementation. This facilitates the use of implementation by multiple objects without concerning the changes at the abstraction level.

Which design pattern will be helpful when one wants to add a new functionality to an existing object?

The **decorator pattern** is the best choice when the developers want to add a new functionality to an existing object without changing its structure.

Which design pattern is useful in case of passing data with multiple attributes from the client to the server in one shot?

The **transfer object pattern** is useful in case one has to pass the data with multiple attributes from the client to the server in one shot.

When to use the intercepting pattern?

The **intercepting pattern** can be used when we wish to perform pre- or post-processing of data in a request response. This is also termed as the intercepting filter pattern.

What is a factory design pattern? When can the factory pattern be used? What are the benefits of the factory design pattern?

The **factory design pattern** is a creational pattern that offers the best ways to create an object. It is also known as a **virtual constructor**. In this pattern, we do not expose the logic of creating objects to the client and a standard interface of using the created object. It enables the subclasses to choose the type of objects to create.

One can use the factory pattern when we have to create an object of the parent or any one of subclasses depending on the given data. The factory design pattern can be used in the following situations:

- When a class is not aware of which class of objects needs to be created
- When the class specifies its subclasses to specify which objects are to be created

The benefits of the factory design pattern are as follows:

- It increases the level of encapsulation while creating the objects.
- It allows to replace the original implementation of classes with more advanced and high-performance functional implementation, that too without making any changes on the client.
- The factory pattern makes the code more robust. The code is less coupled, so it is easy to extend.

Why to use a factory class to instantiate a class when we can use a new operator?

The factory classes provide design flexibility with the following benefits:

- The use of this pattern results in more decoupled code, as it enables to hide the creational logic from the dependent code.
- The pattern enables the introduction of an inversion of control container.
- It provides more flexibility in case one needs to change the application as the creational logic is hidden from the dependent code.

Can you give some examples of the factory design pattern implementation in JDK?

- `java.util.Calendar`
- `java.util.ResourceBundle`
- `java.text.NumberFormat`

What is an abstract factory pattern?

The **abstract factory pattern** is a creational design pattern. This pattern allows defining an abstract class or an interface for creating the families of the related objects without specifying their concrete subclasses. The reason of having the abstract factory pattern is one level higher than the factory pattern, as it defines a class that returns the factory of classes. The abstract factory patterns works around the super classes. These super classes are involved in creating other classes. Each of the generated factories is responsible for giving the objects according to the factory pattern. In the abstract factory pattern, an interface is liable for creating a factory of related objects without explicitly identifying their classes.

Differentiate between the factory and abstract factory design pattern?

The factory pattern deals with the creation of objects that are delegated to a separate factory class, and the abstract factory pattern works around a superset of the factory that is involved in creation of other factories.

Explain the singleton pattern?

The **singleton pattern** is a creational design a pattern that offers a single instance creation within an application. JDK class **`java.lang.Runtime`** is based on the singleton pattern. The singleton pattern enables defining a class that has only one instance and provides a global point of access to that instance. It means, it is the responsibility of the class to offer a mechanism that should create a single instance, and all other classes can use that single object.

How to implement the singleton pattern?

- The two ways of creating a singleton pattern are as follows:

- **Early instantiation:** In early instantiation, the instance will be created at load time. The following code represents how to implement the singleton design pattern for early instantiation:

```
public class EarlySingleton
{
  private static EarlySingleton earlySingleton = new
      EarlySingleton();
  private EarlySingleton() {}
  public static EarlySingleton getInstance()
  {
     return earlySingleton;
  }
}
```

- **Lazy instantiation:** In lazy initialization, the instance is created only when required. The following code represents how to implement the singleton design pattern for lazy instantiation:

```
public class LazySingleton
{
  private static LazySingleton lazySingleton;
  private LazySingleton() {}
  public static LazySingleton getInstance()
 {
    if (lazySingleton==null)
    lazySingleton = new LazySingleton();
    return lazySingleton;
  }
}
```

What are the limitations and disadvantages of the singleton Pattern?

Limitation of the singleton design pattern:

The singleton pattern ensures the class has only one instance along with providing a global point of access to it. This single instance becomes the limitation because most of the classes in the application might need to create multiple instances.

Disadvantages of the singleton design pattern:

- The pattern does not follow the single repository principle as it controls its own logic of creating an instance and how to manage the object lifecycle.

- As it will have a shared global instance, it stops the de-allocation of the objects and the resources accessed by the global instance.

Can you give some examples of implementation of the singleton design pattern by JDK?

- The **getRuntime()** method of **java.lnag.Runtime,** which returns the runtime object that is associated with the current Java application.

- The **getSecurityManager()** method of **java.lang.System** class. The method returns **SecurityManager**.

- The **getDesktop()** method of **java.awt.Desktop** class. The method **getDesktop()** returns the Desktop instance, which is associated with the current desktop context.

Can you write thread-safe singleton? Why do we need that?

Even if we implement the private constructor for implementation of the singleton pattern, there are few situations in which multiple threads can access the class to create an object. In such cases, even if the singleton pattern is implemented, multiple objects can be created. To control this, we can create a synchronized or thread-safe singleton object.

There are many ways to write a thread-safe singleton as follows:

- The most straight forward way is by using the enum to create a thread-safe singleton.

- By writing the singleton with the help of double checked locking.

- By using a static singleton instance, which is initialized during class loading.

You can make the following change to the *getInstance()* method to make it thread-safe:

```
public static synchronized LazySingleton getInstance()
{
  if (lazySingleton==null)
    lazySingleton = new LazySingleton();
  return lazySingleton;
}
```

Can we create a clone of a singleton object?

Yes, it is possible to create a clone of a singleton object.

Is it better to make the whole getInstance() method synchronized, or will it be better to synchronize only the critical section? Which one will you prefer?

When the complete method is synchronized, the monitor will be locked until the complete method is executed. So, synchronization of the **getInstance()** method is costly, and it is only needed during the initialization on a singleton instance to stop creating another instance of singleton. So, it is better to prefer synchronization of the section and not the complete method.

Can you name a few design patterns used in the standard JDK library?

The following are some of the examples of design pattern implementations in the JDK library:

- **Decorator design pattern:** It is used in various Java IO classes.

- **Singleton pattern:** It is used in the **Runtime**, **Calendar** class.

- **Factory pattern:** It is used with immutable classes likes **Long**. For example, the **Long.valueOf()** method.

- **Observer pattern:** It is used in Swing programming and many of the event listener frameworks.

What are the adapter patterns?

In the **adapter pattern**, based upon the requirements, one converts the interface of one class into another interface. It means the pattern allows the developers to convert the interface according to requirement while using the class service with some other different interface. The pattern is also called as a **wrapper pattern**. Using such pattern, we can create an object that will be a hybrid object, which can use the services from two interfaces at a time as and when needed.

Explain the decorator pattern. Give some examples from JDK which implements Decorator Design pattern

The **decorator pattern** is one of the popular design patterns. It facilitates to change the behavior of an existing object, which changes the code. This pattern creates a new class, which is termed as a decorator class. This decorator class wraps the original class within it with additional methods. Obviously, this keeps the original class as it is, but along with that, because of the decorator, you will be able to use the new features as well.

JDK's **java.io** package does heavy usage of it. The decorator pattern uses composition instead of inheritance to extend the functionality of an object during runtime.

The examples of decorator pattern are as follows:

- `java.io.InputStream`, `java.io.OutputStream`, `java.io.Reader` and `java.io.Writer`
- `java.io.BufferedReader`
- `java.io.BufferedWriter`
- `synchronizedXXX()` from `java.util.Collections`
- `unmodifiableXXX()` from `java.util.Collections`

When to use the template method design pattern in Java?

The **template method pattern** is also among one of the most popular design patterns. The template method is written in super class, which declares the structure and sequence in which the operations can be performed. The subclass extends this super class and uses this template method to follow the sequence strictly declared in the super class. One of the most important thing to control in this pattern is the template method must be declared as final. This will make sure that the child class will not be able to override this method to change the steps or sequence for algorithm implementation. At the same time, some individual steps can be abstract, so the child classes can implement them in their own way.

Differentiate between the strategy and state design pattern in Java?

Both the strategy and state design pattern have the same structure. The UML class diagram of both looks the same, but their intent is very different. The **state design**

pattern allows managing and defining the state of an object. However, the **strategy pattern** allows describing the set of an interchangeable algorithm.

What is a proxy design pattern?

The **proxy design pattern** is a structural pattern. As the name itself indicates, it serves as a proxy for some other class, which in turn accesses the functionality of other class. So, instead of talking to object directly, the client talks to the proxy object, which wraps the actual object inside that to provide the functionality.

Explain the difference between the decorator and proxy pattern

Both the decorator and proxy design patterns implement the interface of an object they decorate or encapsulate, which is very similar. But, the decorator pattern is used to implement the functionality on an object that is already created. And, the proxy pattern is used to control access to an object.

State the difference between proxy and adapter?

The proxy object has the same input as that of the actual object. However, the adapter object has a different input than the actual object.

Explain the difference between factory and abstract factory

The **abstract factory pattern** creates a factory, and the **Factory pattern** creates the objects. Though both abstract the logic of creation, one abstracts the logic for creating a factory and the other for items.

When to use the strategy design pattern in Java?

The **strategy pattern** is useful for implementing a set of related algorithms such as compression algorithms, filtering strategies, and so on. The pattern enables to create context classes that use the implementation of the strategy in order to apply the business rules. The **sort()** method of collections and comparator has a strategy of sorting, and the comparator interface provides a way of comparing objects. Due to the strategy, the **sort()** method does not need modification. At the same time, one can define the comparing strategy by overriding the **compare()** method of the comparator interface. The Strategy pattern is a good example of the open–closed principle. We override the method of comparator. So, it is open for implementation but no need to override the **sort()** method as it does not change.

State the advantages of the composite design pattern in Java?

The following are the advantages of the composite design pattern:

- The composite design pattern allows the clients to operate collectively on a bunch of objects that may or may not represent the same hierarchy.

- The pattern provides an easy way to add new kind of the components.

- The pattern provides the flexibility of structure, which will have manageable class or interface.

Explain the uses of the composite pattern? When to use the composite design pattern in Java? Have you used it previously in your project?

The **composite pattern** allows us to treat the container and the object similarly. The best example of the composite pattern from JDK is the **JPanel** class. **JPanel** is a class that works as both the component and container. Whenever some modification in the presentation of the panel is required, one calls its **paint()** method. The **paint()** method internally will call individual component's **paint()** and allows them draw themselves.

The composite pattern is used when in the application one needs to represent a partial or full hierarchy of objects. We can also use this pattern when we need to add the responsibilities dynamically to the individual object, without affecting other objects one can use the pattern.

What is the observer design pattern in Java? When do you use the observer design pattern in Java?

The observer pattern is based on the concept of observation and notification. Our objects are always connecting with something in the application. And, these objects are interested to know if any change occurs in the component they are connected with. In such cases, we can use the observer design pattern, in which a notification is given to an object if the there is a change in the component state to which they are connected to.

Can you give any typical example of the observer design pattern?

One of the most common real-time examples of the observer patter is publisher–subscriber. Let us assume that you have subscribed to a new channel that releases the news updates. So, the news channel acts as a publisher, and you act as a subscriber. Any new update that is released by news channel will reach to you as you are a subscriber.

What is the builder design pattern in Java? When do you use the builder design pattern? What problems does the builder design pattern solve? State the advantages of the builder design pattern

The **builder pattern** is a creational design pattern. Whenever we are in need of creating a complex object, which is result of different processes, this pattern achieves it by building simpler small objects.

Advantages of the builder pattern:

- The pattern supports enhanced control over the construction process.

- The pattern facilitates a clear separation between the construction of an object and its representation.

- In this pattern, the object is always instantiated in its complete state.

- It facilitates the objects of immutable objects to be created quickly in the object building process.

Scenarios to use the builder pattern:

- When we want the algorithm for creating a complex object, independent of the parts that will make up the object and the way by which they are assembled.

- When the construction process should allow the different representations for the objects that are constructed.

The pattern addresses the following problem:

- When any object has many attributes. Many of these attributes can be optional, or they may have an inconsistent state. The pattern provides a solution by providing a way by which the object can be built in a step-wise manner. It provides a method that will actually return the final object.

Give the examples from JDK that implements the builder design pattern

- `java.lang.StringBuilder`
- `java.lang.StringBuffer`
- `java.nio.ByteBuffer`
- `java.nio.FloatBuffer`
- `java.nio.IntBuffer`

What is the proxy pattern? What does it do? What are the types of proxies? What are the use cases of the proxy pattern?

Proxy means a dummy, an object that represents some other object. The proxy pattern offers a substitute for some other purpose to control access to it.

According to GOF, the proxy pattern offers a control for accessing the original object.

It allows performing security operations by hiding the information of the original object. It also allows on-demand loading of object.

There are different types of proxies, which are as follows:

- **Protection proxy:** The protection proxy controls the access to the original object depending upon some condition.

- **Caching proxies:** The caching proxies preferred to cache the expensive calls to the real object to enhance the performance. These caching strategies are read-through, write-through, cache-aside, and time-based.

- **Virtual proxies:** The virtual proxies are used for instantiating the expensive object by managing the lifetime of the real object in the implementation. It optimizes performance by deciding the need of instance creation and when to reuse

- **Remote proxies:** The remote proxies are used under the distributed object communication. The remote proxy invokes a local object method to make an execution of the remote object.

- **Smart proxies:** The smart proxies are used for implementing log calls and reference the counting to the object.

The proxy pattern can be used under the scenarios in which we want to provide the following services:

- Lazy initialization

- Implementation of logging

- Facilitation of the network connection

- A way to count references to an object

Explain the chain of responsibility pattern and its advantages

In the chain of responsibility pattern, the sender sends a request to a chain of objects. Then any object in the chain can handle this request.

A **chain of responsibility pattern** avoids the coupling of the sender of a request to the request receiver. Let us consider an example of an ATM service. The ATM service uses the pattern in monetary transactions. Each receiver contains the reference of another receiver. When one object fails to handle the request, it sends it to the next receiver, and the process continues.

Following are the advantages of this pattern:

- The pattern minimizes the coupling.

- The pattern provides the flexibility in assigning the responsibilities to objects.

- The pattern permits a set of classes to act as one unit. The events produced in one of the class can be sent to the other handler classes with the help of composition.

How is the bridge pattern different from the adapter pattern?

The **bridge pattern** is designed for the isolation of an implementation of the interface from the class. It allows one to change the implementation without changing the client code.

On the other hand, the **adapter pattern** allows removing the need of having two class implementations so as to work with incompatible interfaces.

Under which scenarios can one can the adapter pattern?

One can use the adapter pattern when he/she needs to make two classes working with incompatible interfaces. The pattern can be used to encapsulate the third-party code in such a way that your application only depends on the adapter. The adapter can adapt itself when the third-party code changes or when one moves to a different third-party library.

Explain the dependency injection and service locator patterns. Also state their differences

In **the dependency injection pattern,** the class that has dependencies will not be aware of them and also it does not care where they came from. The **service locator pattern** is used to create class dependencies. The class is still responsible for creating its dependencies irrespective of whether it is using a service locator or not. The service locators can also be used to hide dependencies. One cannot decide by looking at an object whether it connects with a database or not while obtaining the connections from a locator.

The difference between a dependency injection and service locator:

The **dependency injection** is much easier to unit test than the service locator because we can pass in the mock implementations of its dependent objects. Also, it is possible to combine the two objects and apply the service locator.

When to use the setter and constructor injection in the dependency injection pattern?

The **setter injection** is used to provide the optional dependencies of an object and the constructor used to provide a mandatory dependency of an object.

The Spring framework provides an IOC container, which provides the ways for using the setter methods or constructors for the injection of the dependencies.

What is the MVC pattern?

- This is one of the most-used design patterns in J2EE Design. In MVC, *M stands for model, V stands for view,* and *C stands for controller.*

- The models are the objects, used as the blueprints for all of the objects, which will be used in the application.

- The views are the presentational aspect of the data mostly to the user

- The controllers are the control point. The controller acts as the connection between the model and view. The controller accepts the incoming requests and then may forward it to the next point, which might be the business logic layer or the view layer.

Explain the intercepting filter design pattern along with its benefits?

The **intercepting filter design** pattern is used to intercept and manipulate the response before and after processing the request. Such filters can perform the security check using the authentication and authorization of the request, logging the requests, tracking the request, and after logging or tracking forwarding the requests to the corresponding handlers. These handlers can be another filter in the chain or a controller.

The components involved are the filter, filter chain, target, filter manager, and client.

- **Filter**: The filter is a unit that is involved in performing a certain task before or after the execution of request by the request handler.

- **Filter chain**: A filter chain plays a very important role. Under certain circumstances, a single controller might not be able to perform the desired task, or sometimes, more than one task is divided into multiple steps performed in different filters. The filter chain contains multiple filters, which will be executed in a defined order on the target.

- **Target**: The target is the request handler.

- **Filter manager**: The filter manager manages the filters and filter chain.

- **Client**: The client is an object who sends a request to the target object.

Benefits of the intercepting filter design pattern

- The pattern offers a central control over the request with loosely coupled handlers.

- It enables and expands reusability.

- Any time a new filter can be added without affecting the client code.

- The selection of the filters can be selected dynamically during the program execution.

Explain the data access object or DAO pattern?

The data access object or DAO pattern is used to isolate the high-level business services from the low-level data accessing APIs or the actions. The DAO has the following components:

- **Data access interface:** The DAO interface describes the standard actions that can be performed on a model object.

- **The data access implementation or the concrete class:** This class is the implementation of the DAO interface. This class is responsible to get the data from the data source. This data source can be an XML file, some database, or any other storage mechanism.

- **The model object:** The model object is a POJO containing the getters and setter methods, which allows storing of data retrieved from the data source using DAO class.

What is a front controller design pattern? Can you give an example of a front controller?

The **front controller design pattern** provides a centralized request handling mechanism in which all the requests will be handled by a central handler. This centralized handler can be used for authentication, authorization, logging, and tracking the requests. Once it is done, the front controller forwards the requests to corresponding handlers.

The following are the entities involved in the front controller pattern:

- **Front controller:** A single handler for all kinds of requests to be attended by the application.

- **The dispatcher:** A front controller may use a dispatcher object that can dispatch the request to corresponding specific handler.

- **The view:** The views are the objects for which the requests are made.

Which design pattern will you use to create a complex object?

The builder design pattern is most suitable to construct a complex object. The builder pattern is designed to solve the issues with the factory and the abstract design pattern.

What is the null object pattern?

The **null object pattern** is a design pattern in which the null object replaces the NULL check for the instance variable. Instead of putting a check for a null value, the null object reflects a do nothing relationship. It can also be used to provide default behavior in case data is not available.

What is the open–closed design principle?

The **open–closed design principle** is one of the SOLID principles defined by Robert C. Martin in his most popular book, *Clean Code*. This principle states that the code should be open for an extension but closed for the modification. Once in the beginning of coding we explore the power of polymorphism, we will find the patterns that can provide the stability and flexibility of this principle. The state and strategy design pattern is one of the critical examples of the pattern where the context class is closed for modification, and one can add new functionalities by implementing a new state of strategy.

What are the SOLID design principles? Can you give an example of the SOLID design principles?

The SOLID design principles are actually a short form that is made up of taking the first letter of the actual principle as:

- Single responsibility principle or SRP
- Open–closed design principle or OCD
- Liskov substitution principle
- Interface segregation principle
- Dependency inversion principle

Conclusion

In this chapter, we discussed about the different design patterns and their importance in the overall software development approach. We discussed many questions that could be asked on these patterns, which will help you to clear your Java interview. Though one may feel that the design patterns may not be that important as far as Java is concerned, knowledge of this is surely going to be one of the added flavors to your profile. In the next chapter, we will enter in the world of Web and will learn the basics of Web application development.

CHAPTER 12

The Basics of Web

Introduction

For years, the developers were busy in developing standalone applications. But, standalone applications were always a headache to users as well as developers. There is no second opinion about whether software makes the job of users easier and reliable. But, the developers need to invest a log of efforts in installing, maintaining, and updating standalone applications, which could be sometimes more than developing an application. This approach was a bit simplified in later stages by implementing the network applications. In this architecture, the actual program or software was installed on a server that is accessed by the client machines in the network. Though this approached reduced the efforts, it has its own limitation of the distance to which the systems can be connected and can communicate with each other. Along with this, the pure networking applications are homogenous in nature, which means that the server application and client applications must communicate with each other using a common programming language, which is not always feasible. We need some language-independent approach by which the data can be shared between different applications. The solution to this is Web technology. In Web technology, the application resides on a server machine within a Web container, and it can communicate with client using the language independent protocol like HTTP. Different programming languages have developed different APIs to work with the Web architecture. Java uses Servlet and JSPs to develop such application. We will talk about different features of a Servlet and JSPs in this chapter.

Structure

Understanding the Web technology might look simpler than advance technologies like Spring and Hibernate. But, if you do not know the basics of Web programming, then it will be difficult for you to face the interface questions based on the Web technology.

In this chapter, we will discuss the basics of Web application development. We will learn:

- Different interview question with possible answers
- Life cycle of a Servlet and JSP
- Reading and processing a request and response
- Session management

Objective

At the end of this chapter, you will be able to answer the different interview questions that are based on the Web technology in Java. You also learn how use a Servlet and JSP to handle the requests and responses.

What are types of enterprise architecture? Which architectures have you worked with?

An enterprise application can be built up by implementing different architectures as:

- Single-tier architecture
- Two-tier architecture
- Three-tier architecture
- N-tier architecture

Single-tier architecture

The single-tier architecture is useful for small applications. It consists of the presentation layer, business logic layer, and data layer in a single computing system or platform. Applications such as MP3 player, MS Office come under one-tier application.

Two-tier architecture

This was the traditional way of developing an enterprise application. In the **two-tier architecture,** the data layer is separated from other two layers. Here, the application entirely exists on one local machine while the database is deployed on a separate secure system. The load of processing is taken by the client. However, the server handles the traffic between the application and the data access layer. As the data is centralized, multiple users can access it at a given time.

The two-tier architecture is commonly called as client–server communication.

The communication between the client and server is established by providing the implementation of the UI, business logic, and data access layers.

Three-tier architecture

In the **three-tier architecture,** we will have three separate tiers consisting of the presentation layer in one tier, business logic in second tier, while the data layer is handled by the third tier. As the presentation and business logic is separated from each other, it adds a lot of flexibility. For one business logic depending upon the client requirement, more than one presentation layers can also be developed.

N-tier architecture

As the name suggests, the **n-tier architecture** has enormous layers facilitating developers to create flexible and reusable applications. It is suitable for developing enterprise applications. The architecture enables to provide solutions for scalability, security, reusability, fault tolerance, interoperability, and maintainability.

What is role of containers in Java EE?

Containers acts as the interface between the components and the low-level, platform-specific functionalities that supports the component. It facilitates the deployment of applications and provides ways of managing and executing the deployed application components.

Explain different types of containers

Following are the different types of containers:

- **Web container:** It allows the deployment of applications containing a Servlet and JSP pages along with all its components. All the Web components and their services run on Web containers.

- **Application client container:** The application client container is used to host application components and clients. As the name suggests, it runs on the client computer. It enables robust Java applications development along with the support of accessing J2EE resources such as data sources.

- **Applet container:** An applet container provides the support for the applet programming model. This container is a mixture of Java plug-in on client machine and Web browser. It uses the sandbox security model for preventing the applets from accessing the system resources to stop any damage.

- **EJB containers:** The container is used to deploy EJB applications. It allows the execution of all enterprise beans. These are also called as application containers. There are different types of EJB containers such as Glassfish and JBOSS.

Which are different application developments and deployment roles?

Deploying the applications and its management is a very complex process. Many people are involved in this process who play different roles. These roles are defined as per the Java EE specifications. The roles are:

- Java EE product providers
- The tool providers
- The application component providers
- The application assemblers
- The application deployers and administrators

What is the process of deploying application?

Deployment is the process of installing the application and all its components to the containers.

What are protocols? Which protocols have you worked with?

The set of the rules that are agreed by the parties that communicate with each other are called as **protocols**.

For example, network protocol. The **network protocol** establishes the set of rules that determine the way by which the data is transmitted between different devices in the same network regardless of any differences in their internal processes, structure, or design.

We also have the protocols for:

- **Communication:** FTP, IP, Bluetooth, routing are some of examples

- **Security:** Encryption protocols, transportation protocol

- **Network management:** Connection protocol, link aggregation protocols

- **Network:** HTTP, SSH, SMS, and so on

Can you explain different Http methods?

The most commonly used HTTP methods are **GET**, **POST**, **PUT**, **PATCH**, and **DELETE,** which correspond to create, read, update, and delete operations, respectively.

- **GET**

    The **GET** method requests for a specific resource. It is used preliminary to retrieve data. In such case, the client data is sent to the server by appending it to the URL. This approach is secure as someone may copy the URL and reuse it later. You can send only 2047 characters at the max in query string generated by this method.

- **HEAD**

    The **HEAD** method requests for some response from application deployed on server. It is very much identical to that of a **GET** request. However, when we use **HEAD** method, the server *MUST NOT* return a message body in the response.

- **POST**

    The **POST** method is used to submit data to the specified resource on server. The method causes a change in state. It means it has side effects on the server. The data from the client is sent to the server from the request body, making it very secure. Unlike the **GET** method, there is no data restriction for this method.

- **PUT**

    The **PUT** method is used to replace all current representations of the target resource with the request payload.

- **DELETE**

    The **DELETE** method is used to delete the specified resource on server.

- **OPTIONS**

    The **OPTIONS** method is used to describe the communication options for the target resource by the request URI. This method facilitates the client to determine the options or the requirements associated with a resource, the capabilities of a server, without implying a resource action or initiating resource retrieval. The responses to this method are not cacheable by client.

- **TRACE**

  The **TRACE** method is used specifically for diagnostic purpose. It is used to invoke a remote application layer loop-back test along the path to the target resource.

- **PATCH**

  The **PATCH** method is used to perform partial updates to a resource using the URI.

- **CONNECT**

  The **CONNECT** method establishes a channel to the server identified by the URI.

What is status code?

When a client sends a request to the server, the server sends the response back to the client. Along with the actual content of the requested data, the server also issues a specific number back to the client. This specific number issued by the server in response to the client is called as **status code**. These status codes are separated into five categories. The first digit of the status code defines the class of response. Following are the different categories of status codes:

- **1xx**: It denotes informational response. For example, Request was received, continuing process.

- **2xx**: It denotes that the task is successful. For example, Request was successfully received, accepted, and processed.

- **3xx**: It denotes redirection is in process.

- **4xx**: It denotes client error. For example, Request contains bad syntax or cannot be fulfilled.

- **5xx**: It denotes server error. For example, Server failed to fulfil an apparently valid request.

Can you explain the components of the Web application?

There are three major components of the Web application as:

- View layer

- Business logic layer

- Data access layer

    1. **View layer or user interface**

        The **view layer** acts as a user interface (UI component). The view layer can be considered as one of the most important components as it acts as a bridge between the user of a system and the application. This component is only responsible for the presentation of the data or ways for accepting the data from the user. It never takes part in any business logic or database communication. However, as per the application demand, it can be responsible for user data validation.

    2. **Business logic layer**

        The business logic layer is the most important layer of an application. The components of this layer are responsible for applying the business logic or algorithms to solve the problem. It never directly communicates with the database, but usually it acts on the data retrieved from the DB. It also never decides how the data will be presented, this decision is always be taken care by UI

    3. **Data access layer**

        The **data access layer** has the code to communicate with the persistence components such as database or files. It is quite possible to migrate from one DB to another. Under such scenario if the layer is not coded properly, lots of rework is required. So, a developer has to take care of writing loosely coupled classes.

Can you explain the MVC 1 and MVC 2 architecture?

Note: The interviewer might also interested know if you are aware of the terminology MVC.

MVC is application development architecture where your components are divided into three types:

- M – Model
- V – View
- C – Controller

The model component is responsible for business logic. This is typically pure Java code. The **view** component is responsible for presentation. Normally this is HTML or JSP code.

The **controller** controls flow of application. It normally transfers the user data to the model, and once the model generates a response, it is transferred to view to present the same to end user.

MVC1 is also termed as *single-page request-response application*. In this architecture, JSP page acts as only an accountable component for handling the request. All the HTTP requests are mapped to JSP pages. The JSP page accepts the requests data, processes it, and also generates the response with presentation. So, a single page acts a controller as well as the presentation layer.

MVC2, on the other hand, introduced *Servlet as a controller*. It accepts the request and delegates it to model for the business logic implementation, which is pure Java code. The model generates the data/response, which is transferred to the presentation layer. This presentation layer could be HTML or JSP or any other template that can generate the presentation like FreeMarker, and so on.

What is a Servlet and its use?

A **Servlet** is a Java program that is hosted or deployed on a server as a part of a Web application. It extends the capabilities of the server so that a response can be generated for the request. It provides different methods like **doGet()** and **doPost()** to handle the corresponding requests. To create a Servlet, you can either implement the Servlet interface from the **javax.servlet** package or extend the **HttpServlet** class from the **javax.serlet.http** package.

Explain the Servlet life cycle

The Servlet is managed by a Servlet container. The life cycle of a Servlet is different than the normal object's life cycle. It has the following stages:

- **Loading and instantiation of a Servlet**

  In this stage, the Servlet is loaded in memory and instantiated by a Servlet container. To achieve this, the container uses the no-argument constructor of a Servlet.

- **Initialization of a Servlet**

  After instantiation, the Servlet is initialized by using the **init()** method. During this process, the object of **ServletConfig** is generated, which can be used to read the initialization parameters. You can also initialize other resource if required by overriding this method. This makes the Servlet ready to serve the request.

- **Servicing the request**

  In this stage, the Servlet generates objects of **HttpServletRequest** and **HttpServletResponse** through the methods like **doGet()** and **doPost()**. These methods internally invokes the **service()** method, which is responsible for services different the requests coming from clients.

- **Destroy**

  When the Servlet finishes the task of servicing the client, the container destroys the instance of the Servlet. All the threads, which are running for the objects are forced to complete their task and then the **destroy()** method is called. You can release all the resources which are connected to this Servlet in this method. After this, the Servlet instant becomes eligible for garbage collection.

Did you develop a Servlet-based application? Explain the steps to develop a Servlet application. Explain the ways to configure Servlets?

To develop a servlet-based application, we need to create a Servlet and configure it so that it can be accessed by other resources.

- **Creating a Servlet**

  To create a Servlet, you need to create a class that can either extend **HttpServlet** or implement the **Servlet** interface. The recommended practice is to create it by extending **HttpServletRequest** and override the methods **doGet()** or **doPost()** based on the requirement of the request type. The following code snippet shows how to do this task:

```
public class Simple Servlet extends HttpServlet{
  public void doGet(HttpServletRequest req,HttpServletResponse res)
                    throws ServletException,IOException  {
    //Reading request parameters
  }
}
```

- **Configuring a Servlet**

  A servlet can be configured either by using the XML file, which is a deployment descriptor file or by applying annotations on the Servlet class.

o   By configuring XML

To declare the URL pattern and other initialization values for a Servlet, we can configure the Web deployment descriptor file, that is, **web.xml** is shown as follows:

```
<web-app>
  <servlet>
    <servlet-name>SimpleServlet</servlet-name>
    <servlet-class>SimpleServlet</servlet-class>
  </servlet>
  <servlet-mapping>
    <servlet-name>SimpleServlet</servlet-name>
    <url-pattern>simple.com</url-pattern>
  </servlet-mapping>
</web-app>
```

o   Using annotations

In Servlet 3.0 API, we can annotate the Servlet class instead of the XML file to define URL pattern:

```
@WebServlet(value = "/Simple")
public class Simple extends HttpServlet {


}
```

We can also have multiple URL patterns for a single servlet.

How to read request parameters?

To read the request parameter, the **HttpServletRequest** object gives different methods as described in the following table:

Method	Description
getParameter()	Returns the single value for the parameter declared in the argument.
getParameterValues()	Returns array of values from parameter. This method can be used if we want to know the selected items from checkbox.
getParameterNames()	Returns all the names of parameters available in current request object in enumeration format.

Table 12.1: Reading request parameter

What is the difference between the getRequestDispatcher() method of ServletRequest and ServletContext?

The **getRequestDispatcher()** method is used to forward the request to a location specified by the String argument provided in the method.

getRequestDispatcher() of **ServletContext** accepts only absolute path as an argument. **getRequestDispatcher()** of **ServletRequest** accepts both absolute and relative path as an argument.

How to define the custom init() method?

The **init()** method of a **HttpServlet** is called only once before a servlet handles the first incoming request. As the name suggests this method is used to initialize the Servlet. The **init()** method can save the instance of **ServletConfig** using **super. init()** method.

Differentiate between the GET and POST method?

When one uses the **GET** method in form submission, the submitted form parameters will be added to the **URL**. This **URL** is visible to everyone, and anyone can use the values. It means **GET** is not secure, and one should not use it to pass request parameters of type username and password. Also, it has an upper limit of how much data can be transferred. **GET** is faster as well as easier to use and can preferred to fetch the data from server.

The **POST** method passes the parameters to the server from the request body, and hence, those are not visible. **POST** is secure and always used to pass data such as username and password between the client and server. As the data is getting passed from the request body, there is no limit on how much data to be transferred between.

How a client can send the information to a server?

The client information can be sent to the server using request parameters. We have two ways to send request parameters to the server:

- **Form submission:**

    The HTML **<form>** tag can be used to collect the information from the client and on submission of the form the information will be sent to the resource, which is mapped in the action attribute of form, which is shown as follows:

```
<form action="senddata">
```

- **URL rewriting:**

    URL rewriting can be used to send the data between a client and server as follows:

```
<a href="senddata?username='myname'">CLICK HERE</a>
```

Whenever the client clicks on the link **CLICK HERE** request parameter, **username** will be sent to the server with the value **myname**.

What is the difference between attribute and parameters?

In Web application development, sometimes, we need to share the data between different components of the application, such as Servlets, JSPs, filters.

A request parameter is one way by which a data can be shared between the components, especially from the requested page to the requested target. For example, sending form data from a client to other resource. Along with the request parameters, we also have **context** parameters and **config** parameters.

The attributes facilitate the developers to share the data as an object event of type collection between different components. However, the parameters share the data only of type String.

The attributes can be added, updated, or even removed from a scope, but the parameters cannot be set using any such method. It is only possible to send the data in request parameters either by form submission or **URL** rewriting.

What are headers and different types of headers?

The Http headers enable developers to exchange some extra information between the client and server. We have two types of headers, request headers and response headers. Headers use a key–value pair, which is separated by the colon. The end of the header section is denoted by an empty field header.

- Context wise, we have the following four types of headers:
    - o **General headers:** These types of headers are applied on both request and response.

o **Request headers:** This type of headers contains the information about the request fetched by the client.

o **Response headers:** This type of headers contains the information about the source location.

o **Entity headers:** This type of headers contains the information about the resource body such as content length, MIME type, and so on.

The **HTTP** headers provide the information about the request context so that the server can utilize it to generate an appropriate response. There are different types of request headers as:

- From
- Accept
- Accept-Encoding
- Accept-Language
- Authorization
- Charge-To
- If-Modified-Since
- User-Agent
- Referrer
- Pragma

We can use the headers to:

- Communicate authentication information, caching information.
- Request a specific type of response from the server, using the content negotiation headers.
- Handle session using cookies.
- Communicate with a third-party application using cross-origin resource sharing (CORS).

What is a scope? What are the different types of scopes?

Scope is the life time for which something can be used. The scope is used in terms of a Web application to explain how long an attribute can be utilized. The following are the different scopes available in a Web application:

- **Request scope:** The request scope is initialized at the point when the request hits the servlet and ends when the servlet delivers the response. The request attributes can be available to Servlets as well as JSPs that are taking part in serving the request.

- **Session scope:** The session scope is initialized at the point when the client establishes a communication with the Web application. The session scope spans across multiple request and response pairs unless the session is not inactivated. The session attributes can be available to servlets as well as JSPs that are taking part in serving the client and that are part of one session.

- **Context or application scope:** The context scope starts at the point when the application is started. The request attributes can be available to all the requests and sessions from the point the attribute is added to the context. This attribute is available till the application is shutdown or reloaded.

- **Page scope:** The page scope is a much specialized scope that is only available in the JSP pages. The page scope is restricted to the same page from the point it is initialized till the end of the page. The implicit object **pageScope** demotes the page scope in JSP pages.

Explain the difference between ServletConfig and ServletContext

The **ServletContext** and **ServletConfig** instances are used to perform the initialization of a Servlet through initial parameters or configuration.

- **ServletContext:** The instance of **ServletContext** is created by a servlet container. The instance shares the initial parameters or configuration information to the entire application. It means all the servlets, JSPs, filters can use the data stored in the **ServletContext** instance. Only one instance of **ServletContext** is created per application, and the same is utilized by all the Web components. One can configure the context parameters as follows:

```
<context-param>

    <param-name>company_name</param-name>

    <param-value>Company1</param-value>

</context-param>
```

We can fetch the name of company as follows:

```
String company_name = getServletContext().

                    getInitParameter("company_name");
```

- **ServletConfig:** The servlet container creates the **ServletConfig** instance using the parameters or configuration information. This information is passed to the servlet during the initialization process. The instance of **ServletConfig** is specific to a particular Servlet. It means information of one **ServletConfig** instance cannot be utilized by another. We will get one **ServletConfig** instance per servlet created. One can configure the context parameters as follows:

```
<servlet>
    <servlet-name>servlet1</servlet-name>
    <servlet-class>MyServlet</servlet-class>
    <init-param>
        <param-name>servlet_name</param-name>
        <param-value>name1</param-value>
    </init-param>
</servlet>
```

We can retrieve the parameter as shown below:

```
String servlet_name  = getServletConfig()
                        .getInitParameter("servlet_name");
```

What is session tracking? What are ways of session tracking? Why session tracking is required? When to use session tracking?

By default, once a request is served and response is sent back to the client, the server does not remember any details about that request. It means, by default, the application cannot establish some relation between two consecutive requests. In other words, the server is stateless. **Session tracking** is a process by which a relationship between consecutive requests is established.

There are different ways of session tracking as follows:

- Hidden form field
- URL rewriting
- Cookie management
- Http session handling

How to work with the HttpSession object in a Servlet?

To instantiate the **HttpSession** object, we need to invoke **request.getSession()**, which returns the current session. In case if current session does not exist, then it will create a new one and return it.

request.getSession() accepts by default Boolean **true** as an argument. So, **request.getSession()** and **request.getSession(true)** are identical internally. **request.getSession(true)** also returns the current session. If in case the current session does not exist, then it will create a new session and return it.

On the other hand, **request.getSession(false)** returns an existing session. If the session is not available, it will not create a new session and return null.

It means from the application perspective, to track the session, the developers need to use **request.getSession(false)**. It will make sure the page is loaded as a part of one session and has all the required information.

What is event handling in a Servlet?

Events denotes occurrence of a user's action, and it might change the state of some object. Nobody knows when this event will occur. So, an event handler methods uses the callback mechanism.

Event classes are as follows:

- ServletRequestEvent
- ServletRequestAttributeEvent
- ServletContextEvent
- ServletContextAttributeEvent
- HttpSessionEvent
- HttpSessionBindingEvent

The event interfaces/listeners are as follows:

- ServletRequestListener
- ServletRequestAttributeListener
- ServletContextListener
- ServletContextAttributeListener
- HttpSessionListener
- HttpSessionAttributeListener

- `HttpSessionBindingListener`

- `HttpSessionActivationListener`

What is JSP? Why to use JSP? How JSP is useful in Web programming?

JSP is acronym for **Java Server Pages**. It is a server-side programming technology that enables the developers to create dynamic, platform-independent Web applications. For every JSP, a servlet class file is generated by the container.

In JSP, one can use HTML tags as well as Java code. To use Java code, one can use different types of tags in JSP as:

- **Scriptlet**: This tag is used to embed the Java source code in HTML page. JSP contains presentation using HTML tags plus Java code in a scriptlet. It has the syntax as follows:

  `<% source code of Java %>`

- **Expression**: The **expression** tag is used to write the code to the output stream with a syntax:

  `<%= statement to display something %>`

- **Directive**: The **directive** tag is used to provide information for the Web container about how the to translate a JSP. We have following three types of directive tags:

  o   page directive

  o   include directive

  o   taglib directive

- **Declaration**: The tag is used to declare the data members and methods. The code written using the declaration tag is placed outside the **service()** method of the auto-generated servlet.

What are the advantages of JSP?

Servlets are written in **.java** files. It is difficult to write the HTML code with a complex design in servlets. The following are the advantages of JSP:

- JSPs are extended servlets, so all the features of servlets are available. Along with servlet features, JSPs also have implicit objects, and they support JSTL tags, custom tags, Els.

- The development using JSPs is faster. It does not require recompilation, and hence, there is no need of redeploying the application after the changes.

- JSPs are easy to maintain.

- The developer needs to write comparatively less code as many predefined tags, implicit objects, JSTL tags, EL functions are supported in JSPs.

Explain the life cycle of JSP?

Each JSP follows the following phases:

- **Translation**: Each JSP is translated to a servlet class by the container.

- **Compilation**: The container compiles the converted servlet and generates the .class file.

- **Loading**: `Classloader` loads the generated class file.

- **Instantiation**: The container instantiates the object of the servlet class using the constructor.

- **Initialization**: After instantiation, the container invokes the `jspInit()` method to perform the initialization of resources.

- **Servicing**: To service the request by client, `_jspService()` is invoked by the container.

- **Destroy**: When the application shuts down, the `jspDestroy()` method is invoked by the container to perform the cleanup.

What are implicit objects in JSP?

Implicit objects are predefined objects of some type, which are created by the container automatically. These objects are created during the translation phase of the JSP. We can directly use these implicit objects in the scriptlets.

We have following implicit objects for the use in JSPs:

- **out**: This is an object of the `javax.servlet.jsp.jspWriter` class, which enables writing the data to the buffer and sending the output to the client in response.

- **request**: This object is an instance of `javax.servlet.http.HttpServletRequest`. It is used to fetch the information about the form parameter, header information, and so on. We can use `request.getParameter()` to fetch the request parameter.

- **response**: This object is an instance of `javax.servlet.http.HttpServletResponse,` which can be used to send the response to the client. This implicit object can be used to set the content type, add cookies to response, and to redirect response to other resource.

- **config**: This object is an instance of **javax.servlet.ServletConfig**. It is created by the container for each JSP. It is used to retrieve the initialization parameters that are configured in **web.xml**.

- **application**: This object is an instance of **javax.servlet.ServletContext**, which is used to retrieve the context information in JSP. The container creates a single application object at the time of deployment of an application.

- **session**: This object is an instance of HttpSession. The session object is used for retrieving, setting, and removing the attributes in the session scope. It also provides the information about the session instance.

- **pageContext**: This object is of type **PageContext**. It is used for retrieving, setting, and removing the attributes in the page scope.

- **page**: The page represents an object for the current JSP page.

- **exception**: This object is an instance of the **Throwable** class. This facilitates exception handling in JSP. The exception object plays important role in creation of the error pages.

What do you mean by action tag? How can you use it?

Action **tags** are used to perform some action from the JSP. Such actions include transfer of control between pages, setting or getting the properties of an instance, including one page into another, and so on. We have the following standard action tags:

- **jsp:useBean**: This enables the use of Java beans in JSP. The tag either creates a new instance of a type or locates some instance from the scope specified. It has the syntax as follows:

```
<jsp:useBean id="reference_value" class="fully_qualified_class_
name" scope="scope_for_which_the_instance_is_available"/>
```

The value of scope will be **page, request, session, or application**. The default value of scope is **page**.

- **jsp:include**: The tag is used to include another resource or file during the request processing phase in the page.

```
<jsp:include page="name_of_page_to_include"/>
```

It allows easy way of reusing the pages such as header pages or footer pages can be created once and added whenever required.

- **jsp:forward**: The forward tag is used to navigate in between the pages. The action of the current page is terminated, and the request is forwarded to the specified resource. This resource can be any other static page, JSP, or even a servlet. The syntax to use forward action is as follows:

```
<jsp:forward page="resource_URL_to_which_request_is_forwarded"/>
```

- **jsp:plugin**: The tag is used to embed another Java component to a page. The tag determines the type of the browser and then inserts the **object** or **embed** as per the needs. The syntax of the tag is as follows:

```
<jsp:plugin type="specified_as_either_applet_or_bean"
            code="class_name_of_applet_or_bean"
            codebase="base_URL_contains_files_of_classes"/>
```

- **jsp:text**: It is used to template the text in the JSP. Its body cannot contain any other element; however, it contains only text or the EL expressions. It has the syntax as follows:

```
<jsp:text> template text </jsp:text> >
```

- **jsp:param**: The tag is child object of the plugin tag. It must contain one or more actions that provide additional parameters. The syntax of the tag is as follows:

```
<jsp:param name="name_of_param" value="value_of_param" />
```

- **jsp:body**: This tag is used to define the XML that is used to generate dynamically element body. The syntax of the tag is as follows:

```
<jsp:body> </jsp:body>
```

- **jsp:attribute**: This tag is used to define the attribute of XML, which will be generated dynamically. It has the following syntax:

```
<jsp:attribute name="name_of_attribute"> </jsp:attribute >
```

What is the difference between include directive and include standard action?

Both include directive and include standard action are useful for including one file into other, with the following differences:

- Include directive includes the file at translation time; however, include standard action includes the file at runtime.

- When the included file is changed, but not the JSP that is including the changed page, then the changes will reflect only if the developers have used the include action tag.

- Both approaches use different syntax as follows:

- Include directive has the syntax as : `<%@ include file="name_of_file"%>`

  And,

- Include action has the syntax as : `<jsp:include page="name_of_file"/>`.

What is EL and EL function?

JSP **Expression Language (EL)** is the easiest possible way to access the application data that is stored in the JavaBeans components. **EL** enables to create arithmetic as well as logical expressions. **EL** allows the use of integers, floating point numbers, strings, Boolean values, or even null. EL is very useful when one wants to display the data. Along with EL, the *out* tag of JSTL is also used to display the data. However, if the data to be displayed might have no value, the out tag still displays **null** on the page. But, if the value of the data is **null, EL** will not display anything.

The *EL* function is a function that is mapped to a static function of a Java class. The **EL** function can be used in the template text or in the attribute of a custom tags. The *Tag Library Descriptive (TLD)* is used for EL function mapping.

Explain JSTL

JSTL is known as **Java Standard Tag Library**. It is a set of tags that simplifies faster JSP development. JSTL contains the following tags:

- Core tags
- Function tags
- SQL tags
- Formatting tags
- XML tags.

A JSTL tag has the following advantages:

- JSTL tags make the development faster and more simplified.
- It enables code reusability.

It takes away the need of using scriptlets in JSP.

How to create a custom tag in JSP?

The following are the steps to create and use custom tags in JSP:

- **Creating a Tag-Handler class:**

  In this step, we need to create a class that implements the **JspTag/Tag/ IterationTag** interface, or we can also write a class that extends the **TagSupport** class. In this class, we need to implement the method, which will be invoked when the tag is used.

- **Configuring a Tag Lib Descriptor (TLD) file:**

  In this step, the class is mapped with the tag, which can be referred by the JSP file.

- **Using a custom tag in JSP file:**

  In this step, we refer the tag that is configured in the **TLD** file. To do this, we also need to assign the prefix for the **TLD** file so that the tags can be located easily by JSP.

What are filters? When to use filters? How to configure filters?

In Web development, sometimes, a request needs a pre- or post-processing. The servlet acts as a controller that accepts the request data and forwards it to the model for further business logic. The **filters** are the Web components that allow the pre- or post-processing of the request. The filters are used for logging, performing some conversions, compressions of files, encryption or decryption of the data, or to perform input data validations.

- To develop a filter, we need to follow the steps as follows:

  o Write a class implementing the **Filter** interface.

  o Override the **init()**, **doFilter()** and **destroy()** methods.

  o The **doFilter()** method contains the logic for pre- or post-processing of request data. Once the pre- or post-processing is done, the request can be forwarded to the next filter in the filter chain or to a servlet. The **doFilter()** method of **FilterChain** delegates the control to the next component in chain. The code before **chain. doFilter()** is used for pre-processing, and the code written after **chain.doFilter()** is used for post-processing of the request.

  o Now, map the filter in the **web.xml,** which is shown as follows:

  ```
  <filter>
  ```

```
    <filter-name>...</filter-name>
    <filter-class>...</filter-class>
</filter>

<filter-mapping>
    <filter-name>...</filter-name>
    <url-pattern>...</url-pattern>
</filter-mapping>
```

Conclusion

In this chapter, we talked about the Web technology in Java. We started the discussion with what is need for the Web technology and how it is better than a standalone application. We discussed different interview questions that can be asked during the interview process. While discussing these questions, we learned many components of a Servlet and JSP. Of course, the Web technology is one of the small segments of J2EE; there are other technologies like Spring and Hibernate, which we will discuss in the later stages of this book. In the next chapter, we will discuss about one of most in-demand frameworks Spring. Get ready to be flexible guys, see you in the next chapter.

CHAPTER 13

Spring and Spring Boot

Introduction

Application development is becoming complex day by day. Expectations of clients are increasing, and business scenarios are also becoming challenging. Apart from writing only business logic, a developer needs to also think of other perspectives of the application like flow of application data and other cross-cutting concerns. While servicing all these needs, a developer also has to make sure that he/she delivers the software in the given timeframe. Traditionally, a developer was solely responsible to develop everything that was time-consuming, and it was difficult to maintain the software as well. So, to make things little bit simpler for the developer, frameworks were introduced. Frameworks are the semi-complete applications, with some readymade code or configurations, which can be customized by developers to create customized applications as per the need.

There are different frameworks for different tasks. The Spring framework is one of such frameworks, which is known for its concepts like dependency injection and IoC technique. In this chapter, we will walk through about all the common questions that might be asked based on the Spring and Spring Boot frameworks.

The Spring framework is one of the most demanding frameworks in the industry. Typically, if you are targeting financial institutions, Spring is the most preferred frameworks because of the high performance. The Spring framework is always a sweet dish for an interviewer. You can literally see the eyes of interviewer glow up when he/she reads "Spring Framework" in your profile.

Structure

This chapter will gradually walk through different concepts of the Spring framework to Spring Boot by discussing different interview questions. You will learn the following concepts during this chapter.

- Spring Framework
- Modules of Spring
- DI and IoC in Spring
- Different configurations of Spring bean
- Spring Boot configurations

Objective

At the end of this chapter, you will be able to learn the Spring framework and Spring Boot. You will be also able to answer different interview questions based on this framework, which nowadays have become an integral part of interview process.

Tell me something about the Spring framework?

Spring is a lightweight framework that comprises of some modules that enables a developer to develop console as well as Web applications rapidly.

So many times we seen the blogs, books, or references claiming that the Spring framework makes the development easy. Can you explain how?

The following are the main features implemented by the Spring framework, to enable the rapid or easy application development:

- Spring development is focused on developing decoupled code.
- **Easy configuration:** Spring provides both XML- and annotation-based configuration. Both of these ways are easy and self-explanatory.

- **Focus on development:** The main concern of a developer is to provide a solution to a problem by some business logic, algorithm, and so on. But, in reality, many times, while developing Java enterprise applications, the developer needs to think about and code for configuration, logging along with the logic. These configurations, loggings are time-consuming and repetitive. The framework manages bean, provides AOPs for the developers, which allows them to focus on the logical aspects of an application.

- Reduces the plumbing code.

- **Reduces boiler-plated code:** In the process of development, the developers have to write similar kind of code again and again, which is termed as boiler-plated code. Spring provides templates such as `JdbcTemplate`, `JMSTemplate`, `RestTemplate` components to get rid of the boilerplate code.

What do you mean by boiler-plated code?

In a process of development, at multiple situations, we need to write similar kind of code again and again, and we cannot get rid of that easily. Let us take an example of fetching data from the tables. We know **ResultSet** is a collection of objects, but we cannot obtain an object or list of objects directly. When we get **ResultSet**, we need to write the code to convert each row from **ResultSet** to an object. However, the way we get an Employee object from **ResultSet** is similar to the way we get object of Book from **ResultSet**. The only difference in this process is each of them has different data members or data types. So, this kind of the code is considered as boilerplate code.

Can you provide some examples of boilerplate codes?

Yes! As I already mentioned, the JDBC codes are the best examples of boilerplate code. Along with that, when we do exception handling, transaction management, and logging, we need to write boilerplate code.

How many modules of Spring you have used?

(This question is asked to find out how much comfortable you are with the framework, how much practical exposure you have. The answer of this question will decide the journey of your Spring framework interview. So, be real and answer very genuinely. You might not have the real-time experience for a couple of modules, which is still fine. Spring is really huge to cover everything. It will be very difficult for you to escape if you pretend to be experienced in some modules that you have not worked with. So, be real. Here, I am providing an ideal answer. A couple of these modules you might not have worked with. So, please choose the modules as per experience.

Now, the question is, "If I am practicing Spring on my own, what shall I do?" In this situation, you can mention the modules you are aware of, and then, tell them the modules you have used.)

Spring provides around 20 modules as shown in *Figure 13.1*, which supports different features:

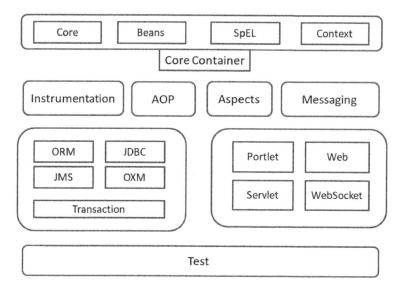

Figure 13.1: Spring modules

Core container

A. The core container consists of the modules for *spring-beans, spring-core, spring-context,* and *Spring Expression Language*.

B. The features such as dependency injection and IoC are supported by *spring-core* and *spring-beans* modules.

C. The *spring-context* module provides the means to access objects from the container.

D. The *spring-expression* module provides a way for querying and manipulating an object graph.

Spring AOP and instrumentation

A. The *Spring AOP* module supports integration of the aspect-oriented programming approach. By using *AOP,* cross-cutting concerns can be integrated in the application.

B. The *Spring Aspects* module provides the integration of *AspectJ* in the application.

C. Data access or integration module.

D. The *JDBC, ORM, JMS, OXM*, and *Transaction* modules can be integrated using the data-access module.

E. The integration of JDBC is supported by *Spring-Jdbc* module.

F. The support for integrating Object Relational Mapping (ORM) is provided by *Spring*

ORM

A. The *Spring-TX* module supports programmatic and declarative transaction management.

B. The *JAXB, Castor, XStream* provides the Object/XML mapping. The *Spring-OXM* module supports integration of these mappings

C. The *Spring-JMS* module was added in Spring 4.1 version. This module provides the features for producing and consuming messages.

Messaging

The *Spring-Messaging* module has been included in Spring 4. The module provides support for integrating *Message, MessageChannel, MessageHandler* in messaging applications.

Web

A. The Web Module layer consists of *Spring-Web, Spring-Web MVC, Spring-WebSocket.*

B. The *Spring-Web* Module supports web-oriented development.

C. *Spring-Web MVC* supports application development for Spring MVC and REST-based Web services.

Test

The support for integrating unit testing and integration testing in the application with *JUnit* or *TestNG* is provided by the Spring-Test Module.

What is DI in Spring?

Spring uses dependency injection for managing the dependencies of a bean.

Please explain a dependency injection

Dependency injection is a process by which the values of data members are pushed in an object by the container.

What are the ways of dependency injection in Spring? Spring provides two ways for dependency injection:

1. **Setter injection**

   When the setter functions are used to set the values for data members, it is termed as a setter injection. In XML, we can use the **`<property>`** tag, which is an instruction to container to use setters/setter functions for setting values.

2. **Constructor injection**

   When a parameterized constructor is used to push values for the data members, it is called as constructor injection. The **`<constructor-arg>`** tag is used for generating a constructor injection.

Explain dependency injection with a relevant example

Note: Here, the interviewer wants to check the theoretical as well as practical knowledge of the participants. So, it is better to go with bit of theory about what is DI, types of DIs, and then explain the practical implementation. We have already discussed the theoretical answer about dependency injection in the earlier question.

Let us take an example of database communication for DI. If we are not using Spring, we need to obtain a Connection object with the singleton or factory design pattern implementation. When we use Spring, we can write a bean of type **`DriverManagerDataSource`** in XML or Java code. Here, the container will create an object according to the configurations provided by the developer.

Is DriverManagerDataSource the only implementation provided by the framework?

No, **`BasicDataSource`**, **`ComboPooledDataSource`**, and **`SingleConnectionData Source`** also are provided by the framework.

Consider a scenario in which multiple requests for obtaining connections are fired. Will it be feasible to use DriverManagerDataSource?

In the practical scenarios, the application may need to obtain multiple database connections. However, **DriverManagerDataSource** does not provide facility for connection pooling and may affect the application performance. So, alternatives such as **BasicDataSource**, **ComboPooledDataSource** can be used.

What is IoC/inversion of controller?

A very simple meaning of **IoC** is inverting the responsibility.

The major task of a Java developer is to create an object by setting values of the data members. Now, instead of developers creating objects themselves, here the developers get objects from the containers. So, the developers are inverting their responsibilities and letting the container to create, manage an object.

In more technical words, you can explain the concepts as:

We have objects with some dependencies. These dependencies are injected to the beans through the process of instantiation by the container; this process is called IoC.

Please explain about Spring IoC container

The IoC container is responsible for instantiating bean, managing the life cycle of bean, and injecting its dependencies. Spring has **BeanFactory** and **ApplicationContext** as containers. **BeanFactory** provides the basic functionalities and configuration. **ApplicationContextInterface** is an extension of the **BeanFactory** interface.

ApplicationContext makes easy message resource handlings for internationalization support, integration of AOP features and publishing of the events.

What is a bean according to you? Or, explain bean with reference to the Spring framework

Bean is an object that is instantiated or managed by the container depending upon the configuration provided.

You just mentioned about the ApplicationContext interface. If it is an interface, do we need to provide its implementation?

Note: An interviewer might ask this question differently like let me know the implementation classes of `ApplicationContext`. Or, which are the classes implemented by `ApplicationContext`, and so on.

Though there are different flavors of a question, the answer will remain same as follows:

The **`ApplicationContext`** interface is implemented by:

- **`ClassPathXmlApplicationContext`**

  This class is used to load the bean configuration file from the class path.

- **`FileSystemXmlApplicationContext`**

  This class is used to load the bean configuration file from file system.

- **`AnnotationConfigApplicationContext`**

  The class is used to create the Spring IoC container and the instantiation of beans from annotation-based configuration.

Ideally, the preceding answer is sufficient. But, sometimes, if the interviewer finds you confident and having sound knowledge, he/she can go in further details. He might want to know the differentiation between console and Web-based implementations.

Note: The preceding implemented classes discussed in the previous question play an important role in console-based applications. We also have Web implementations for Web applications. So, you might expect some questions on Web-based containers as well.

Did you work with Web-based containers? Can you explain about Web containers as well?

- **`XmlWebApplicationContext`**

  This class is used for containers used in Web-based applications. It loads the XML file containing bean definition from **WEB-INF/applicationContext.xml**.

- **`AnnotationConfigWebApplicationContext`**

  The class facilitates application context for the Web-based application with annotation-based configuration for bean definitions.

Can you tell us an overall process to use ClassPathXmlApplicationContext?

- We can define a bean configuration file in **classpath**. For example, the **beans.xml** file using the **\<bean\>** tag.

- Now, we can load this file using **ClassPathXmlApplicationContext** as follows:

```
ApplicationContext context = new ClassPathXmlApplicationContext("beans.xml")
```

Now, using this context, we can get the beans from the containers as follows:

```
context.getBean("mybean")
```

Where **mybean** is an ID of one of the beans defined in the **beans.xml** file. The following code snippet shows the contents of **beans.xml**:

```xml
<?xml version="1.0" encoding="UTF-8"?>
<beans xmlns="http://www.springframework.org/schema/beans"
    xmlns:xsi="http://www.w3.org/2001/XMLSchema-instance"
    xmlns:context="http://www.springframework.org/schema/context"
    xsi:schemaLocation="http://www.springframework.org/schema/beans
      http://www.springframework.org/schema/beans/spring-beans.xsd
      http://www.springframework.org/schema/context/
      http://www.springframework.org/schema/context/spring-context.xsd»>
    <bean id="mybean" class="com.beans.Employee">
    </bean>
</beans>
```

Can we use a different file name for the bean configuration? Or, is it mandatory to use beans.xml as the file name?

We can use any valid name to the bean confirmation file. The only thing we need to do is to use the changed name while creating the container instance.

Is the location of the beans.xml file fixed? Can we change the location of the file?

The location of the file is the choice of the developer. While instantiating the container, we need to load the configuration file from the relevant location. If the file is in classpath or relative to classpath, we can use **ClassPathXmlApplicationContext**; if the file is not relevant to classpath, we can use **FileSystemXmlApplicationContext**.

Can we use more than one configuration file? Is it possible to distribute the beans in more than one configuration file in a single application?

Yes, we can use more than one configuration file to configure the beans. The files then can be loaded at the time of Spring container initialization.

What are the ways to get the container instantiation for more than one bean configuration files? How to load more than one bean configuration file while creating the container?

The following are the different ways to load beans from multiple configuration files in the Spring framework.

- We can use the constructor of **ClassPathXmlApplicationContext** to load the XML files containing the configuration as follows:

```
ApplicationContext context = new
  ClassPathXmlApplicationContext("beans.xml","beans1.xml","beans2.
xml");
```

- We can write more than one files containing bean configuration, and then use the **<import>** tag to load the bean definitions from other files.

You can also get some questions on how to get the configured beans from XML. So, be ready for them as well.

Please write a standard way of configuring bean in an XML file

We can configure the bean either using the setter injection or the constructor injection.

- **For setter-based injection:**

```
<bean id="valid_bean_id" class="fully_qualified_class_name">
        <property name="name_of_data_member"
                    value="value_of_the_data_member"/>
</bean>
```

- **For constructor-based configuration:**

```
<bean id="valid_bean_id" class="fully_qualified_class_name">
        <constructor-arg value="value_of_the_data_member"/>
</bean>
```

What is the way to configure a bean having has-a-kind relation?

An interviewer might give a class definition as shown in the following code and ask you to configure them:

```
1. package com.pojo;
2. class Address{
3.      long pincode;
4.      String cityName;
5.      //getters and setters
6. }
7.
8. class Publication{
9.      Address add;
10.     String publicationName;
11.     //default and parameterized constructor
12. }
```

Here, we need to define two beans as follows:

```
1. <bean id="add" class="com.pojo.Address">
2.    <property name="pincode" value="12345"/>
```

```
3.    <property name="cityName" value="city1"/>
4. <bean>
5.
6. <bean id="obj" class="com.pojo.Publication">
7.    <constructor-arg ref="add"/>
8. <bean>
```

When we are using a has-a-kind of relationship, we need to use the ref attribute in configuration file. In the preceding snippet, we have used **<constructor-arg ref=" ">** instead of **<constructor-arg value=" "">**.

You just mentioned a couple of bean configurations; I would like to know how many instances the container will create for such a bean configuration?

The same question can be reframed as:

- **When you define a bean configuration, how many instances a container creates?**

Spring by default supports singleton scope of beans, which means bean will be instantiated only once by Spring. The Spring container merely returns the same instance again and again for multiple requests for that bean.

Or, on a simple note, only one object is created for one bean configured in XML.

Does that mean the developer gets only one instance to work with from the container?

This question can be reframed into different flavors as:

- **Is there a possibility to get more than one instance from the same bean configuration?**

- **What is the scope of a bean?**

- **What are the scopes available in Spring?**

The scope of a bean defines how many instances for a bean configuration to create or how long a bean instance will live.

The following five scopes are provided by the Spring framework:

- **singleton**: The Spring IoC container creates only one instance for the configured bean. This is the default scope of a bean.

- **prototype**: The Spring IoC container creates a new instance for every new request made.

- **request**: The Spring IoC container creates a new instance for every new HTTP request made. The request scope is valid only when the context is Web-aware.

- **session**: The Spring IoC container creates a new instance for a new creation of *HttpSession*. The session scope is valid only when the context is Web-aware.

- **application**: The application scopes a single bean definition to the life cycle of a *ServletContext*. The scope is valid only when the context is Web-aware.

- **websocket**: The application scopes a single bean definition to the life cycle of a *WebSocket*. This scope is also valid only when the context is Web-aware.

What is the default scope of a bean?

The default scope of bean is singleton.

You just said beans are singleton. Can we change the default singleton scope?

This question can be reframed with two types of questions by the interviewer as shown below as well:

- **How to change the scope of a bean?**
- **How to configure the scope of a bean?**

Yes, we can change the scope by modifying the configuration, as shown in the following code:

```
1. <bean id="add" class="com.pojo.Address" scope="prototype">
2. <property name="pincode" value="12345"/>
3. <property name="city_name" value="city1"/>
4. <bean>
```

Instead of prototype, we can specify singleton, request, session, or global-session.

Is it possible to define the bean scopes using annotations?

Yes, it is. We can define the request scope using annotation-driven components by using **@RequestScope**, session scope with **@SessionScope,** and application scope by **@ApplicationScope**.

Is it possible to create user-defined scopes?

Yes, a developer can develop a new scope, which is called as custom scope.

Note: If you are aware of how to create it, you can explain how to create custom scope. But, go for it only when you know the process and you are not explaining just to impress the panel. They are only making sure you are aware of the framework features. Being smart is perfectly fine, but do not try to be extra-smart, that too when you have limited knowledge.

To define a custom scope, one needs to implement the **org.springframework. beans.factory.config.Scope** interface and override the following methods:

- `Object get(String name, ObjectFactoryobjectFactory)`
- `Object remove(String name)`
- `void registerDestructionCallback(String name, Runnable destructionCallback)`
- `String getConversationId()`

When does the instantiation process take place by the container? Whether the bean is initialized eagerly or lazily?

By default, the Spring container (**ApplicationContext** implementation) eagerly creates the instance for each one of the configured bean.

Is it possible to change the default mechanism of bean instantiation?

Again, this question can be reframed differently as follows:

- **Can we instruct the container for lazy initialization?**
- **How is the lazy initialization configured?**

The default mechanism of eager initialization can be changed by configuring the **lazy-init** attribute in XML configuration. The configuration can be written as follows:

```
1.  <bean id="valid_bean_id" class="fully_qualified_class_name"
2.       lazy-init="true">
3.  <property  name="name_of_data_member"  value="value_of_the_data_
    member"/>
4.  <bean>
```

Can a bean be initialized lazily? Is it possible to control lazy initialization at the controller layer?

Yes, it is possible to initialize beans lazily at the container level.

In your opinion, which initialization is desired, eager or lazy, and why?

The errors in the configuration or problems in environment can be discovered immediately at the time of XML configuration instead of discovering the issues in the later phase. Under the situation when it is not desired to create an instance eagerly, we can configure the attribute **lazy-init=true** to create the instance when asked.

What is auto-wiring? Can we use auto-wiring for primary dependencies?

Usually, while defining the bean configuration, we need to mention all the dependencies of the bean explicitly. **Auto-wiring** facilitates us to inject the object dependencies explicitly automatically.

Auto-wiring is used for a has-a-kind relation where one object needs to be injected in another. It is not applicable to primary dependencies of an object of type **int**, **float**, **long,** and so on as well as dependencies of type String.

What are the types of auto-wiring, and how to configure them?

Different types of auto-wiring are:

- **no**: The default mode of auto-wiring is no. It means the developer needs to mention a way to inject the required object dependencies implicitly.

- **byName**: The *byName* auto-wiring mode facilitates the injection of the missing object depending upon the name of data member.

- **byType**: The *byType* auto-wiring mode facilitates the injection of the missing object depending upon the type of data member.

- **constructor**: The *constructor* auto-wiring mode injects the dependency by calling the parameterized constructor of that class.

Explain the bean life cycle

The interviewer might ask the following questions on the similar concepts:

- **What are the callback methods in bean life cycle?**

- **Is it possible to customize the nature of bean?**

Yes, certain callbacks can be used to customize the bean nature. The following figure shows the life cycle of bean:

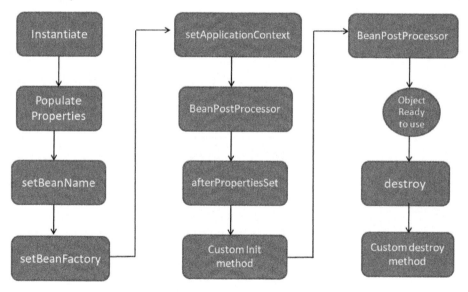

Figure 13.2: Spring life cycle

Is it possible to set some mechanism to modify the bean properties after its instantiation?

This question can take multiple forms as follows:

- **What is use of init-method attribute?**

- **When we can use the InitializingBean interface?**

- **What is the use of InitializingBean?**

After instantiation, in case we need to modify the properties of the bean, then we can use the `init` method.

There are different ways to do this:

1. Declare a public void method with no arguments in the class and use the attribute `init-method=method_name`.

2. We can implement the `InitializingBean` interface in the class and override the `afterPropertiesSet` method to modify the properties of the bean.

3. Alternatively, we can write a generic method and annotate it by @ `PostConstruct`.

Using init-method as an attribute and the InitializingBean interface are two ways for modifying the bean properties after instantiation. Which one is preferable?

I will not say good or bad, rather I would put some points that will help to take decision which one to choose. A good thing about implementing the interface is that we do not need to specify the method to be invoked by the container after instantiation of the bean. But, at the same time, we need to remember one thing. When we implement an interface, the code is tightly coupled.

At the same time, if we are writing an X,ML-based configuration we can use `init-method`. The configuration file can be changed at any moment. So, it is a good choice, if we do not want to prefer tightly coupled classes.

Can we have custom cleanup methods?

This question can be reframed in different flavors as:

- **Is it possible to write a method that will release resources before destroying the bean?**

- **What is the use of destroy-method attribute? Why to use the DisposableBean interface?**

- **Can you tell an elegant way to provide a cleanup mechanism?**

Yes, we can have custom cleanup mechanism.

This cleanup method allows a developer to provide a way to close all the open resources or to perform some back steps before the container containing the bean is destroyed.

There are three ways by which the cleanup mechanism can be provided:

1. In a class, provide a void no argument cleanup method and configure `destroy-method=method_name` for the bean configuration in XML.

2. The second way to achieve this is by implementing the **DisposableBean** interface by a class and overriding the destroy method to provide the cleanup mechanism.

3. Alternatively, we can also write a general method and annotate it by **@ PreDestroy**

Providing each time init-method or destroy-method in every individual bean configuration is repetitive as well as time-consuming. Can we have an alternative way to provide default initialization or destroy method?

Yes, configuring each bean for initializing and destroy method is repetitive. To avoid this, we can add the same methods in every class, which will represent the **init()** and **destroy()** methods. Now, we can configure the attribute **default-init-method="method-name"** or **default-destroy-method="method-name"** in the **<beans>** configuration by the names of the method that we have declared with the classes.

ApplicationContextAware, BeanFactoryAware, or BeanNameAware are used for?

Sometimes, beans need to access the **ApplicationContext** to look up for some other beans. **ApplicationContextAware**, **BeanFactoryAware** allow to look up for the configured bean.

Sometimes, the beans expects that the **BeanFactory** should be aware of their name. In such case, the class can implement **BeanNameAware**.

What is the parent attribute in the bean configuration used for?

This question can be reframed as:

- **Why to use the "parent" attribute?**

- **Explain the use of the "parent" attribute.**

Spring always supports reduction in boilerplate code. And, it is applicable even to an XML configuration. Suppose we have two bean definitions whose properties are same along with their values. Instead of repeating the same configuration, we can reuse first in another by providing the **parent** attribute. We can either use all the property values from the parent, but at the same time, overriding values for a couple of properties is also allowed.

The best part is, the child bean definition inherits scope, method overrides from the parent, constructor argument values, along with property values, and the option to add new values is still open.

XML and annotation based are two different ways of configuration; which one do you prefer?

Both of these approaches are available, and both have some pros and cons. It totally depends upon the situation/scenario which one is better and which is not.

An XML-based configuration is decoupled from the source code. So, one can modify the configuration without touching the source code.

When we use annotation-based configuration, it provides a context in the declaration. No extra configuration file needs to be maintained. Annotation-based configuration is more concise.

One more thing to consider is XML enables placing the configuration at a centralized location. It means controlling the changes become easier. However, when we use annotations for the configuration, they are distributed all over the code and then to control such a decentralized configuration.

Are the annotations by default enabled?

Or interviewer might ask:

- **How to enable annotation-based configurations?**

When we consider an XML-based configuration, annotations are disabled. When we want to enable annotations, we need to configure `<context:annotation-config>` or `<context:component-scan>` on top of our XML file.

Both <context:annotation-config> and <context:component-scan>, which are written on the top of our XML file, activate annotation-based configurations. Are they same? Or, are they different?

The `<context:annotation-config>` annotation is mainly used to enable the annotations for the dependency injections. The configuration activates the annotations for the beans that are already registered in the application context.

The configuration `<context:component-scan>` scan the packages to detect the annotations from the classes.

Which annotation activates package scanning for annotation?

This can be also asked as:

- **What is achieved by applying the @ComponantScan annotation?**

@ComponantScan allows scanning of packages to for the classes and interfaces for the annotations applied for stereotype and auto-wiring.

Explain stereotype annotation?

Stereotype annotations, when applied to a class, register it in the application context. As the class is registered in the context, it is now available for dependency injection in the other classes.

Which are the stereotype annotations? Explain different stereotype annotations in Spring

The following are the different stereotype annotations present in the Spring framework.

- **@Component**: This is a generic annotation that can be applied to any Spring-managed component.

- **@Service**: This annotation is applied to the classes that perform some business logic or API calls to perform some functionalities.

- **@Controller**: This annotation is applied to the classes that are responsible for handling an Http request and responses.

- **@Repository**: The **@Repository** annotation is applied to the classes that are involved in database communication.

Explain @Configuration

The **@Configuration** is a class-level annotation. When a class is applied with **@Configuration**, it indicates that a class is used by the Spring container as the source for bean definitions.

Explain @Bean configuration

The **@Bean** annotation is applied to the methods. The annotation indicates that the bean returned from this method is registered with the Spring context.

Why to use @Autowired? Explain the @Autowired annotation

This annotation is used for auto-wiring of the dependencies. **@Autowired** can be used on data member, constructor, or setter functionality.

When to use the @Qualifier annotation? What does the @Qualifier annotation signify?

The **@Autowired** annotation when applied to the dependency usually indicates auto-wiring by type. **@Qualifier** is applied when we want the name of the property to be used for discovering the missing property for injection. (It is same as **autowire=byName.**)

What does the @Required annotation signify?

@Required is a method-level annotation. When it is applied on a setter method, it indicates that the property must be injected to the bean at the time of configuration.

Are @Autowired and @Required same? Which one is recommended to use?

@Autowired and **@Required** annotations plays different roles in a Spring-based application.

- **@Autowired** is used for denoting the auto-wiring of the dependencies. However, **@Required** is useful to check whether the property has been set or not.

- **@Autowired** can be applied to data member, constructor, or setter functionality, but **@Required** is applied to setter methods.

- When **@Autowired** is applied on a dependency, it indicates the injection of the property. If the dependency is not discovered or available, then exception will be thrown. Under the uncertain situation when it is not must to inject the bean, we can configure **@Autowired(required=false)** to overlook the default behavior of injection.

Why to use the @Scope annotation?

By default, beans configured in spring are singleton. When the developers want to change the default scope, the class is applied with the annotation as **@ Scope("prototype")**.

Can you explain some features of Spring MVC framework?

1. It is designed around the front controller MVC design pattern.

2. It supports clear separation of the roles with Controllers, Validators, Model and View objects.

3. Easy binding and validation of the data.

4. Provides JSTL tags for easy binding of the data

Explain Spring MVC framework

The Spring MVC framework can be explained with the help of *Figure 13.3*:

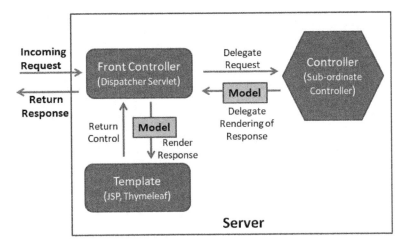

***Figure 13.3:** Spring MVC framework*

Spring MVC is designed around the front controller MVC design pattern. Each time a request is made, it is attended by the front controller. Depending upon the request pattern, the request is delegated to the respective controllers. The controller is responsible for reading the data from the incoming request and then performing logic on it. Once the logical part is done, it is time to communicate the response with the user. The data that the controller wants to send to the user is bounded to a Model object. This Model object now will be bounded in the view template by the front controller. This response containing template with data is returned to the user.

Please explain the components of the Spring MVC design pattern

Spring MVC is designed around the front controller MVC design pattern. MVC stands for model view and controller.

- *Model* is an object with data. This data may be fetched from the database or an object created using some logic.

- *View* is played by a simple JSP containing JSTL code; it can also be of the **Thymeleaf** template.

- *Controller* is a class annotated by **@Controller** responsible for handling request and generating a model which the bounded in view.

- The front controller is the most important part of the framework, which attends all the incoming requests and then delegates them to the subsequent controller. The front controller is also responsible for returning the response back to the user. **DispatcherServlet** provided by the Spring framework acts as the front controller.

Which annotations have you worked with while dealing with the Spring MVC framework?

Different annotations that are present in Spring MVC framework are:

- **@Controller**: The class that handles an Http request and response is annotated by *@Controller*.

- **@RequestMapping:** This annotation is used to map Web requests onto specific handler classes and/or handler methods where some logic is performed so as to generate some data that can be returned back as a response.

- **@Valid**: This annotation is applied to an input parameter whose validation needs to be performed.

- **@ModelAttribute**: This annotation is applied to a method parameter or the returned value from a method. The annotated parameter is then exposed to the Web view.

How does the front controller the controller to delegate the request?

The front controller is mapped in **web.xml** or Deployment Descriptor(DD) with the **<servlet>** tag. The mapping to discover the controllers to dispatch the request is available in **WEB-INF/servlet_name-servlet.xml** file.

Note: Try to hold yourself from giving more information on mapping. Do not go ahead with mapping.

You just told the request mapping is available in WEB-INF/servlet_name-servlet.xml file. Is this location fixed? Can we change the location or name of the file?

By default, the **WEB-INF/servlet_name-servlet.xml** file is the location. However, it is possible to change the location or even name of the file. We can configure the **init** parameter to the **<servlet>** tag in DD to change the location as:

```
1.  <init-param>
2.  <param-name>contextConfigLocation</param-name>
3.  <param-value>
4.     /WEB-INF/sub_folder_name/file_name_with_extension
```

```
5.    </param-value>
6.    </init-param>
```

Did you configure <load-on-startup>1</load-on-startup>?

What <load-on-startup>1</load-on-startup> does?

The tag `<load-on-startup>` in DD specifies whether the servlet will be loaded at the project deployment time or server start. The container loads the servlets in ascending order of the integer values, which are declared within the `<load-on-startup>` tag. If we do not specify this tag, then the servlets will be loaded on demand.

Which are the different beans contained within WebApplicationContext?

The following beans are present in **WebApplicationContext**:

- **HandlerMapping**: This bean is responsible for mapping the incoming request to the respective handlers.

- **ViewResolver**: This bean helps in resolving local name to the actual view file name. **ViewResolver** defines the prefix and postfix attributes, which can be applied to local file name, based on which the actual view file is located by framework.

Did you work with message resource bundle? What is its use?

Yes, I did. **ResourceBundleMessageSource** helps in resolving the messages from the properties file. This implements **MessageSource** and uses **ResourceBundle**. One of the main uses of **ResourceBundleMessage** is to store the messages that can be used in the process of internationalization.

Did you work with validation? What are the ways of providing validation? Why do we need validation?

Interaction with a user is what software is meant for. The user interacts with software by providing some inputs, based on which software generates some output. But, whenever a user inputs some data, there are chances of irrelevant data being entered by the user. For example, let us say the application expects to enter the email address from a user, and the user does not provide email address in a proper format, or imagine you ask a user to enter age and the user enters a value less than 0 or greater than 100. In these cases, the business logic that is written (assuming user is smart) will fail. So, there has to be a way to ensure the correctness of the user's data. The process to ensure this correctness is validation. Validation can be done at the client or server side. Client-side validation can be done using JavaScript. Spring provides **Validators** to perform server-side validations.

In case of writing custom validators, we need to write a class implementing **Validator** and override the **support** and **validate** methods. The **support** method checks if the object that we want to validate is of the expected type or not. The **validate** method has the logic to apply validation rules. To perform such validation, **validator** has to be registered to the container as a bean.

Writing a custom validator is one of the ways to perform validation. Another way to perform validation is to use Hibernate validators. We can apply **@NotNull, @Min, @Max, @Size** annotations to the POJO data members. Now, we can use *@Valid* annotation to the argument of the request handler method of the controller that we want to validate.

What is AOP?

AOP is **Aspect-Oriented Programming** to write cross cutting concerns and facilitates getting rid from code duplication.

Under which circumstances will you prefer AOP? What are the use cases to choose AOP? Can you explain the situations to refer AOP?

The most important responsibility of the developer is to provide a confined solution to the client to solve a certain issue or problem. Along with developing the solution, the developer also needs to think and implement the exception handling, transaction management, and logging. These concerns are distributed through all the layers of the application and lead to duplication of the code. AOP allows us to write the code at one place, and according to *pointcut*, it will be applied on to the join point.

Explain the concepts of AOP

AOP consists of different terminologies as:

- **Aspects**: Aspect is a component containing cross-cutting concerns such as transaction management or logging.

- **JoinPoint**: A point in the application where the aspect can be applied.

- **Advice**: Advice is the action to be taken on a particular JoinPoint.

- **PointCut**: An expression that allows selection of the JoinPoint where the advice is to be applied.

- **Target Object**: The object on which the advice is going to be applied is a target object.

- **Weaving**: It is the process of linking aspects with other application objects to create an advised object.

What is an advice, and what type of advice are available?

Advice is the action to be taken on a particular *JoinPoint*.

Types of advices:
- **Before advice**: Advice that executes before the join point.

- **After advice**: Advice that executes after the join point.

- **After returning advice**: Advice that executes after the join point completes normally.

- **After throwing advice**: Advice that executes after the method throws an exception.

- **Around advice**: The advice executes before and after the join point.

In what ways weaving can be done? Which types of weaving are supported by Spring AOP?

Weaving can be done at compile time, load time, or runtime. Spring AOP performs runtime weaving.

Explain how to write the pointcut expression using a couple of examples. Can you write pointcut expression to track all the methods from the package com.dao?

We can write the pointcut expressions such as:

- **@Pointcut("execution(public * *(..))")** is used for tracking all the join point from all the methods from all the packages.

- **@Pointcut("within(com.dao.MyClass.*(..))")** is used for tracking join points for all the methods from the class com.dao.MyClass.

- **@Pointcut("within(com.dao.*.*(..))")** expression to track all the methods from the package com.dao.

You can refer to the following expressions to write pointcut as well:

- Any public method: *execution*(public * *(..))

- Any method with a name beginning with "set": *execution*(* set*(..))

- Any method with a name beginning with "get": *execution*(* get*(..))

- Any method defined by the MyService interface:
  execution(* com.service.MyService.*(..))

- Any method defined in the dao package or a sub-package:
  execution(* com.dao..*.*(..))

- Any join point within the dao package:*within*(com.dao.*)

- Any join point within the dao package or a sub-package:*within*(com.dao..*)

- Any join point where the proxy implements the MyService interface:

- this(com.xyz.service.AccountService)

Explain the pointcut designators you have used, or explain the pointcut designators you know

I have worked with the different pointcut designators as:

- **execution**: The execution designator is used for matching method execution join points.

- **within**: To limit matching to join points within certain types such as packages, the within designator is used.

- **this**: It is used to limit matching to join points where the bean reference is an instance of the given type.

- **target**: The target designator is used to limit matching to join points where the target object is an instance of the given type.

- **@target**: The @target annotation limits matching to join points where the class of the executing object has an annotation of the given type.

- **@args**: The annotation limits matching to join points where the runtime type of the actual arguments passed has annotations of the given type.

- **@within**: The designator limits matching to join points within types that have the @within annotation

- **@annotation**: This annotation is used to limit matching to join points where the subject of the join point has the given annotation.

Can you explain Around advice?

This question can also be re-framed as:

- **In what ways does Around advice differ from other advices?**
- **When can we use Around advice?**

Around advice runs at matched point cut. It enables to perform the work both before and after the method execution. It also allows us to determine when and how the method actually gets executed. It is said to be powerful whenever we need to share the state. The around advice is often used whenever we need to share the state before the method execution and then after a method execution. For example, it can used to calculate the time taken to complete the method execution.

Did you work with Spring Boot? Explain Spring Boot. What is Spring boot?

Spring Boot is Java-based framework that facilitates creation of production-grade standalone as well as Web application.

Can you tell us some features of Spring Boot?

Spring boot has different features as:

- It helps or facilitates the creation of standalone as well as Web applications.

- It provides inbuilt support for servers like *Tomcat, Jetty, Underflow* directly.

- It enables the features such as *Metrics Creation, Health Checks* to create production-ready applications.

- Allows externalizing application supports that help in managing application from a single point.

- The application can be configured from simple properties file instead of XML-based configuration.

- It provides many starters for enabling easy application configuration.

Did you work with Spring Boot projects? Which starters you worked with?

Yes, I have worked with following Spring Boot starters:

- `spring-boot-starter`
- `spring-boot-starter-web`
- `spring-boot-starter-jdbc`
- `spring-boot-starter-data-jpa`
- `spring-boot-starter-hateoas`
- `spring-boot-starter-security`
- `spring-boot-starter-data-rest`

Note: If you did not work with all of them, then do not worry. You can only list of all the starters and then let interviewer know that though you know the list, you have worked with only a couple of them.

There are many ways to create Spring Boot applications. How many have you worked with? Can you tell us the ways of creating a Spring Boot project?

The Spring Boot application can be created by:

- Spring Initializer
- Spring Boot CLI
- Spring Tool suites

Which annotations have you worked for creating REST applications?

This question can be also reframed as:

- Can you explain the couple of annotations used in REST applications?
- Explain annotations used for REST application development?

Different annotations that are used in REST applications are:

- **@RestController**: It provides a convenient way to declare a class responsible for creating *REST* Web services. The annotation is introduced in 4.0, which combines **@Controller** and **@ResponseBody**.

- **@RequestMapping**: **@RequestMapping** is very commonly used annotation. It allows mapping HTTP requests to handler methods of REST controllers.

- **@GetMapping**: The annotation enables mapping HTTP GET requests to specific handler methods. It is a shortcut for **@RequestMapping(method = RequestMethod.GET)**.

- **@PostMapping, @PutMapping, @DeleteMapping,** and **@PatchMapping** are the annotations introduced for mapping method handlers for POST, PUT, DELETE, and PATCH methods.

- **@ResponseBody**: The **@ResponseBody** annotation tells a controller that the object returned is automatically serialized into JSON and passed back into the response object.

Can you explain about the @PutMapping and @ PatchMapping annotations?

This can be also reframed as:

- **Can you explain when to use the PUT and PATCH methods?**

We can create different methods that will represent PUT and PATCH methods. And, we can apply **@PutMapping** and **@PatchMapping** on those methods, respectively.

Whenever we have a resource and a client needs to replace the existing resource entirely, it is feasible to use the **PUT** method.

Whenever we have a resource and a client needs to replace the existing resource partially, it is feasible to use **HTTP PATCH.**

Which are the annotations to map handler methods?

Different annotations that can be used to map handler methods are:

- The **@GetMapping** annotation enables mapping HTTP GET requests to specific handler methods. It is a shortcut for **@RequestMapping(method = RequestMethod.GET)**.

- The **@PostMapping, @PutMapping, @DeleteMapping,** and **@PatchMapping** are the annotations introduced for mapping method handlers for POST, PUT, DELETE, and PATCH methods.

What are runners in Boot?

You can get different questions in connection with this question:

- **Which runners does Spring Boot provide?**
- **What is CommnadlineRunner?**
- **Can you create a standalone application using Spring Boot?**
- **How to create a standalone application in Spring Boot?**

Runner is an interface that facilitates the execution of the code after the application starts. Spring Boot provides **ApplicationRunner** and **CommandLineRunner**.

CommandLineRunner is an interface. It is used to indicate that a bean should run when it is contained within a **SpringApplication**. It allows creation of standalone applications.

How you can read the input from a request? Which annotations have you used to read request input?

We can read the input from request by using annotations like:

- **@RequestParam**: This annotation is used to read the data from request such as form data and then bind it automatically to the method argument.

- **@RequestBody**: This annotation maps the request body to *Transfer Domain Object* to the method argument of a type.

What is the difference between @RequestParam and @QueryParam?

Both of these annotations are used to read request parameters.

@QueryParam is an annotation provided by the JAX-RS framework, and **@RequestParam** is an annotation from the Spring framework.

Did you work with Spring Boot's internal database?

The answer to this question will be followed by different questions like:

- **How to configure H2 database?**
- **Is it good to use H2 DB?**
- **When and how to use H2 DB?**

H2 is an in-memory database written in Java. It can be embedded in Java applications. Spring Boot supports integration of H2 in Spring Boot application.

To configure H2 in Spring Boot, we need to add H2 dependency in the **pom.xml** file and then configure database properties in the **application.properties** file. Now, configure, **spring.h2.console.enabled=true** and *spring.h2.console.path=/h2* in the properties file. Sometimes, installing a DB on a system is not possible or not feasible. Then, we can use an internal DB for testing the code without having to worry about installing and managing a dedicated database server upfront.

When H2 is going to be used for production as well, using H2 is a better choice. However, when we are using a different DB in production, testing code against H2 is a bad choice.

How to execute database schemas to create a table or insert records in table?

Spring Boot allows an easy way to create a table and manipulate data in it. To do this, you can create **.sql** files containing DML or DDL statements to execute. You have to create this file in directory **/src/main/resources/**.

The file will be loaded at startup and executed to create a table or insert records in it according to SQL statements written within it.

What is the use of *RestTemplate*? How to use *RestTemplate*?

- **RestTemplate** is used for consuming REST applications. **RestTemplate** provides different methods for Web communication as follows:

- **exchange**: This method executes a specified HTTP method as GET or POST, and it returns **ResponseEntity**. **ResponseEntity** can contain HTTP status code, the resource as an object, or both.

- **execute**: This method expects **RequestCallback** and a **ResultSetExtractor** as parameters. It facilitates creation of complex requests or may process complex responses.

- **getForEntity**: This method executes a GET request and returns **ResponseEntity** containing the status code and the resource as an object.

- **getForObject**: This method executes a GET request and returns the resource directly.

Note: Though this answer is enough, you can add the extra spoon of sugar by adding information as: Same as getForEntity and getForObject for GET, we have counterpart methods for post and put.

What is HATEAOS?

HATEAOS is acronym for *Hypertext As the Engine of Application State.*

Usually, in HTML pages, we can place a hyperlink to browse or link in between two resources. In a Web service, response linking in two resources is provided by HATEAOS. It facilitates creating links between two resources to retrieve relevant information. It enables creating links for model classes for link and resource representation models. It supports the APIs for link builders to create links which point to the methods declared in Spring MVC controller.

How to provide HATEAOS support in an application?

To enable *HATEAOS*, we have to follow different steps as:

- Add dependency for *HATEAOS* in the **pom.xml** file.

- Create POJO class extended by **RepresentationModel**.

- In the controller, create the links between resources by using the **linkTo()** method of **WebMvcLinkBuilder**.

What is Swagger, and why to use it?

In REST applications, there are many handler methods mapped for different request parameters and response types. It is important to properly communicate the REST API documentation to the client. **Swagger2** is an open-source project that is used to generate the REST API documentation. It also provides a user interface to access our RESTful Web services via the Web browser.

Finally, this interesting journey had reached to the destination. The Spring framework is huge in size, and the features to cover in a single chapter is difficult. But, we have covered almost every concept that may be required to answer the questions based on Spring and Spring Boot.

Conclusion

In this chapter, we explored the entire Spring framework. We discussed about different component of the Spring framework and what interview questions could be asked on those components. We also discussed through different questions how spring is useful in application development and how we can customize the behavior of an application using XML files and annotations.

We also talked about how Spring Boot helps to create a REST-based Web application, which is becoming the need of the current era of software development.

In the next chapter, we will be expanding our knowledge to understand another interesting framework, Hibernate. We will discuss how an interviewer will test your skills on Hibernate.

CHAPTER 14
Hibernate

Introduction

Storing data in database is one of the most important aspects of application development. Whatever may be the type of the application, we need to store the data permanently. In our earlier chapter of *JDBC*, we have seen how to store the data in the database using the *JDBC API*. You are also well aware that writing the *JDBC* code is not a cake piece. Often, the developers get frustrated by writing the boiler-plated code to implement different interfaces that are part of *JDBC API*. The *Hibernate* framework is for rescue. It provides a simplified way to persist the data into database. *Hibernate* uses a Java object to represent data, which is mapped with a table where it can be persisted. This approach of storing object to database is termed as **Object Relational Mapping (ORM)**, and *Hibernate* is one of the implementation of it. *Hibernate* makes the job of a developer way simpler by providing configuration to achieve object persistency. We can configure *Hibernate* by writing, and we can also make the use of different annotations provided by the *Hibernate API*.

Structure

Hibernate provides an automotive way to persist the data to database through the concept of *ORM*. Instead of writing the code of the JDBC API, the developer can make the use of XML configuration or annotations that are provided by the *Hibernate* framework. In this chapter, we will discuss:

- The architecture of *Hibernate*
- Working of the *Hibernate* framework
- Different interview questions along with their answers that could be asked in a *Hibernate* interview

Objective

At the end of this chapter, you will be able to understand the automotive approach of persistency, Hibernate. You will be able to work with different configuration settings of Hibernate and also annotations that are used in this framework. Along with this, we will also discuss different interview questions based on Hibernate.

What is ORM?

ORM is Object Relational Mapping.

Which are the different frameworks that support ORM?

ORM tools like *Hibernate*, *TopLink*, and *iBatis* provide an implementation of JPA specifications for data persistency.

What are the features of ORM? How ORM helps developers?

The following are the different features are ORM:

- ORM helps in fast application development.
- ORM takes away all the crude-level details.
- Makes it easy to map inheritance, collection management.
- It manages the transaction.

Are there any drawbacks of ORM or Hibernate?

Though ORM provides many features for an application developer, it has some drawbacks as:

- Development is faster, but the application performance is slower than traditional *JDBC*.

- Debugging of the application becomes difficult.

- Hibernate does not allow multiple inserts.

- It advisable to use pure *JDBC* for batch processing as *Hibernate*. Performance of Hibernate is not good in batch processing.

- The learning curve of *Hibernate* is bit time-consuming.

Explain the architecture of Hibernate?

The following figure shows the different components of *Hibernate* framework:

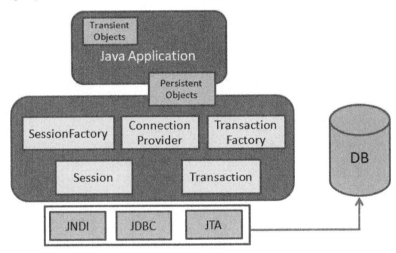

Figure 14.1: *Architecture of Hibernate*

As shown in *Figure 14.1*, the *Hibernate* framework consists of different components as:

- SessionFactory

- Connection Provider

- Transaction Factory

- Session

- Transaction

What is Hibernate? Are JPA and hibernate same or different?

Java Persistence API (JPA) is a specification facilitates accessing, managing, persisting an object to the database. JPA is provides an API and does not provide any implementation and so it requires an implementation.

The ORM tools like *Hibernate, TopLink,* and *iBatis* provides an implementation of *JPA* specifications for data persistency.

Hibernate and JPA are related with each other, but they have some fundamental differences as follows:

Hibernate	JPA
Hibernate is an ORM tool that is used to save the state of an object into the database.	JPA defines the API for managing the relational data in the Java applications.
It uses a `SessionFactory` interface to create Session instances.	It uses the `EntityManagerFactory` interface to interact with the entity manager factory for the persistence unit.
It uses the **Hibernate Query Language** (**HQL**) as an object-oriented query language to perform database operations.	It uses **Java Persistence Query Language** (**JPQL**) as an object-oriented query language to perform database operations.

Table 14.1: Difference between Hibernate and JPA

Explain the interfaces or core components you worked with in Hibernate

The core interfaces of the Hibernate framework are:

- **Configuration**: An instance of *Configuration* facilitates the application to specify properties and mapping documents, which can be used to create **SessionFactory**. Usually, in an application, we create a single *Configuration* to build a single instance of **SessionFactory**. By default, a new *Configuration* will be created from the properties, which are specified in the **hibernate. properties** file.

- **SessionFactory**: Usually, an application has a single **SessionFactory** instance, and the threads those are servicing client requests obtain *Session* instances from this factory.

- The internal state of a **SessionFactory** is always immutable. Once an instance is created, this internal state is set, which includes the metadata about Object/Relational Mapping.

- **Session**: The main purpose of the *Session* is to offer means for creating, reading, and deleting operations for instances of mapped entity classes.

- **Query**: The session interface facilitates to perform CRUD operation, which are performed on database using PK. The Query interface on the other hand provides a way to retrieve the rows without using PK. The Query interface provides the methods such as **executeUpdate()**, **list()**, `setMaxResult(), setFirstResult()` methods to perform operation on DB for processing the data.

The following code snippet describes how to create and use the Query object:

```
Query query=session.createQuery("from Employee");
Query q=session.createQuery("select sum(salary) from Employee");
```

- **Criteria**: **Criteria** helps in building the criteria query objects dynamically. It facilitates another way of data retrieval apart from *HQL* and native SQL queries. The *Criteria* API is designed to manipulate data without using any hardcoded SQL statements.

The following code snippet describes how to create and use a Criteria object:

```
Criteria c2 = session.createCriteria(Employee.class);
c2.add(Restrictions.like("empName", "ABC"));
c2.add(Restrictions.like("projectName","%Java%"));
```

- **Transaction**: Transaction allows the application to define units of work by maintaining abstraction from the underlying transaction implementation such as *JTA, JDBC*. An instance of transaction is associated with a *Session* and is usually instantiated by a call to **Session.beginTransaction()**.

In how many ways a class can be mapped to table/tables? How hibernate does mapping of object to the table?

Hibernate maps a class to the table. We can use two different approaches to do this mapping. Firstly by configuring it in the **XXX.hbm.xml** file and by using predefined annotations on the POJO class.

Which files are needed to maintain the configuration in Hibernate?

Hibernate needs information about how to communicate to the DB and how a class is to be mapped with a table in DB. To achieve this, *Hibernate* uses the **hibernate.cfg.xml** file to configure the properties used to communicate with DB. And, the **XXX.hbm.xml** (*Hibernate Bean Mapping*) file helps in mapping a class to the table.

Can we change the name of the hibernate.cfg. xml file?

By default, **hibernate.cfg.xml** from class path is used to obtain the instance of *Configuration*. However, it is possible to change the location as well as a different name to the file.

We can use the following syntax to use another file name:

```
Configuration configuration = new Configuration();
configuration.configure("New_File_Name.cfg.xml");
```

How to obtain SessionFactory?

We can obtain **SessionFactory,** as shown in the following code snippet:

```
Configuration configuration = new Configuration();
SessionFactory factory=configuration.configure().buildSessionFactory();
```

How many SessionFactory objects are usually created and can be used by a developer in an application?

This question can be reframed as:

- **How many times have you created an instance of SessionFactory?**

- **It is a usual process to create and use a single instance of SessionFactory per database in Hibernate, can you tell us the reason?**

Usually, in an application, a single database is more than sufficient for persistency. However, in some situations, more than one database are used in the application.

- **SessionFactory** is a heavyweight object, and creating more than instance in an application may affect the application performance, so it is recommended to use one instance per application.

- However, *Hibernate* supports configuring more than one databases to work with within the same application.

- If we want to configure more than one database within the application, you need to simply add more configuration files, as one configuration file is used to obtain a single instance of **SessionFactory**.

- The following code can be used to work with two databases.

- The default **hibernate.cfg.xml** for first database can be used for obtaining an instance of **SessionFactory** as:

```
Configuration configuration = new Configuration();
SessionFactory factory=configuration.configure().
buildSessionFactory();
```

The second database can be configured to obtain another **SessionFactory** instance in the same application as:

```
Configuration configuration1 = new Configuration();
SessionFactory factory1=configuration1.configure().
                                      buildSessionFactory();
```

Can we communicate with two different databases in an application using Hibernate? How to create two session factories in Hibernate?

Yes, *Hibernate* supports configuring and using more than one databases within the same application.

The default **hibernate.cfg.xml** for first database can be used for obtaining an instance of **SessionFactory** as:

```
Configuration configuration = new Configuration();
SessionFactory factory=configuration.configure().buildSessionFactory();
```

The second database can be configured to obtain another **SessionFactory** instance in the same application as:

```
Configuration configuration1 = new Configuration();
SessionFactory factory1=configuration1.configure().
                                      buildSessionFactory();
```

Is SessionFactory a thread-safe object?

Yes, **SessionFactory** is a thread-safe object; many threads cannot access it simultaneously.

Is Session a thread-safe object?

No, **Session** is not a thread-safe object; many threads can access it simultaneously. In other words, you can share it between threads.

Please explain the phases of an entity. What is a detached entity? What are the states of an object?

The following figure shows the different phases of an entity:

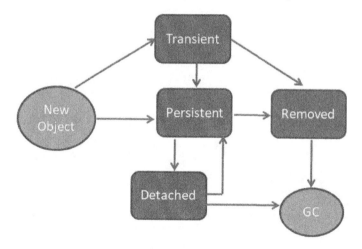

Figure 14.2: Phases of Entity

- **New Object**: The new object state is achieved by the methods like **get()**, **load()**, **uniqeResult**, **iterate()**, and **scroll()**. This newly created object is ready for persistency.

- **Transient state**: The object is in a transient state if it is just created but has no identifier or PK in a table. It does not associate with a session.

- **Persistent state**: The Session object invokes the methods like **save()**, **saveOrUpdate()** on a transient object to convert the transient object to persistent object. In the persistent state, an object in application represents a row in the database within a live session. In this state, it is associated with a unique **Session**. Or, the object is in a persistent state if a session is open, and you just saved the instance in the database or retrieved the instance from the database.

- **Detached state**: In the detached phase, an object in an application is not in live communication with the database. We can achieve this state by invoking the **evict()**, **clear()**, or **close()** method on the persisted object. The object is in a detached state if a session is closed. It is not possible to work with an object being in the detached phase. The object comes to the persistent state if we call the **lock()** or **update()** method.

- **Removed state**: The entity is pushed into removed state when the **delete()** method is invoked on it. The objects in this state are pushed to the garbage collector.

How to map a class to a table? Explain the annotations to map an entity to a row in table

Hibernate supports both XML- and annotation-based confirmation to map an entity to the table.

XML-based configuration:

```
<hibernate-mapping>
    <class name = "Employee" table = "EMPLOYEE">
        <id name = "name_of_data_memember_to_consider_as_
            PK" type = "data_type" column = "column_name">
          <generator class="generator_class_name"/>
        </id>
        <property name = "property_name" column = "column_name"
            type = "data_type"/>
    </class>
</hibernate-mapping>
```

Annotation-based configuration:

- Annotate the POJO class by, **@Entity.**

- Annotate the data member by **@Id,** which needs to be considered as PK in the table.

- Other data members by default become the columns of the table. By default, the name of the data member is considered as name of column. However, the column name can be changed by annotating the data member by **@Column**. The annotation allows customizing properties such as **length**, **constraint**.

What does the @Id annotation do?

When we annotate the data member by **@Id**, that data member value is considered as a PK in the table.

What does @NaturalId do?

The **@Id** annotation is used to denote a data member as a PK. One has to use **@ID** along with **@GeneratedValue** to create primary keys for records in database. But sometimes, instead of using PK as identification, entity may use other property of itself, which can be treated as a natural ID. If you want to assign any property of entity as natural ID, then you can annotate it by **@NaturalId**.

Can you give any real-time example of @Id and @NaturalId?

If you consider the *Employee* entity, then **empId** will be always treated as a property, which is a primary key, which can be annotated by @Id. But, **emailAddress** connected with **Employee** will be also unique, and in some scenarios, the employee can be identified by his email address. So, the **emailAddress** property can be annotated by **@NaturalId**.

Is it possible to stop a data member from being persisted or ignore fields to save in the database?

Yes, it is possible to ignore one or more data members from being persisted in the database. To do this, we need to simply add **@Transient** to annotate a property or field of an entity class, mapped super class, or embeddable class. **@Transient** helps in ignoring field from adding in the DB.

What methods are provided by Session?

Different methods that are provided by **Session** are:

- **save(Object object):** The method saves the given transient instance.

- **saveOrUpdate(Object object):** The method enables either save the new instance or update the given instance in the table.

- **update(Object object):** The method enables updating the persistent instance with the identifier of the given detached instance.

- **delete(Object object):** This method enables removing a persistent instance from the datastore.

- **get(String entity_name, Serializable id):** This method returns the persistent instance of the given named entity with the given identifier. It may return *null* if there is no such persistent instance.

- **getTransaction():** This method gets the *Transaction* instance associated with the current *session*.

- **beginTransaction():** The method begins a unit of work and return the associated *Transaction* object.

- **createCriteria(String entity_name):** The method creates a new *Criteria* instance for the given entity name.

- **createQuery(String query_to_execute):** The method creates a new instance of *Query* for the specified HQL query string.

- **clear():** This method clears the session.

- **close():** This method allows to end the session by releasing the JDBC connection and cleaning up.

Explain the difference between persist() and save() of the Session interface?

The following are the differences between these two methods:

1. Both the methods enable inserting records into the database. However, the return type of **persist()** method is void while that of the **save()** method is a serializable object.

2. Both methods make a transient instance persistent. However, the **persist()** method does not guarantee that the identifier value will be assigned to the persistent instance immediately. It might be performing the assignment at the **flush()** time.

3. Both the methods behave differently on the outside of transaction boundaries. The **persist()** method guarantees that it will not execute an insert statement if it is called outside of transaction boundaries. However, the **save()** method does not guarantee the same; it returns an identifier. If an insertion has to be executed to get the identifier, the insertion happens immediately, no matter whether it is inside or outside of a transaction.

4. The **persist()** method outside the transaction boundary is useful in long-running conversations with an extended *Session* context. On the other hand, the **save()** method is not good in a long-running conversation with an extended **Session** context.

Explain the differences between the save(), saveOrUpdate(), and persist() method of Hibernate. Which one should we use?

- The **persist()** method is useful for adding a new entity instance to the persistence context. We usually invoke it when we want to add a record to the database, that is, when we want to persist an entity instance. The following code snippet shows how to use this method:

```
Employee emp=new Employee(12,"ABC","Java");

session.persist(emp);
```

  When the **persist()** method is invoked on an already persistent instance, nothing happens. When we try to persist a detached instance, the implementation is bound to throw an exception.

- The basic purpose of **save()** is the same as that of **persist()**. But, this method is guaranteed to return the serializable value of this identifier. The following code snippet shows how to use the **save()** method:

```
Employee emp=new Employee(12,"ABC","Java");

Long id= session.save(emp); //long is the data type of PK
```

  When we invoke **save()** on a detached instance, it creates a new persistent instance and assigns it a new identifier. It results in a duplicate record in a database upon committing or flushing.

- The **merge()** method is used to update a persistent entity instance with new field values from a detached entity instance. The **merge()** method finds an entity instance by ID taken from the already passed object and then copies its fields to this new instance. Finally, it returns newly updated instance. The following code snippet shows how to use the **merge()** method:

```
Employee emp=new Employee(12,"ABC","Java");

session.save(emp);

session.evict(emp);


emp.setName("new name");

Employee emp_new=(Employee)session.merge(emp);
```

- The **update()** method is used to update the data. The method acts upon the passed object. The **update()** method transits the already passed object from the detached to persistent state. The method throws an exception if you pass a transient entity to it. The following code snippet shows how to use the **update()** method:

```
Employee emp=new Employee(12,"ABC","Java");

session.save(emp);

session.evict(emp);


emp.setName("new name");

session.update(emp);
```

> **Note: We did not put the result of the update operation in a separate variable because the update takes place on the Employee object itself. It means, we are reattaching the existing entity instance to the persistence context.**

The **saveOrUpdate()** method is a more safe method. This method does not throw an exception when applied to a transient instance. In case we are not sure whether an identifier exists in the table, we can use the **saveOrUpdate()** method. It will add a new row in the table if one does not exist.

What will be the output of the following code?

```
Employee emp=new Employee(12,"ABC","Java");

emp.setName("new name");

session.update(emp);
```

The update call on a transient instance will result in an exception. So, when we run the above code, it will not work.

What is a difference between the get() and load() method?

Both the methods are actually used to pull the object. But, they have some differences as well. These differences are discussed in the following table:

load()	get()
If an object is not found, it throws ObjectNotFoundException.	If an object is not found, the method returns null.
The load() method does not hit the database.	The get() method always hit the database.
It returns the proxy object.	It returns the real object, not the proxy.
It should be used if you are sure that an instance exists.	It should be used if you are not sure about the existence of an instance.

Table 14.2: Difference between get() and load()

Do you know generator classes? How many generator classes have you worked with? Please explain generator classes in Hibernate

Every table in a database will have a primary key. Either the key is assigned by the application for that row, or it can be generated by the underlying database. It is used to generate the unique identifier for the objects of the persistent class. The `<generator>` element or `@GeneratedValue` can be used to generate the PK.

Which generator class has to be used is dependent on the underlying database. Hibernate supports `assigned`, `increment`, `sequence`, `hilo`, `native`, `identity`, `seqhilo`, `uuid`, `select`, `foreign`, `sequence-identity`.

We can use `@GeneratedValue(strategy = )` to generate a PK according to a strategy. We can specify strategies as:

- `GenerationType.AUTO`
- `GenerationType.IDENTITY`
- `GenerationType.SEQUENCE`
- `GenerationType.TABLE`

What does hibernate.hbm2ddl.auto mean?

The property `hbm2ddl.auto` is used to validate and export schema of DDL to the database when `SessionFactory` is created. The possible values are:

- **Create:** creates a schema
- **Update:** updates an existing schema
- **Validate:** validates existing schema
- **Create-drop:** creates and drops the schema automatically when a session starts and ends

What does hibernate.dialect do?

Hibernate takes away the responsibility of writing SQL queries from the developer. Instead of developer, Hibernate generates these queries. However, we cannot over look different data types and the way queries and procedures are written in SQL. The dialect specifies the type of database used in Hibernate to make sure appropriate generation of type of SQL statements. When we connect Hibernate to an application, it is essential to configure the dialect.

List the different mapping strategies to implement inheritance in Hibernate

We can map the hierarchical classified classes with the table of the database using one of the three inheritance mapping strategies:

- Table Per Class Hierarchy
- Table Per Concrete Class
- Table Per Subclass

How to map the Table Per Class Hierarchy, Table Per Concrete Class, and Table Per Subclass?

- **Table Per Class Hierarchy**: In the Table Per Class Hierarchy mapping, a single table is required to map the whole hierarchy. We specify an extra column in the configuration (discriminator column), which is added to identify the class. We can specify the discriminator column as through XML, or we can also provide annotation for it

    o XML file configuration:

    ```
    <discriminator column="type" type="string"></discriminator>
    ```

    ▪ By using annotations:

    ```
    @DiscriminatorColumn(name="type",
              discriminatorType=DiscriminatorType.STRING)
    @DiscriminatorValue(value="employee")
    ```

- **Table Per Concrete Class**: In case of Table Per Concrete Class, tables are created as per the class. Though the data is stored as per class definitions, always duplicate columns are added in subclass tables.

    The strategy can be mapped by two ways:

    o **Using the union-subclass element:**

    ```
    <class name="com.Employee" >
        <id name="id">
            <generator class="increment"></generator>
        </id>
        <property name="name"></property>
    ```

```
    <union-subclass name="com.Child_Employee1">
        <property name="salary"></property>
        <property name="projects"></property>
    </union-subclass>


    <union-subclass name="com.Child_Employee2" >
        <property name="wages_per_hour"></property>
        <property name="contract_duration"></property>
    </union-subclass>
</class>
```

o **Using the self-creating the table for each class:**

```
<class name="com.Employee" >
    <id name="id">
        <generator class="increment"></generator>
    </id>


    <property name="name"></property>
</class>
<class name="com.Child_Employee1">
    <id name="id">
        <generator class="increment"></generator>
    </id>
    <property name="name"></property>
    <property name="salary"></property>
    <property name="projects"></property>
</class>
<class name="com.Child_Employee2" >
    <id name="id">
        <generator class="increment"></generator>
    </id>
    <property name="name"></property>
    <property name="wages_per_hour"></property>
    <property name="contract_duration"></property>
</class>
```

We can also make the use of annotation to set up this relationship. To use the annotation-based configuration, specify **@Inheritance(strategy = InheritanceType.TABLE_PER_CLASS)**. The annotation denotes table per concrete class strategy. It should be specified in the parent class only. The **@AttributeOverrides** annotation defines parent class attributes is overridden in this child class. In the table structure, the parent class table columns will be added in the subclass table.

- **Table Per Subclass**: In this strategy, tables are created as per the class but related by foreign key. In Table Per Subclass, the subclass-mapped tables related to parent class mapped table are joined by the primary key–foreign key relationship.

  o **XML-based configuration**

   We need to use the **<joined-subclass>** element of class is used to map the child class with parent using the primary key and foreign key relation:

```
<class name="com.Employee" >
      <id name="id">
          <generator class="increment"></generator>
      </id>

      <property name="name"></property>

   <joined-subclass name="com.Child_Employee1" >
        <key column="empid"></key>
        <property name="salary"></property>
        <property name="projects"></property>
   </joined-subclass>

   <joined-subclass name="com.Child_Employee2">
        <key column="empid"></key>
        <property name="wages_per_hour"></property>
        <property name="contract_duration"></property>
   </joined-subclass>
</class>
```

  o **Annotation-based configuration**

   To use the annotation-based configuration, we need to specify **@Inheritance(strategy=InheritanceType.JOINED)** in the parent class and the **@PrimaryKeyJoinColumn** annotation in the subclasses.

Can you explain the advantages and disadvantages for inheritance mapping strategies?

The following are the advantages and disadvantages of each of the strategies:

1. **Table Per Class Hierarchy**

    Advantage

    This strategy offers the best performance even for in the deep hierarchy because single select is sufficient.

    Disadvantage

    Whenever there are changes to the members of the hierarchy, it requires the column to be altered, added, or removed from the table.

2. **Table Per Subclass**

    Advantages

    *   This strategy does not require complex changes to the database schema when a parent class is modified.

    *   It works well with shallow hierarchy.

    Disadvantages

    *   With growing hierarchy, it may result in poor performance.

    *   The number of joins required to construct a subclass also grows.

3. **Table Per Concrete Class**

    Advantage

    *   It is the easiest method of inheritance mapping to implement.

    Disadvantages

    *   The data belonging to a parent class is scattered and duplicated across a number of subclass tables, which represents the concrete classes.

    *   Whenever there are changes to a parent class, they are reflected to large number of tables.

    *   It causes a large number of select operations.

What are the different association models available in Hibernate?

The following are the different association models present in Hibernate:

- One-to-one
- Many-to-one
- One-to-many
- Many-to-many

Can you explain how to configure the many-to-one association with a relevant example?

The **many-to-one association** represents two-way relationships between entities where one object refers to multiple references of other object. And, the other object in turn can contain a single reference of the first object. The typical example of this pattern can be represented by Movie and Review. Movie can have multiple Reviews, whereas each Review entity can refer to a single Movie.

The following code snippet shows how to configure the class and Review classes to represent this association:

Movie.java

```
1. @Entity
2. public class Movie{
3.    @Id
4.    @GeneratedValue(strategy = GenerationType.AUTO)
5.    @Column(name = "id", updatable = false, nullable = false)
6.    private Long id;
7.
8.    @OneToMany(mappedBy = "movie")
9.    private List<Review> reviews = new ArrayList<Review>();
10. ...
11. }
```

Review.java

```
1. @Entity
2. public class Review {
```

```
3.    @Id
4.    @GeneratedValue(strategy = GenerationType.AUTO)
5.    @Column(name = "id")
6.    private Long id;
7.
8.    @ManyToOne
9.    @JoinColumn(name = "fk_movie")
10.   private Movie movie
11. ...
12. }
```

Note: This question can also be an answer for the question "How do you map collections in Hibernate?"

Can you explain what is a many-to-many association, and how can you configure that with some real-time example?

When one entity can refer multiple entities and in turn the other entity can also refer multiple references of first entity, such association is termed as many-to-many associations. A real-time example could be **Movie** and **Writer**. Movie can have multiple writers, and multiple writers can write multiple movies.

The following code snippet shows how to write configurations for the same:

Movie.java

```
1. @Entity
2. public class Movie{
3.    @Id
4.    @GeneratedValue(strategy = GenerationType.AUTO)
5.    @Column(name = "id", updatable = false, nullable = false)
6.    private Long id;
7.    @ManyToMany
8.    @JoinTable(
9.    name = "movie_writer",
10.   joinColumns = { @JoinColumn(name = "fk_movie") },
```

```
11.      private List<Writer> authors = new ArrayList<Writer>();
12....
13. }
```

Writer.java

```
1. @Entity
2. public class Writer {
3.    @Id
4.    @GeneratedValue(strategy = GenerationType.AUTO)
5.    @Column(name = "id")
6.    private Long id;
7.    @ManyToMany(mappedBy="movie_writer")
8.    private List<Movie> books = new ArrayList<Movie>();
9. ...
10. }
```

What is unidirectional and bidirectional mapping?

- **Unidirectional mapping**: As the name suggests, it is mapping in one direction. When only one of the entities contains a reference to the other, the association is unidirectional. When only one of the entity supports *"has-a"* kind of relation, it unidirectional mapping. It suggests we can fetch one instance from another, while another instance has no reference to the earlier. Let us consider *User* has an *Address*. The *User* instance can access *address*, update *address*. However, the *address* is not aware *User* is using *address* as the *address* model does not contain any reference to the *User* model.

- **Bidirectional mapping**: When the association between both entities are mutual, it is known as bidirectional mapping. In other words, when both the entities have reference to each other, it is termed as bidirectional mapping. It means one instance can fetch, update another instance easily. The bidirectional mapping provides the navigational access to the both directions. Let us consider the same example. *User* has an *Address*, and now, as we are using the bidirectional mapping, *Address* also has *User*. Both the *User* instance and *Address* can access and update each other.

One of the attribute of entity needs to be calculated by some expression. How can you map such attribute using Hibernate?

To achieve this, we can apply the *@Formula* annotation on that attribute. We can use either SQL expression or normal expression to generate value, which can be used by *Hibernate* for persistency.

What is lazy and eager fetching?

Lazy and Eager are two types of data loading strategies supported by Hibernate in case of association such as one-to-one, one-to-many, and so on.

- **Eager loading/fetching**: In eager fetching, the data loading happens at the time of their parent is fetched. Associations like many-to-one and one-to-one use the eager loading strategy by default. Initial loading of data may take more time as child also need to be loaded when parent is loaded. The use of the `fetch = FetchType.EAGER` attribute enables the use of eager fetching.

- **Lazy loading/fetching**: In lazy fetching, the data loading happens only when developers explicitly call the *get* or *size* method. By default, many-to-many and one-to-many associations use the lazy loading strategy. In this case, the initial loading time is much smaller than eager loading, as children will be loaded only when explicitly asked. To enable lazy fetching, one can use the `fetch = FetchType.LAZY` attribute.

What is cascading? What is CASCADE.ALL means? Which of the cascading options you worked with?

The simplest dictionary meaning of **cascading** is *"A process whereby something, typically information or knowledge, is successively passed on."*

In Hibernate, an entity have some association with another entity. So, when we perform some action on the target entity, that action must be propagated to the other entity, which is having association with it. This can be achieved by cascading. Let us consider User has an address. When one performs updating User, whether to update the address or not is decided by the value provided to the cascading attribute.

We have cascading options as follows:

- **ALL**: This means that "all" the operations performed on the container will be also applied on the contained entity.

- **PERSIST**: In this case, when the parent entity is persisted, then all its related entities will also be persisted. It means that **save()** or **persist()** operations are cascaded to related entities.

- **REMOVE**: In this case if the parent entity is removed, then all its related entity will also be removed.

- **MERGE**: When the parent entity is merged, then all its related entity will also be merged.

- **DETACH**: When the parent entity is detached, then all its related entity will also be detached.

- **REFRESH**: When the parent entity is refreshed, then all its related entities will also be refreshed.

There is no default cascade type in JPA; it means by default no operations are cascaded.

How to map java.util.Date in Hibernate?

When we map **java.util.Date**, which is part of our entity into database, Hibernate, by default, stores the same in the nanoseconds format. However, you can change this format to different types as:

- **TIMESTAMP**: Persists the data of date and time in nanoseconds.

- **TIME**: Persists data of time in nanoseconds.

- **DATE:** Persists data of only date in years, months, and days.

To use these types, you can use the **@Temporal** annotation as **@Temporal (TemporalType.DATE)**.

How can you map enum to database using the Hibernate framework?

To map the **enum** attribute to a database, we can use the *@Enumerated* annotation. We can provide different values to this **enum,** which decides in what way the **enum** element is stored in the database. If we use **@Enumerated(EnumType.ORDINAL)**, then the index number of the **enum** is persisted in the database. But, if we use **@ Enumerated(EnumType.STRING),** then the string value of **enum** is persisted in the database.

What is a transaction? How to manage a transaction in Hibernate?

A **transaction** simply represents a unit of work. It means, if one step fails, the whole unit fails. A transaction can be described by **Atomicity, Consistency, Isolation and Durability** (**ACID**) properties. In Hibernate, the Transaction interface defines the unit of work. It has JTA and JDBC as the implementations of the transaction. The transaction is always associated with Session. `session.beginTransaction()` enables the start of a new session.

The Transaction interface has methods as follows:

- `begin()`: starts a new transaction.
- `commit()`: ends the unit of work unless `FlushMode.NEVER` is setup.
- `rollback()`: forces the transaction to rollback.
- `setTimeout()`: sets a transaction for a certain timeout for any transaction started by a subsequent call to begin on the instance.

What is HQL?

Hibernate Query Language (**HQL**) is very much similar to **Structured Query Language** (**SQL**), with a one important difference. HQL uses the class name in query; on the other hand, SQL uses the table name. It means HQL is independent of any database.

What are the advantages of HQL?

- HQL is database-independent.
- HQL always supports polymorphic queries.
- HQL supports object-oriented features like inheritance, polymorphism, and associations as well.
- HQL is easy to learn for a Java programmer.

Explain the disadvantages of HQL

- DDL operations cannot be performed by HQL.
- As compared to SQL, the HQL query gives negligible performance degradation because of conversions.
- PL/SQL program cannot be called by HQL.

What is caching? Why caching is used?

In Hibernate, when more data is fetched from a database, due to size of data, the performance of an application is impacted. In case of finding of data every time, we need to hit the database. This process takes more time to load the data over the network. Instead of every time hitting the database, it is a good approach to hit temporary local storage. This storage is a buffer memory, which lies between the application, and the database is termed as **cache**. The cache memory stores recently used data to reduce the number of database hits as much as possible.

Explain caching in Hibernate

This question can be reframed as:

- **Can you explain caching architecture in Hibernate?**

- **Explain first-level and second-level caching.**

- **Explain second-level caching.**

  The following figure explains the architecture of caching in Hibernate:

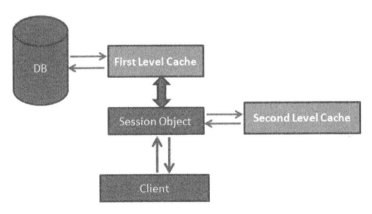

Figure 14.3: Caching Architecture

- **First-level cache**

  Whenever, the data is loaded from a DB, we are unknowingly using *first-level* cache. The *first-level* cache is nothing but the *Session* cache. It is a mandatory cache through which all requests are passed. The *Session* object keeps an object with itself before committing it to the database. One can use the *first-level* cache to store the data locally or the data, which is needed by the *Session*. The *first-level* cache is enabled by default.

- **Second-level cache**

  The *first-level* cache is enabled by default. However, the *second-level* cache is an optional. The *first-level* cache will always be consulted before any attempt is made by the *second-Level* cache to locate an object. One can configure the second-level cache on a per-class and per-collection basis, which is responsible for caching objects across sessions. The *second-level* cache is maintained at the `SessionFactory` level and is available to all sessions.

  The *second-level* cache is disabled by default. *Hibernate* also does not provide any caching implementation for that. *EHCache, OSCache, warmCache, JBossCache* are some third-party caches that can be used with *Hibernate*. To handle cache implementation, we must implement `org.hibernate.cache.CacheProvider`.

Explain the difference between the first- and second-level cache. Or the first-level cache versus second-level cache in Hibernate

- The very basic difference is, *the first-level* cache is maintained at the *Session* level, and the *second-level* cache is maintained at the *SessionFactory* level.

- The *first-level* cache is accessible to the only *Session* that maintains it. However, the *second-level* cache is accessible to all.

- The *first-level* cache is by default enabled, but the *second-level* cache is by default disabled.

What is the similarity between cache and lazy loading?

Both caching and lazy loading help in improving application performance. But, the mechanism is very different and also the concept. Caching is to store the data either in *Session* or using the *second-level* cache locally. Lazy loading loads the data only when requested. Lazy loading is more of concern when the one-to-many association is dealt.

What is an immutable class in Hibernate? How to make an immutable class in Hibernate?

In *Hibernate*, classes or objects are by default mutable, which allows the class or collection to add, update, and delete. Whenever this mutability is set to false, the class and its related collection cannot be changed. We can use **@Immutable** to annotate an entity as immutable.

@Immutable marks an entity as immutable. One can use it when the lists, map, or collection rarely mutate. The updates for the class will be ignored, without any exception is thrown. Only the **add** and **delete** operations are allowed on this class.

Immutability specifies the object cannot be mutated, but sometimes, the object needs to be updated in the DB. How to change the data?

One can annotate the class to stop mutation. It means the states tend to be rarely changed. Because of this, once we make any object as immutable, there is no way, such object can be modified at runtime using the *Hibernate* API. In case the change of data has to be made, it can be done manually, via *SQL* or an administration application.

Note: Hibernate cache must be taken into consideration while we talk about mutability. When the reference data changes, the arrangement has to be made to make sure that the applications using that data is notified. This is done by the refresh() method or by restarting the application.

What is Automatic Dirty checking in Hibernate?

Hibernate provides **Automatic Dirty checking** as one of the very powerful feature. In this concept, the changes made to a persistent object are automatically saved to the database when the session is flushed or the transaction is committed. It enables implicit updates of the object, and the code does not need to invoke an explicit save or update.

What is an inspection strategy?

When an object is loaded from the database, a snapshot of it is kept in memory. Now, when the session is flushed, Hibernate compares the stored snapshot with the current state. In case these differ, the object is marked as dirty, and to update the state, a suitable SQL command is enqueued. This strategy of Hibernate is termed as an **inspection strategy**.

What is the use of the @NamedQuery annotation?

In an application, at many scenarios, we need to find the similar query probably with different parameters. So, the developer would always insist to pull this query from some centralized repository instead of writing it repetitively. The **@NamedQuery** annotation is used to declare such types of query. This annotation takes two parameters, name, which is identification of query and query, which is actual query that you would like to execute.

Conclusion

In this chapter, we discussed the architecture about *Hibernate* through different interview questions. We talked about how Hibernate simplifies the usage of heavyweight JDBC code by providing automotive persistency mechanism. We also discussed how to implement different strategies of *Hibernate* for association and inheritance. Along with it, we also covered different concepts like the *first-level* and *second-level* cache and what role it plays in the persistency mechanism. Most importantly, we discussed most of the questions with answers, which could be asked in an *Hibernate* interview.

Index

Printed by Amazon Italia Logistica S.r.l.
Torrazza Piemonte (TO), Italy

24410598R00224